9) GAN II15 £2.50

CW00850834

Deliberative

Deliberative Democracy

Issues and Cases

Edited by
Stephen Elstub and Peter McLaverty

EDINBURGH
University Press

© editorial matter and organisation Stephen Elstub and Peter McLaverty, 2014
© the chapters their several authors, 2014

Edinburgh University Press Ltd
22 George Square, Edinburgh EH8 9LF
www.euppublishing.com

Typeset in Monotype Baskerville by
Servis Filmsetting Ltd, Stockport, Cheshire,
and printed and bound in Great Britain by
CPI Group (UK) Ltd, Croydon CR0 4YY

A CIP record for this book is available from the British Library

ISBN 978 0 7486 4349 3 (hardback)
ISBN 978 0 7486 4348 6 (paperback)
ISBN 978 0 7486 4350 9 (webready PDF)
ISBN 978 0 7486 7806 8 (epub)

Contents

Tables and figures

Tables

Figures

Preface

Deliberative democracy increasingly dominates discussions of democracy and governance. Its progress is still held back by many key issues, however, and ten of the most pertinent are addressed in this volume. The concept of this book was devised during a conversation between Darren Halpin and Peter McLaverty in 2009. During their conversation, Halpin suggested to McLaverty that he should consider producing an edited book in which authors would address the problems and controversies that still surround the theory and practice of deliberative democracy. McLaverty was taken with the idea but was unsure about the viability of the proposed book and the best way to proceed. As the founding convenor of the British Political Studies Association Participatory and Deliberative Democracy Specialist Group, McLaverty decided to get another view on the desirability and practicality of the proposed book by talking with Stephen Elstub, the current convenor of the specialist group. Elstub strongly supported the book idea and agreed to become joint editor. Building on McLaverty's initial thoughts, Elstub and McLaverty together produced what they considered were the main theoretical issues that were holding back the development of deliberative democracy. They agreed that each of the issues would form the basis for a chapter of the book. Owing to the considerable amount of empirical evidence now available on deliberative democracy, they also agreed that, while the chapters of the book would start from theoretical considerations, each chapter would also address the impact of empirical insights on the issue in question. In that way, it was expected that each chapter would advance an understanding of the complexity of each issue and offer possible ways forward. They were fortunate to have invitations to contribute chapters accepted by many of the leading lights in the field of deliberative democracy. The authors of the chapters address deliberative democracy from different theoretical, analytical and normative perspectives, and there has been no effort to impose or to achieve a uniformity of approach towards the study of deliberative democracy. A number of approaches to deliberative democracy are therefore to be found in the book which has no single or overriding theoretical perspective. In this manner, the book certainly reflects the eclecticism currently present in the study of deliberative democracy. As the chapters in the book contain original research and reflections on key issues, the book should be of interest to all scholars of deliberative democracy. The book is also aimed at students at an advanced stage in their undergraduate studies as well as those engaged in relevant postgraduate study.

We should like to thank all the contributors to the book for their willingness to write the chapters and to address points that were raised by us as editors. We should also like to thank all those at Edinburgh University Press with whom we worked in producing the book. Their flexibility and their help are much appreciated. Out thanks also go to Ian O'Flynn and Jenny Pearce for their specific comments on the issues addressed in the book at a round table held at the 'Deepening democracy: Participation, deliberation or both?' conference held at the University of Bradford in September 2012. Elements of the 'Introduction' are drawn from a previous publication: Elstub, S. (2010), 'The Third Generation of Deliberative Democracy', *Political Studies Review*, 8: 3, 291–307. We should like to thank the publisher for permission to use this material.

Peter McLaverty, Aberdeen
Stephen Elstub, Glasgow
January 2013

The editors and contributors

The editors

Stephen Elstub is a Senior Lecturer in Politics at the University of the West of Scotland. His main research interests are in deliberative democracy, with a particular focus on its institutionalisation and comparative institutional analysis, and he has published numerous articles on these topics. He is the author of *Towards a Deliberative and Associational Democracy* (Edinburgh University Press, 2008) and editor of *Democracy in Theory and Practice* (2012). He convenes the British Political Studies Association Specialist Group on Participatory and Deliberative Democracy (http://deliberativehub.wordpress.com/) and is Executive Editor of the *Journal of Deliberative and Participatory Democracy*.

Peter McLaverty is a Reader in Public Policy at Robert Gordon University, Aberdeen Scotland. He was the founding convenor of the British Political Studies Association Participatory and Deliberative Democracy Specialist Group. He has written widely on democratic theory and political participation. He has published in a number of journals, including the *International Political Science Review* and the *Journal of Political Ideologies*. He was the editor of the book *Public Participation and Innovations in Community Governance* (2002).

The contributors

André Bächtiger is currently Swiss National Science Research Professor at the University of Lucerne. He received his doctorate in 2004 and his habilitation in 2010 from the University of Bern. He was Swiss Chair/Jean Monnet Fellow at the European University Institute (Florence) and visiting scholar at the University of North Carolina (Chapel Hill) and the Australian National University. He has published widely on deliberative democracy, including *Deliberative Politics in Action. Analysing Parliamentary Discourse* (2004) and a forthcoming book on *Mapping and Measuring Deliberation. Micro and Macro Knowledge of Deliberative Quality, Dynamics and Contexts*.

Georgina Blakeley is a lecturer in Politics at the Open University. She researches in two key areas. The first area covers issues of democracy and democratisation in Spanish politics. Recent themes include electoral politics (e.g. 'It's politics stupid. The Spanish general election 2004', *Parliamentary Affairs* 2006) and historical memory (e.g. 'Digging up Spain's past: consequences of truth and reconciliation', *Democratization* 2005, and 'Evaluating Spain's reparation law?, *Democratization*, iFirst 2012). The second area covers issues of participation and urban governance drawing on case studies in Spain (e.g. 'Local governance and local democracy: the Barcelona model?, *Local Government Studies* 2005) and in the UK (e.g. 'Governing ourselves: citizen participation in Barcelona and Manchester?, *International Journal of Urban and Regional Research* 2010, and with Brendan Evans, *The Regeneration of East Manchester: A Political Analysis*, 2013).

Mark B. Brown is professor in the Department of Government at California State University, Sacramento. He was previously a postdoctoral fellow at the Institute for Science and Technology Studies, Bielefeld University. He studied at UC Santa Cruz and the University of Göttingen, and received a PhD in political science from Rutgers University. He is the author of *Science in Democracy: Expertise, Institutions, and Representation* (2009), as well as numerous book chapters and journal articles on the politics of expertise, citizen engagement, bioethics, climate change and related topics.

Manlio Cinalli is associate research professor at Sciences Po Paris. His research focuses on comparative political behaviour, the politics of ethnic relations, exclusion and integration, networks, and multilevel public policies. He has published numerous articles in scholarly journals and volumes and is currently research director of the French projects for YOUNEX and EURISLAM (EU Framework Seven Programme).

Juraj Cintula is a PhD student, researching deliberative democracy, in the Department of Political Science, Matej Bel University, Banská Bystrica Slovakia.

Darren R. Halpin is Associate Professor of Policy Studies at the Research School of Social Sciences, the Australian National University. He has held positions previously at Aarhus University and the Robert Gordon University. Darren has published widely on the topics of interest groups and organised interests, including recent articles in *Governance, British Journal of Political Science, Journal of European Public Policy* and *Public Administration*. He has recently authored a book, *Groups, Representation and Democracy: Between Promise and Practice* (2010). He is Founding Book Series Editor for 'Interest Groups, Advocacy and Democracy' and is on the Founding Editorial Team for the journal *Interest Groups and Advocacy*.

Ian O'Flynn is Senior Lecturer in Political Theory at Newcastle University. He is a former Visiting Scholar at Harvard University and Summer Institute

Fellow at the University of Pennsylvania. His current research focuses on questions concerning the nature and requirements of democracy in multicultural and multinational societies. He is the author of *Deliberative Democracy and Divided Societies* (Edinburgh University Press, 2006) and of articles in scholarly journals such as *British Journal of Political Science* and *Political Studies*.

Shawn W. Rosenberg is Professor of Political Science and Psychology and Director of the Graduate Program in Political Psychology at the University of California, Irvine. Rosenberg did graduate work in psychology at Harvard University and in political sociology at Nuffield College, Oxford. He has been a visiting professor at the University of California, Berkeley, Princeton University, Lund University, the University of Amsterdam and Leiden University. He is an author of *Political Cognition and Reasoning* (1988), *Reason Ideology and Politics* (1988), *The Not So Common Sense: How People Judge Social and Political Life* (2002) and editor of *Deliberation, Participation and Democracy: Can the People Govern?* (2007).

Maija Setälä is Professor of Political Science at the University of Turku, Finland. She received her doctorate from the LSE in 1997. Setälä has been a visiting research fellow at Columbia University and the Australian National University. She specialises in democratic theory, especially theories of deliberative democracy, issues of political trust and democratic innovations such as referendums, popular initiatives and deliberative mini-publics. Setälä has published several books and journal articles on these topics.

Jürg Steiner is emeritus professor of political science at both the University of North Carolina at Chapel Hill and the University of Bern. His most recent scholarly book is *The Foundations of Deliberative Democracy. Empirical Research and Normative Implications* (2012). Together with Markus Crepaz, he is also the author of the textbook *European Democracies* (8th edn, 2013). He is currently working on a project about the potential for deliberation across deep divisions.

Alda Wegmann is a research assistant at the University of Lucerne. Her research interests lie in deliberative democracy and peace and development research.

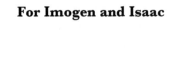

For Imogen and Isaac

Introduction: issues and cases in deliberative democracy

Stephen Elstub and Peter McLaverty

Liberal democracy around the world is in crisis (Galbraith, 1993; Dalton, 2004: 28 and 30; 2006: 59; Stoker 2006, Hay 2007) and deliberative democracy is increasingly seen as the solution. If deliberative democracy really is to be the saviour, however, there are a number of vital issues that still need to be addressed and resolved. This book will consider these key issues facing deliberative democracy today, in theory by drawing on evidence from relevant cases.

Deliberative democracy is very much the zeitgeist not just of democratic theory but political theory per se. Indeed, Gutmann and Thompson (2004: vii) are correct to note that: 'No subject has been more discussed in political theory in the last two decades than deliberative democracy,' while Dryzek (2007: 237) suggests that it is now 'the most active area of political theory in its entirety'. The normative claim which unites this body of thought is that political decision-making should be talk-centric rather than vote-centric. Rather than merely constituting the aggregation of individual preferences, collective decisions should emerge from public reasoned discussion and debate. There are a variety of different ways in which this claim may be justified, including that: it represents the fairest of decision-making procedures; leads to decisions that are more just and in the public good; or that it leads to more prudent, informed, rational and autonomous citizens (Festenstein, 2002; Elstub, 2008).

The recent history of deliberative democracy has been particularly auspicious, to the extent that it not only dominates theoretical discussions of democracy but is starting to receive broad coverage in practical discussions of democracy. Not only does this suggest that deliberative democracy has 'come of age' (Bohman, 1998), and taken an 'empirical turn' (Dryzek, 2008), but that deliberative democracy is now in its third generation (Elstub, 2010a). First-generation deliberative democrats, such as Habermas (1996) and Rawls (1993), debated the normative justifications of deliberative democracy, interpretations, and necessary components of the theory but failed to take account of the sheer complexity of contemporary societies (Elstub, 2010a).

In considering the institutionalisation of deliberative democracy, second-generation deliberative democrats, particularly Bohman (1996) and Gutmann and Thompson (1996), took complexity seriously and reformed the theory of deliberative democracy in the process. They still offered little substantive detail, however, in terms of the type of institutions required to ensure deliberative democracy could be actualised in complex societies (Elstub, 2010a).

This has paved the way for a third generation to emerge who have sought to establish the nature of the institutions required to achieve this reconciliation in practice (Elstub, 2010a). This shift has led to a proliferation of diverse interpretations regarding the institutional features of a deliberative model of democracy. It is apparent that, within its third generation, deliberative democracy is perhaps at its most pluralistic when it comes to the question of institutional design. Following this array of suggestions for the institutionalisation of deliberative democracy, experiments are increasing throughout Europe, the United States, Australia, South East Asia and South America, making deliberative democracy a theory of international importance.

Despite the meteoric growth in popularity of deliberative democracy, and its maturation through its various generations, there are a number of issues that plague its study and are hindering the further development of deliberative democracy and its approximation in practice. A number of these issues perennially affects democracy per se, not just the deliberative variant. In this sense, the book makes a contribution to the discussion of democracy in the twenty-first century more generally. The unique focus on public debate that is found in deliberative theory, however, accentuates many of these problems and/ or provides distinct interpretations of the issues. There is now a considerable amount of empirical evidence on deliberative democracy which is enabling new perspectives on these key issues to emerge. In particular, this evidence has been crucial in determining the conditions in which deliberative democracy can operate effectively and the tensions that exist between key elements of deliberative democracy. In short, the empirical evidence on democracy gives us 'a sense of what may work, how, when, and why – and what may be difficult' (Dryzek, 2007: 240). Though the empirical evidence can tell us the tensions that exist in democracy in practice, the answers to how trade-offs should be made between these concepts ultimately need to be determined by normative theory. For this reason democratic theory still has 'the upper hand' (Thompson, 2008: 513; see also Chambers, 2003: 320; Steiner et al., 2004: 42; Habermas, 2006). These key issues in deliberative democracy therefore need to be addressed by normative theory that is grounded in the empirical evidence available.

Consequently, in this book a number of leading democratic theorists and empiricists, who have written widely about 'deliberative democracy', will address a number of the crucial questions that surround the theory and practice of deliberative democracy. In outlining these problems, surveying the solutions suggested to them, and providing new and innovative ideas to resolve these issues for deliberative democracy, it is hoped that the book will make a profound contribution to the development of deliberative democracy in theory and practice. As an introduction to the individual chapters and the topic each will address, we shall put the chapters in a broad context. We shall briefly, and fairly schematically, outline the historical interest in the relationship between democracy and deliberation, briefly outlining the positive views of some key writers. We shall then show how and why other writers have criticised either the theory or the practice behind ideas of deliberative democracy. This consideration will provide the background against which we shall show why the topics to be examined in this book are crucial both for a coherent theoretical approach to deliberative democracy and for the practice of democracy in the twenty-first century.

Historical overview

An interest of philosophers and others in the relationship between democracy and deliberation can be found in ancient Greece. Ancient Athenian democracy was not a form of 'deliberative democracy' as it would be defined by academics today. For one thing, it was not inclusive of all adults (it excluded all women, slaves and foreign males) and, for another, there is no evidence that major governmental decisions were made after open and egalitarian deliberation between the people or that public deliberation played a large part in people's everyday lives. Deliberation did play some part in Athenian democracy, however, and, while he supported a mixed system that would include elements of democracy and have non-democratic features, Aristotle nonetheless argued from his experience that the people deliberating together could often produce better decisions than an expert on a subject (cf. Barker, 1978: 142). This idea that public deliberation improves decision-making has been a major argument used in favour of a deliberative democracy.

Though there were some elements in the Roman republic that were similar to democratic Athens, the form of government applied in republican Rome cannot really be called a democracy, and ideas supporting democracy went largely out of fashion for a long time following the collapse of Athenian democracy, as the class systems that existed around the world did not find the thinking behind democracy, with its ideas of political equality, at all conducive. It was only in the eighteenth and nineteenth centuries that interest in 'democracy' began to grow among ruling strata. Along with the revival of interest in a form of democracy which was very different from that found in ancient Athens went an interest in deliberation. This interest is epitomised in the thinking of two British writers, Edmund Burke (1854) and John Stuart Mill (1951). Both these intellectuals argued that, within elected parliaments and assemblies, the representatives should engage in deliberation before making decisions. As with the argument of Aristotle, for Burke and Mill, deliberation among elected representatives was desirable because it would produce better decisions. While Aristotle wrote about deliberation between the people, however, both Burke and Mill saw deliberation between elected representatives and the educated as desirable, not deliberation among the mass of the people. This limiting of deliberation to an elected or educated elite is far removed from the commitments of today's supporters of deliberative democracy, whatever other differences there may be between them.

The nineteenth-century supporters of deliberation expressed a limited, class-based and often male-focused approach (though J. S. Mill (2009) supported equality between the sexes) which ultimately calls into question the connection their approaches have with any ideas of deliberative democracy. Early twentieth-century approaches to deliberation had a more democratic focus than their nineteenth-century predecessors. Academics, such as John Dewey (1927), A. D. Lindsay (1929) and Ernest Barker (1951), argued that public deliberation was an essential element of democracy. For Dewey, the people should become aware of their common, collective position, and could become aware of who they were through deliberating together and devise collective solutions to their common problems. Considering the needs and interests of others enabled us to develop as human beings (cf. Festenstein, 2004). A democracy based on elections, where people were treated as isolated individuals, was inadequate. Dewey's approach added a new dimension to arguments in favour of public deliberation and a deliberative form of democracy. Lindsay also stressed the importance of collective discussion, over aggregation, to collective decision-making:

> Government by consent, if taken strictly, is and must be an illusion; that it is an entire mistake to suppose that there exists at any moment a ready made will of the people. The process of discovering what may be called the will of the society is a process of making it, and to that process discussion is essential. (Lindsay, 1929: 430)

Barker saw democracy as basically about common debate between the people which would result in an agreement that would be accepted by the vast majority, if not all, of those involved; he did not see democracy as primarily about the aggregation of votes.

Despite the promotion of key ideas of public discussion and deliberation, however, the theory of deliberative democracy did not exist in the early twentieth century. In fact, the first use of the term 'deliberative democracy' was by Bessette (1980) in his discussion of the American Congress. Following this, the argument that democratic deliberation should aim for consensus among participants was taken up by perhaps the most seminal early, and first generational, writer on deliberative democracy, Jürgen Habermas (1986; 1989). Habermas's approach to deliberation or discourse has changed over time and we shall not attempt to set out the changing nuances in his approach. Central to Habermas's early work on 'deliberative democracy' is a commitment to consensus decisions, which would be based on free and equal deliberation between participants, a communication that was based on the giving of reasons that all could accept, an open-minded approach by those involved, and a willingness by participants to be swayed only by the force of the better argument as they strove to achieve the public interest. This was best reflected in Habermas's ideal speech situation. Here, communication is undistorted, as all participants are free and equal, with no power discrepancies, and unconstrained from subjection, self-delusion and strategic activity. All views are aired in an unlimited discourse, creating open participation aimed at rational consensus where the 'unforced force of the better argument' is decisive (Habermas, 1990: 56–8). Nevertheless the ideal speech situation was a counterfactual ideal, with limited practical relevance, beyond a set of normative values. In his more early but applied work, Habermas focused on deliberation among the public in the public sphere. His concern with the potential of the public sphere came out of his work on the eighteenth-century bourgeois public sphere in Britain (Habermas, 1992). In later work, Habermas (1996) developed a two-track approach to the working of deliberative democracy, arguing that the public opinion which came out of the deliberation of the people in the public sphere would be taken up by the people's elected political representatives and would feed, through these representatives, into the public policy process. The work carried out by Habermas and others in the 1970s and 1980s, which represents what is seen as the first generation of work on deliberative democracy, was concerned with setting out the normative and theoretical case for deliberative democracy. First-generation deliberative democrats thought reason exchange to be the only applicable form of communication, which would result in uniform preference change, ending in consensus (Elstub, 2010a). This phrase might well be seen as laying the foundations on which ideas of deliberative democracy could subsequently be refined.

This refinement continued apace during the second generation. It is essentially the features of complexity, mainly diversity, scale and socio-economic inequality, the need for specialists, and globalisation that motivated Bohman (1996) and Gutmann and Thompson (1996) to attempt to diverge from, and fuse, the theories of Habermas and Rawls (Baber and Bartlett, 2005; Elstub, 2010a). In doing this, a second generation of deliberative democracy was born. For Bohman, in particular, a realistic conception of deliberative democracy must acknowledge cultural pluralism and its challenge to common goods and unitary public reason; social inequalities would mean the exclusion of permanent minorities from public deliberation; that large-scale public organisations are inevitable; and finally, owing to community bias, there is a restriction on the problems that will be acknowledged and solutions that are considered feasible (Baber and Bartlett, 2005: 107). In the second-generational view reasons are public and successful if citizens are willing to accept the resulting majority decisions, or that these decisions are at least sufficiently acceptable that citizens continue to participate in deliberation. Bohman calls this 'plural agreement' (1996: 34, 89) while Gutmann and Thompson term it 'deliberative disagreement'

(1996: 73–9). The second-generational approach also assumes that people are motivated by their own interests (Gutmann and Thompson, 1996: 176–7) and that these interests can be temporarily reconciled through public deliberation but never resolved (Bohman, 1996: 72–3). Consequently, the second genera-tionalists argue that, owing to pre-deliberative commitments, preference change will be limited; that, owing to pluralism, consensus is unlikely to be achieved (Bohman, 1996: 85–9; Gutmann and Thompson, 1996: 42); and that reason exchange is not the only applicable form of communicating in debate but greet-ing, rhetoric and storytelling should, and will, also be included (Bohman, 1996: 116–23; Gutmann and Thompson, 1996: 132–7).

According to James Bohman (1998), through accommodating social com-plexity in its theory, by 1998, deliberative democracy had 'come of age'. This paved the way for the third, and current, generation of deliberative democracy to emerge. Essentially, the third-generation deliberative democratic theorists attempt to put second-generation deliberative democracy into practice. There is now less concern about justifying deliberative democracy normatively and philosophically, and more concern with making deliberative democracy work in practice, by analysing how the existing structures of democracy might be made compatible with deliberative democracy and how deliberative democracy could be institutionalised in practice (Elstub, 2010a).

Within this third generation of deliberative democracy there is a prevalent distinction, derived from Hendriks (2006), between micro and macro strategies for institutionalising deliberative democracy. Micro deliberative democracy focuses on ideal deliberative procedures, within small-scale structured arenas within the state, orientated to decision-making, with impartial participants delib-erating together in one place and at one time. Alternatively, macro deliberative democracy favours informal and unstructured, and spontaneous, discursive communication that occurs across space and time, aimed at opinion formation, within civil society, outside and often against the formal decision-making institu-tions of the state, with partisan deliberators. Micro deliberation tends to be too elitist, excluding too many participants while, in macro deliberation, communi-cation can be easily distorted by inequality and self-interest, and there is a failure to empower citizens sufficiently and make their participation effective, unless this deliberative communication is linked to decision-making and micro venues (Elstub, 2010a). Therefore, Hendriks (2006) rightly argues that it is essential for both micro and macro deliberative democracy to be integrated.

The third generation of deliberative democracy has resulted in the initiation of a range of mechanisms for the promotion of public deliberation and the adop-tion of an 'empirical' turn in thinking about deliberative democracy (Dryzek, 2010). Proposals have ranged from the radical restructuring and decentralisa-tion of the state (Fung, 2003; Baber and Bartlett 2005; Hendriks 2006; Elstub 2008) to discourses emerging from transnational civil society (Dryzek, 2006) to the supplementing of existing structures with participatory mechanisms such as citizens' juries (Smith and Wales, 2000; Leib, 2004; Parkinson, 2006), deliberative opinion polls (Fishkin, 1991; 1997; 2009), and citizen assemblies (Warren and Pearse, 2008; Fournier et al., 2011), to a focus on making current legislative arenas, such as parliaments and their associated committees, more deliberative (Uhr, 1998; Steiner et al., 2004; Davidson and Stark, 2011; Davidson et al., 2011). Mechanisms have been taken up and promoted by states and public organisations, as well as by academics and civil society organisations, in a number of countries, such as citizens' juries, consensus conferences, deliberative polls, deliberative mapping, and national issues forums (Smith, 2005). Other mechanisms, such as citizen assemblies, which have been used in two Canadian provinces and the Netherlands to consider the voting system, also included a strong element of deliberation between members of the public (Warren and Pearse, 2008; Fournier et al., 2011).

It is apparent that, within its third generation, deliberative democracy is perhaps at its most pluralistic when it comes to the question of institutional design. The pluralism of deliberative democracy continues to increase and it is losing its original normative core (Elstub, 2006). Recently, there have been a number of efforts to refine what is meant by deliberative democracy and to think about what public deliberation might practically mean in the twenty-first century. This rethinking has led to some arguing that the emphasis on the exchange of reasons that all can accept between deliberators may be too onerous a requirement and that the distinction between the public interest, which should always be pursued in deliberation, and self-interest, which should be avoided, is untenable (Mansbridge et al., 2010). With a raft of empirical evidence now available on deliberative democracy in practice, in a variety of contexts, the number and variety of interpretations of what deliberative democracy is, should be and can be are growing exponentially. This indicates that there are a number of key issues that still must be addressed right now to determine what deliberative democracy is, what we can expect from it, and how it can be approximated in practice. Despite the incredible advancement of deliberative democracy, it is now at a crossroads, and these issues must be addressed and resolved if the theory and practice of deliberative democracy are to continue to progress. It is the key issues related to these big questions that this book intends to address by drawing on evidence from relevant cases.

Issues in deliberative democracy

As we have seen, John Dryzek (2000) has talked about the deliberative turn in democratic theory and argued that this has changed thinking on democracy. Despite this and the large amount of academic work that has been completed on deliberative democracy, there are a number of questions and issues about both the theory and practice of deliberation that continue to be raised, both by critics of the idea of deliberative democracy and by those who are more sympathetic to this model of democracy. We would suggest that the issues can be arranged around ten areas which we shall outline in turn.

Conflict and deliberation

Does political deliberation emasculate politics? Deliberation demands reasonableness by participants. A certain approach has to be adopted by participants for deliberation to occur: they need to abide by deliberative obligations (Festenstein, 2002). Certain implied, if not always explicit, rules have to be observed during deliberation. These can work reasonably well, it might be argued, where the differences between participants are not large or where participants do not feel strongly about the subject under review, such as in mini-publics. Where the issues are of major importance to the participants, however, and where the views of the participants are very different, deliberation may be seen as impossible or undesirable. Some writers (such as Shapiro, 2003) have argued that, in some circumstances, deliberation, by exacerbating differences, can make reaching acceptable decisions more difficult. In response, it might be argued that issues and circumstances where that is likely to be the case are not suitable for deliberative processes. But, if deliberation cannot work for the important issues in society, why should people support a *deliberative* democracy? Moreover, it can be argued that the essence of politics is the clash of opposing opinions and views of the world. Politics is about people making decisions not only between conflicting policy positions but also between conflicting philosophies and theoretical approaches to how the social world should be. Politics should be passionate. Some radical democrats have criticised deliberative democrats for failing to recognise that democratic politics necessarily involves the clash of opposites and produces winners and losers (cf. Mouffe, 2005). Would a deliberative democracy really be desirable if it avoided conflict? Is it mistaken in its fundamental approach to politics? Does deliberative democracy have to be like this or can good deliberation occur between partisan participants, too? Georgina Blakeley addresses this issue in Chapter 1, by considering the 15-M social movement in Spain with respect to its contribution to the public sphere and macro deliberation. She uses this to identify the limits of deliberative democracy in dealing with conflict.

Inequality and deliberative democracy

Does social inequality make public deliberation impossible? Writers argue that a key element of democracy is the idea of political equality. There are debates about how the commitment to political equality relates to social equality. On the whole, it has been accepted that social equality is not a precondition for political equality and democracy. The link between levels of participation and socio-economic status, particularly education, however, have been firmly established and continue to cause problems for deliberative democrats who also want to see more opportunities for citizen participation. Moreover, writers such as Joshua Cohen and Joel Rogers (2003), and Iris Young (2000) have argued that, for the achievement of *deliberative* democracy, social inequality may be potentially a major impediment. For Young, deliberation in western societies privileges those who are able to talk and construct reasons in line with the dominant paradigm and who feel comfortable speaking in public. Moreover, in as much as it aims to promote the public interest, or the common good, in practice, deliberative democracy underpins the status quo and benefits those who gain from the status quo. This means in practice that the well educated, who tend to be middle-class, white men, will be advantaged by the development of deliberative democracy, and the less well educated – those who tend to be members of the working class, from ethic minority groups and women – will be disadvantaged. Cohen and Rogers also question whether inequalities in the distribution of power fundamentally undermine the practice of deliberation. Marxists and neo-Marxists refer to democracy in capitalist society as 'capitalist democracy'. In this reading, those who own and control the means of production are able to exercise disproportionate influence and power in the democratic political process. For Marxists, this economic basis of inequality limits the exercise of democracy and undermines the achievement of a deliberative democracy. Unless the structural bases of inequality are tackled, on this approach, democracy is likely to remain limited. Why should the already powerful, those who are gaining from existing decision-making processes, subscribe to, or allow, widespread public deliberation in the public policy process? Can satisfactory ways be found to limit the impact of power and social inequality on the workings of deliberative democracy? In Chapter 2 Peter McLaverty raises concerns about the potential of approximating deliberative democracy across a political system owing to a range of prevalent social, economic and political inequalities.

Expertise and deliberative democracy

Is expert knowledge compatible with deliberation among the public? In a complex, technologically advanced society, it is argued that expertise is crucial for effective public administration and the resolution of public problems. Complexity makes us all dependent on experts of one kind or another. There are many issues that the vast majority of people simply lack the knowledge to consider seriously. If this is the case, some argue that it is sensible to privilege experts in the making of public policy. In some senses, this argument is a variant on the criticisms of democracy, that can be traced back to Plato, that the people are too stupid and uneducated to govern themselves. Instead, we should rely on impartial experts to govern benignly on our behalf. Supporters of deliberation between members of the public argue that public deliberation will produce better decisions. But if, in the modern world, we are so reliant on experts, given the complexity of the social and natural world, is that the case? What role should experts play in public policy today and can their role be made compatible with ideas of deliberative democracy? Can the public form epistemic communities of their own through deliberation? If so, can they interact with scientific epistemic communities? Is it possible for lay citizens and scientific experts to deliberate together and exchange reasons that each can understand? What type of institutions might facilitate this? These issues and others are reflected on in Chapter 3 by Mark Brown who argues that appropriate roles of experts in deliberative democracy comprise a political question, and are determined by various social and cultural factors, but that these should be interpreted by lay deliberation.

Interests and deliberative democracy

Does deliberation in the public policy process undermine democracy within groups? Much political activity involves people who represent certain groups or interests coming together and trying to reach agreements on specific matters. Such activity is on the increase, with trends towards an increasing reliance on governance networks made up of a range of civil society actors. A deliberative democracy would encourage the different group or interest representatives to deliberate in an effort to reach agreements that all will find acceptable. While this would promote one kind of deliberation, however, it might also undermine another form of deliberation. A group which has a representative on a committee may reach a decision on what they think their representative should support on the committee after deliberation within the group. If the representative, after deliberation with others on the committee, however, ends up supporting decisions that the group rejected in its own deliberations, where does that leave deliberative democracy? Political deliberation between representatives may be achieved at the expense of intra-group deliberation and democracy. Can these conflicting forms of deliberation be effectively combined or will one always win out over the other? Moreover, what does this tension mean for the relationship between deliberative democracy, private interests and the common good? What are the implications for partisan deliberation and the role of civil society within a deliberative system? In Chapter 4, Darren Halpin and Juraj Cintula reflect on these issues in the context of public policy orthodoxy, assessing what deliberative democracy can contribute to our understanding of public policy, and vice versa.

Pluralism and deliberative democracy

Given the diversity of identities, cultures, interests and opinions that exist in societies today, is deliberation possible? It can be argued that for deliberation to occur there needs to be either some sense of community among those participating or, at least, a degree of trust among participants to ground deliberative obligations (Festenstein, 2002). Increasingly, societies are becoming multi-ethnic and multicultural, and contain people with a variety of different opinions and interests. Societies are seen as having become more heterogeneous. People from different backgrounds and with different experiences are mixing and living together. For some, this will become increasingly normal around the world as a result of developments associated with globalisation. Some would see heterogeneity as a potential threat to deliberation among members of the public, as participants may lack common referral points produced by a similar background and strongly shared experiences. This makes it increasingly difficult for diverse groups to communicate effectively their preferences and to offer reasons that all can accept. In addition, heterogeneity may be seen as potentially exacerbating the tendency for people only to communicate about politics with those who share their views and social position, which was mentioned as a problem for the public sphere as a site of public deliberation. It is for such reasons that radical democrats such as Mouffe (2005) have criticised the possibility of their being fruitful, meaningful and inclusive deliberation. Does deliberative democracy demand some common background among participants for it to be viable? Or is deliberation among those with very different backgrounds and experiences possible? What types of institutions are required to reconcile the theory of deliberative democracy with the empirical reality of diverse, plural and even divided societies? Manlio Cinalli and Ian O'Flynn, in Chapter 5, further our understanding of these complex problems by utilising empirical data from British newspaper articles to provide quantitative and network analysis on ethnic relations in Britain and their connection to deliberative democracy.

Psychological attributes and deliberative democracy
Do people have the necessary psychological perceptions and skills to deliberate successfully? Critics of deliberative democracy argue that individuals simply do not have the psychological attributes that deliberative democracy demands. People are said to lack the ability to appreciate others' perceptions and approaches to political issues and to engage in non-instrumental deliberation. Various empirical studies of people's psychological approaches when engaged in group activity, including activity which is set up to be deliberative, raise questions about the abilities of individuals to deliberate with one another. Psychological theory also gives understandings into the psychological capacity of people to engage in deliberation. If it is difficult for people to deliberate with others, are there any reasons for thinking that the deliberative difficulties that people face might be overcome? Are there mechanisms that can be applied to increase the prospects of deliberation between people? Are there reasons to think that, as larger proportions of the world's population attain higher educational standards, the ability of more and more people to engage in deliberation will also increase? Can people grow psychologically so that they gain the ability to deliberate together? Chapter 6 is dedicated to these issues, where Shawn Rosenberg considers much

empirical evidence, from deliberative experiments and deliberative innovations, to present a realistic understanding of the nature of citizen deliberators and the likely quality of their deliberative practices.

Scale and deliberative democracy

Can deliberative democracy overcome problems of scale so it can be achieved in practice? Democracy in the modern world has developed largely within nation states with geographically constrained boundaries. There are significant challenges to achieving a deliberatively democratic system across a whole national political system, given the problem of scale. There are specific legitimacy problems deliberative democracy faces in adapting to scale (Parkinson, 2006). Is deliberative democracy viable in the nation state? If so, how can this be done? Moreover, over the last forty years there has been a growing interest in whether democracy can and should be extended into geographical areas that are larger than the nation state, including at the global level, in response to changes associated with 'globalisation'. It is argued that an increasing number of decisions that affect people's lives in important ways are taken by bodies standing above nation states. At present, in many of these bodies there is at best only a limited democratic input into their decisions. For some (for example, Held, 1995, Bohman, 2007) democracy needs to be more fully extended into the institutions that stand above the nation state. The problems of scale are, however, even more acute at the transnational level. Most of the initiatives that hope to promote deliberation among members of the public are small-scale (as has been shown). Is deliberative democracy viable if democracy is extended into the different levels above the nation state? If so, how can this be done? Do we need to expect different things from deliberatively democratic institutions at the transnational level? What type of institutions are required to reconcile the theory of deliberative democracy with the reality of scale at the national and transnational level? How can these national and transnational institutions be effectively integrated with one another? In Chapter 7 André Bächtiger and Alda Wegmann consider the potentials and pitfalls of scaling up deliberation in the nation state and to the global level through elected representative and legislative assemblies and a variety of citizen forums, and draw on the latest empirical evidence available on both. In doing so they map under what conditions deliberation 'scales up' and when it does not.

Deliberative democracy and public openness

Is deliberation among the public compatible with political representation? How can participatory and representative mechanisms be appropriately sequenced to foster deliberative norms? Representation has been central to the growth of democracy over the past two hundred or more years. Extending the vote has been central to the development of democracy within nation states, as have limits on the length of time parliaments, assemblies and local councils can sit before there have to be elections where the people can choose who they want to represent them. Ideas of the people having a say in public policy developments through their elected representatives have been crucial to the development of 'parliamentary' or representative democracy. Writers such as Joseph Schumpeter (1952: 209–83) argued that representative democracy, where the people choose between a set of elites in periodic elections and then leave those they have elected to get on with their job until the next election, was the most workable form of democracy. Some, such as Weale (1999: 84–105), have argued that representative democracy represents a workable division of labour and that we should be wary of making too many demands on people for participation in politics, as people have limited time, and commitments to activities that go far beyond politics. Despite evidence of disenchantment with the actual workings of representative democracy in a number of states (cf. Dalton, 2004: 28 and 30; and 2006: 59), there is little evidence that, in most countries where it exists, the people are looking to ditch representative democracy and replace it with a different form of democracy. There have been some 'theoretical' efforts by academics to try to combine elements of deliberation with traditional forms of political representation. But, if they were implemented, would any of the 'models' really create a deliberative democracy or would they produce a bastardised from of democracy that pleases neither advocates of deliberative democracy nor those who support representative democracy? Is there an inherent tension between the preference change sought by deliberative democrats and political representation? Under what circumstances can the two-way deliberative relationship, where reasons and information are exchanged between representative and represented, sought by Young (2000), be achieved? After considering these issues from a systemic standpoint, Jürg Steiner in Chapter 8, offers some innovative suggestions to sequence participatory and representative mechanisms to foster public openness in a multilevel governance system.

The public sphere

Can the public sphere be the site of widespread political deliberation among the public? As we have seen, for Habermas, the public sphere was central to any moves towards deliberative democracy. This commitment to the public sphere would involve people with different views deliberating with each other in an open and egalitarian manner. This deliberation was seen as the basis on which a clear and informed public opinion could influence the development of public policy. Empirical research suggests, however, that it is becoming increasingly unusual for people with different political opinions to discuss politics together in the local community (cf. Mutz, 2006 on the United States's experience). People tend to socialise only with those who share their political positions and, as a result, have their existing views reinforced. This can be seen as reducing the role that the public sphere can play in the development of a deliberative democracy. Does this fundamentally undermine the whole project of deliberative democracy and does it reduce the quality of democracy generally? Will the public sphere inevitably be a vastly unequal arena for the contestation of discourses that is inadequate to approximate the inclusive norms of deliberative democracy? Can the media be reformed to facilitate a more inclusive public sphere? In an era where transnational and global decisions and institutions are thought essential, can inclusive public spheres be formed around these institutions and foster cross-border deliberation? Given the need to link macro and micro deliberation within a political system, to what extent does and can macro deliberation occurring in public spheres influence decision-making? In Chapter 9 Maija Setälä reflects particularly on the desirability and possibility that the public sphere can be inclusive and deliberative.

Mini-publics

What role can mini-publics play in institutionalising deliberative democracy? Are deliberative mini-publics excessively open to manipulation? How can mini-publics contribute to the other nine issues covered in the book? Mini-publics are bodies that are established as representative samples of the wider population. Mechanisms, such as citizens' juries, consensus conferences, deliberative polls and citizen assemblies, can all be seen as mini-publics. Mini-publics have become one of the main mechanisms advocated for, and employed to, institutionalise deliberative democracy. It is thought that non-partisan participants are more likely to transform their preferences in the light of new reasons, and this is an essential element of deliberative democracy. A number of mini-publics has been instituted in different parts of the world and they provide useful information about how such mechanisms operate in practice. It is important to consider how the theory of deliberative democracy relates to the practice, and some progress in this area can be achieved by assessing the available evidence from practical events. One aspect of these mechanisms is that they all make use of facilitators or moderators to ensure that the proceedings reflect deliberative norms and practices. Facilitators have the role of ensuring that participant discussion is not dominated by a few members of the group, that each person is able to have a fair say, and that participants do not engage in abusive, dismissive or domineering activity. They have the role of ensuring that, as far as possible, the rules of deliberation are observed by all members of the group throughout the process. As a result, the participants do not control the discussion in the way, for example, that jurors do in a legal jury where there is no external facilitator. Moreover, in most cases, participants do not decide on the subject on which they will deliberate but follow an agenda set by the sponsoring body. This has led some critics (for example, Furedi, 2005: 118–19) to argue that these types of 'deliberative' mechanisms are open to manipulation and are unlikely to reflect the freely arrived-at views of the participants. In particular, the facilitator can be seen as potentially having the power to control the process and to direct the deliberation in a specific direction. Evidence does not suggest that facilitators engage in widespread manipulation but, for some, the question of potential manipulation remains in need of satisfactory answers.

Moreover, even if mini-publics are representative of the wider public, the number of people who can participate in deliberative initiatives is small. Most people will never participate in a deliberative mechanism. This would be a particular problem if deliberative mechanisms had responsibility for final policy decisions. As long as the outcomes of the mechanisms remain advisory, with final decisions taken elsewhere, as in most cases they are, this may not be a problem, though some might argue that those taking part in a deliberative mechanism may have an unacceptable impact on ultimate policy decisions that the rest of the public lacks. This can be seen as sitting uneasily with ideas of political equality, enshrined, for example, in the idea of 'one person, one vote'. Moreover, if the mini-publics themselves are not linked to decision-making then this undermines the increased legitimacy that the mini-publics are said to bring to public policy-making. Furthermore, it again points to the potential of mini-publics to be co-opted and manipulated. If we are concerned about creating a deliberative *democracy*, then, it might be argued, ways should be found to give the people as a whole greater control over public policy, rather than a small fraction of the people, however representative they may be. Nevertheless, mini-publics have been the most commonly and widespread means employed to implement deliberative democracy. It seems apparent that they do have a significant role to play within a deliberatively democratic polity but, given the issues discussed above, further thinking is required to determine exactly what role that can and should be. Mini-publics are examples of micro deliberation but more research is required on how these can be linked with processes of macro deliberation in the public sphere. In Chapter 10 Stephen Elstub reviews a range of empirical evidence from a variety of mini-publics to consider the contribution they can make to overcoming the associated problems presented to deliberative democracy by the other nine issues raised in this book.

In the concluding chapter, we predict the future of deliberative democracy and start to consider the ten issues in the context of the deliberative system, the key emerging theme in the latest work on deliberative democracy (Parkinson and Mansbridge, 2012; Steiner, 2012). The welcome and necessary attention given to a systemic analysis of deliberative democracy creates distinct interpretations of these issues but also generates new potential solutions.

Conclusion

We support the broad idea of deliberative democracy. Extensive political deliberation between members of the public, which feeds into the public policy process, is, in principle, extremely desirable. There are, however, certain gaps or lacunae in the case for deliberative democracy as it has developed over the years. We think the ten areas outlined above provide key questions where further work is needed to make the case for deliberative democracy convincing. Given the disenchantment with 'actually existing democracy' in a number of countries, if not with the underlying values and principles of democracy (cf. Dalton, 2004; 2006), this is a very good time to consider the key questions surrounding the concept of deliberative democracy. By bringing together leading academic writers to analyse those questions, this book can make a serious contribution to the ongoing, and increasingly urgent, debates about the meaning, desirability and practicality of deliberative democracy.

CHAPTER 1

Conflict and deliberation

Georgina Blakeley

Introduction

This chapter, like many endeavours in recent research on deliberative democracy, aims to bridge the gap between theorising and empirical practice. It bucks the trend in recent empirical research, however, by focusing on the wider process of deliberation within the public sphere rather than micro-deliberative procedures. Specifically, a case study of a social movement – the 15-M movement or *los indignados* (the indignant) – which appeared in Spain before the local and regional elections in May 2011, is used to examine the relationship between deliberation and conflict.

The chapter begins with a brief overview of the current state of play with regard to deliberative democracy. It then examines the reasons for focusing on the macro at the expense of the micro in contrast to the majority of empirical studies of deliberation. The third section defines conflict for the purposes of this chapter. It uses Mouffe's (2000) critique of deliberative democracy as a starting point but develops this framework further. The fourth section provides a brief description of the 15-M movement before analysing the problems of democracy its participants face in practice and its future possibilities. The final section draws lessons from this case study about the limits of deliberative theory and practice.

The current state of play

The 'coming of age' (Bohman, 1998) of deliberative democracy has been characterised by two broad trends in the literature which are motivated by the concern to overcome the gap between the ideal of deliberation and its practice. The first trend moves away from earlier attempts to contrast deliberative democratic ideals and mechanisms with aggregative ones in order to argue for the complementarity and compatibility of the two. This approach is best represented by the work of Mansbridge et al. (2010) which argues for the place of self-interest, power and voting within deliberative democracy. This broadening of deliberative democracy builds on Mansbridge's (1999) earlier arguments about the importance of everyday talk to democracy, which may or may not be deliberative, and on Young's (2002) expansive theory of communicative democracy. The argument for a complementary relationship between deliberative and aggregative mechanisms of democracy is a welcome step in moving beyond 'exclusive' models of democracy. The primacy of the ideal and practice of deliberation, however, remains in their argument for the role of self-interest, fair bargaining, negotiation on the basis that 'they can and must be justified deliberatively' (Mansbridge et al., 2010: 64).

The second trend attempts to bridge the gap between ideal and practice by 'sequencing'. Authors in this mode include Goodin (2005: 194) who argues for 'a staged deliberative process', which allows for the pluralism of different forms of deliberation in different forums, and Landwehr (2010: 118) who proposes a 'cyclical and combinatory model of democratic decision-making' in which 'discussion, deliberation, bargaining and debate fulfil complementary functions'. Bächtiger et al. (2010) attempt to strengthen the empirical usefulness of deliberative democracy by finding a third way between two ideal types. They regard Type 1 deliberative democracy, exemplified by Habermas's theory of communicative action, as too narrow while they regard Type 2 deliberative democracy, exemplified by writers such as Young (2002) and Mansbridge (1999: 2010), as too broad. For them, a 'via media' can be achieved by means of an 'integrative approach' which would draw on elements of both Type 1 and Type 2 deliberation. This would occur via 'a sequential approach whereby debates and communication processes are partitioned in smaller sequences ... we would expect that different sequences fulfil different deliberative virtues' (Bächtiger et al., 2010: 55). Sequencing is a useful approach but it, too, rests on the assumption that deliberation should be accorded primacy over other democratic ideals and practices.

Attempts to bridge the gap between ideal and practice are fruitful and they have contributed significantly to recent developments in deliberative democracy. This chapter, however, takes a different tack. It argues that the usefulness of bridging the gap between ideal and practice is determined, to some extent at least, by the ideal and the practice in question. With regard to the ideal, this chapter, following Kohn (2000), questions the primacy of the ideal of deliberation as the normative basis for functioning democracies. With regard to practice, as will be discussed in the next section, this chapter questions what we can learn from empirical work which focuses almost entirely on micro-deliberative experiments which are often relatively isolated from the real world of politics in which they take place.

Macro or micro – that is the question?

The case study upon which this chapter is based corresponds to what Hendriks labels a macro approach to deliberative democracy. Hendriks distinguishes between two streams of thought in deliberative democracy, each of which envisages a different role for civil society. For Hendriks (2006: 491) micro-theories of deliberative democracy are those that focus on civil society actors who 'take on communicative forms of action through collaborating with the state' through mechanisms such as citizens' juries or deliberative polls, while 'macro-accounts are concerned with the messy forms of deliberation that take place in the public sphere. Here the focus is on how informal, open and unstructured deliberation in civil society can shape public opinion and, in turn, political institutions.'

For a while now the micro-theorists have been winning the day, with empirical literature focusing more on deliberative experiments such as citizens' juries, planning cells and deliberation days than on macro deliberation in the public sphere. Such micro-deliberative experiments have tended overwhelmingly to be consultative rather than binding upon policy officials (Ryfe, 2005: 61), and empirical studies have shown overwhelmingly that contextual variables are highly significant in determining the advantages and disadvantages of deliberation in these micro settings (Delli Carpini et al., 2004). This growth in the academic analysis of micro experiments is also matched by the growth of a 'consultation industry' and a 'deliberative profession' with its conferences, training and formal networks. (Carson and Hendriks, 2008: 300–2) Carson and Hendriks (2008: 294) highlight the commercialisation and professionalisation of deliberative practice, particularly micro deliberation, and write that 'Along with other community consultation activities, deliberative procedures have become a market commodity that are bought and sold by governments and political organizations.'

While such micro experiments have their place, the danger is that the more specialised and professionalised they become, the less able they are to shed light on the quality of functioning democracies in any wider sense. (But see Chapter 10, 'Mini-publics: issues and cases', by Stephen Elstub.) In particular, micro-deliberative experiments represent a shift away from the original premise of deliberative democracy as conceptualised by Habermas which accorded the public sphere its prominent role in democratic politics, 'namely that of forming public opinion and will on matters of common concern' (McAfee, 2000: 96). Carson and Hendriks agree that a 'fundamental risk for the commercialization of deliberative democracy is that the meaning and practice of public deliberation is reduced to one-off procedures'. (2008: 307–8)

The justification for a macro approach in this chapter, therefore, is that it allows us to explore discourse in the public sphere: in other words, the 'insisted spaces' of democracy in contrast to the particular and often artificially created instances of deliberation which Carson and Hendriks (2008) label the 'invited spaces' of deliberative democracy. In particular, its focus is justified by an attempt to work from practice to theory by taking on Blaug's (1997: 116) suggestion that critical theory should 'inspect the problems of democracy from the point of view of participants in a practical discourse'.

The place of conflict

Mouffe criticises deliberative democracy for not taking seriously the paradox at the heart of democracy which results from the tension between the two distinct logics of liberal democracy. The liberal tradition, with its emphasis on the rule of law, human rights and individual liberties, exists in constant tension with the democratic tradition which gives primacy to equality and popular sovereignty. For Mouffe (2000: 50) the fact that 'liberal democracy results from the articulation of two logics which are incompatible in the last instance' produces 'the conflictual nature of politics and the ineradicability of antagonism'. Mouffe (2000: 7) argues that it is conflict in this constitutive sense that the 'consensus model of democracy', which underpins deliberative democracy and Third Way politics, is unable to grasp.

Conflict is understood here in the sense advocated by Mouffe as something which is 'ineradicable' because it is 'constitutive *at the conceptual level* of the very nature of modern democracy' (Mouffe, 2000: 19; italics in the original). Nevertheless, it is argued that the tension between liberalism and democracy needs to be specified more clearly than occurs in Mouffe's discussion. In particular, liberalism as a political form of society, whose principles such as the rule of law and individual liberties are necessary for any version of democracy to be possible, needs to be distinguished from liberalism as an economic system where social inequality as a result of the market conflicts with democratic principles of equality. (See also Chapter 2, 'Inequality and deliberative democracy', by Peter McLaverty.) Thus, *pace* Mouffe, this chapter argues that it is not helpful to define liberal democracy as 'a political form of society that is defined exclusively at the level of the political, leaving aside its possible articulation with an economic system'. (Mouffe, 2000: 18) By contrast, it is the articulation of democracy with capitalism that explains what Walzer (1999: 67; italics in the original) describes as 'the permanence of conflict' in liberal democratic politics which results from the 'endless repetition' of the 'story of the establishment *and partial disestablishment* of inequality'. Streeck (2011: 6) similarly points to 'the normal condition of democratic capitalism' as 'ruled by an endemic conflict between capitalist markets and democratic politics'. Streeck's (2012: 63–4) sequential description of the ways in which the tension between democracy and capitalism 'had been successively displaced by an unsustainable process of "borrowing from the future", decade by decade: from the inflation of the 1970s, through the public debt of the 1980s, to the private debt of the 1990s and early 2000s, finally exploding in the financial crisis of 2008' can be questioned. His argument that the political tools available to manage the tension between democratic politics and capitalism have become less successful, however, is convincing. As the case study will show, politicians are struggling to respond to the 15-M movement precisely because its critique focuses on the weakness of the political system of democracy vis-à-vis the strength of the economic system of liberalism.

The 15-M movement – *los indignados*

The inspiration behind the 15-M movement comes from numerous sources. It has links to movements such as *Vde Vivienda*, which began in 2006 in support of the right to reasonably priced housing, and *Precarios en movimiento*, a loose network of groups struggling against the lack of certainty (*precariedad*) in employment, housing, pensions, health and education. Two movements provide more recent antecedents: *Juventud Sin Futuro* (Youth without a Future), which coalesced in Madrid's universities in April 2011 around the slogan 'no house, no job, no pension, no fear', and *Democracia Real Ya* (DRY – Real Democracy Now), which is 'critical of the lack of real democracy and the tendency towards an institutionalised bi-partism' in Spain (Alcaide, 2011). A pamphlet by Stéphane Hessel, *Get Indignant*, and a book entitled *React: 10 Reasons why you should act in the face of the economic, political and social crisis*, provided inspiration while, months before the movement formed, activity on the Internet in blogs and social networks calling for solutions to the crisis was high. Finally, the Arab Spring and demonstrations by young people in Greece and Portugal inspired young people in Spain.

On 15 May 2011, demonstrations occurred in around fifty Spanish cities organised entirely over the internet by DRY in protest against the economic crisis, the austerity measures imposed by the socialist government, youth unemployment which is estimated to be as high as 45 per cent, and the political system in the light of the local and regional elections on 22 May. The arrest of twenty-four demonstrators at the end of the march in Madrid led to a spontaneous sit-down on the evening of 15 May in Madrid's main square, the Plaza del Sol. On Monday, Facebook, Twitter and other social media were used to call for a mass sit-down that same evening which then converted into a more permanent camp.

The level of self-organisation during the occupation of the Plaza del Sol was impressive. According to participants, there were ordered alleyways between stands and tents in the square.[1] The square, and the eight donated portable lavatories, were kept spotless so that the local council was not required to service the square (Saleh and Pérez-Lanzac, 2011). Solar panels provided energy and computers were donated to help participants sustain the movement. Various committees were created, including food, infrastructure, communication, internal co-ordination, legal advice and cleaning (Barroso, 2011). These were supplemented by working groups on diverse issues from feminism, culture, health and education to spirituality, respect and economy. Suggestion boxes all over the square were emptied daily: the suggestions were sorted, considered and sometimes adopted. Donated food and water were dispensed free every day. No alcohol was consumed and the movement's 'Respect Commission' ensured that there were no disorderly or violent incidents.

The 15-M movement subsequently decided to abandon the square and continue through a mix of demonstrations, other protest activities and the sporadic occupation of public squares across Spain, including the Plaza del Sol, which remains symbolic for the movement. Mass demonstrations on 19 June 2011 were followed by many groups deciding to march on foot through Spain, stopping in village and town squares to explain their ideas and discuss them with residents. Marches from the north, the north-east, the north-west, the east, the south and the south-east (15-M News Special: the 'Arrival of the Popular Indignant March') converged once more on Madrid's Plaza de Sol on 27 July, bringing with them the experiences of those they had talked with along the way. Inspired by the 15-M movement, protests took place internationally on 15 October 2011 with 951 cities in eighty-two countries taking part (Galarraga, 2011).

The movement still holds weekly assemblies in Madrid's Plaza del Sol in addition to assemblies at the neighbourhood level across Spain. It has established a virtual community which unites all the different websites set up under the 15-M movement under the main portal of www.madrid.tomalaplaza.net (Muñoz Lara, 2011). There are three blogs: madrid.tomalaplaza.net (providing information about the Sol General Assembly and its different commissions and working groups); actasmadrid.tomalaplaza.net (publishes the acts of the general assemblies, commissions and working groups); and madrid.tomalosbarrios.net (provides information about the assemblies taking place in Madrid's neighbourhoods and municipalities). There are two twitter accounts – @acampadasol (in Spanish) and @takethesquare (in English) – and three Facebook communities – Acampada Sol (on the Sol occupation and its assemblies), Spanish Revolution (on the movement in general) and Take the Square (on the internationalisation of the movement).

15-M – deliberation in the public sphere?

The 15-M movement illustrates Habermas's (1996) two-track democracy where public opinion is formed discursively in the public sphere through public dialogue and debate about matters of collective concern which mirror people's personal life experiences within private spheres. In turn, this opinion puts pressure on more formal deliberative bodies, namely legislatures, where the discursively formed public opinion is formed into public will in the shape of laws. In terms of the discursive formation of public opinion in the public sphere, various characteristics of the 15-M movement stand out.

First, the movement used the Internet to constitute itself and to constitute a new public sphere. The Internet is its main communication method and space.

According to Saíz, on the afternoon of the 15 May demonstrations #15mani was the third most important conversation topic on Twitter in the world. In the days following the demonstrations, #nonosvamos (we're not leaving), #acampadasol (sit-down in the Plaza del Sol) or #spanishrevolution were the most popular topics on Twitter worldwide (2011). The movement also has its own channel on YouTube – Spanishrevolutionsol – which provides information about the movement as well as educational videos. It is estimated that DRY, one of the key organisations underpinning the 15-M movement, has 430,000 followers on Facebook and 120,000 followers on Twitter (Elola, 2012a) while 1,037 collectives contribute content to the tomalaplaza.net website (Elola, 2012b). Caution is necessary, however, in extrapolating the impact of the movement from its Internet presence. Gladwell's (2010: 49) reminder that the Internet 'makes it easier for activists to express themselves, and harder for that expression to have any impact' is prescient. The 15-M movement, however, does not rely solely on virtual communication, thereby avoiding the problem that 'the platforms of social media are built around weak ties' (Gladwell, 2010: 45). During the occupation of the Sol square, the different committees met at 1 p.m., followed by a general assembly and public demonstration of protest at 8 p.m. every evening. People gathered to hear the assembly opinions and news and decisions were made by majority. Everyone had the right to speak and to vote but not to veto.[2]

The movement placed great emphasis on getting its message heard and in getting it heard accurately. In terms of ensuring that its message has resonance, it is no coincidence that, in addition to committees organised around practical tasks such as cleaning and food, other committees included: a communication committee to manage the movement's social networks and voice; a dissemination committee to explain the movement to others; and a materials committee to produce banners (Pérez-Lanzac, 2011). In short, of the eight committees originally organised, three concerned communication. In addition, spokespersons were elected to speak to the media in a co-ordinated way as well as to anyone who approached the camp to find out what was going on. The democratic way in which each of the thirty-six spokespersons take turns to represent the 'public' face of the movement avoids anyone becoming too much of a 'protagonist' with regard to public opinion and democratises the power to communicate (González, 2011). The publication of its message via social network sites is complemented by its message in physical form via banners and a newspaper. The last is published twice weekly with the exhortation to 'Print, Distribute, Participate'. The reach of the movement was beyond doubt: according to an Ipsos Public Affairs survey, 78 per cent of Spaniards were aware of the 15-M movement and between six and 8.5 million Spaniards claimed to have participated in the movement either by visiting one of its camps, attending an assembly or joining one of its demonstrations (El País, 2011b).

With regard to ensuring the accuracy of its message, the movement analysed media reports to correct misinformation or bias. For example, the slogan '*No les votes*' (Don't vote for them) was interpreted by many in the mainstream media as a call to abstention when, in fact, it was a call to not vote for parties whom voters feel have not represented them (Limón, 2011). On the day of the 2011 municipal and regional elections, DRY issued a communiqué to clarify to citizens that they had never advocated abstention nor had they called for people to spoil their ballot paper or to vote for any particular party. The communiqué said that:

> *Democracia Real Ya* encourages people to inform themselves and to decide for themselves who to vote for according to their ideology because being a plural platform the diversity of voting intentions is also wide. Our aim is to improve our current electoral system, but until this model changes, we believe that each person should participate in whatever way they feel is best. (http://www.democraciarealya.es/presensa/ 2011)

Second, this was not just a dialogue among young people. Public dialogue about matters of collective concern which mirror people's personal life experiences occurred throughout Spain as the movement passed through towns and villages across the peninsula. In a Habermasian sense, the movement has shaped public opinion and consciousness. Opinion polls indicate broad social support for the movement because it reflects the concerns of ordinary people. In the June 2011 Metroscopia Barometer for *El País* newspaper, 66 per cent felt sympathy with the movement. Though this differed between right-wing PP and left-wing PSOE voters with 46 per cent of the former expressing sympathy with the movement compared to 78 per cent of the latter, that 46 per cent of PP voters expressed sympathy with the movement suggests that this is not a purely left-wing movement. A high 88 per cent felt that the indignant were right while only 9 per cent felt they lacked arguments; 84 per cent felt that the movement was concerned with problems that affected citizens compared to 70 per cent who felt that their interests were not represented by any political party (Garea, 2011b).

It is this broad support that has helped the movement to put pressure on the legislature in the way that Habermas suggests. Though the direct link between actions taken by the legislature and the influence of the movement is hard to verify, three examples suggest that politicians were being forced to heed the public opinion which the movement helped to form and to shape. First, one of the responses of the Socialist Party to the movement's pressure is the idea of 'Seat 351'. This is the suggestion to have an additional seat in the Spanish lower house (currently it has 350) for popular representation. The aim of Seat 351 is to allow citizens to intervene in the Congress plenary as representatives of those signing popular legislative initiatives (Garea, 2011a). This idea has been replicated in the Andalusian Parliament which proposes an additional 'Seat 110'. Perhaps of more significance is the adoption by the Andalusian Parliament of the movement's proposal to reduce the number of signatures required to set in motion a popular legislative initiative. Currently in Andalusía, the number of signatures required is 75,000 while the 15-M movement want it reducing to 41,000 (El País, 2011a).

Second, it also seems to be the case that the public opinion created by the movement put pressure on the legislature to be more transparent and open. On 8 September 2011, details of the income and assets of 614 MPs and senators were made public. Information about MPs' salaries, investments, properties, pension schemes, cars and parking spaces was disclosed. The socialist government 'hoped that the measure would help to restore credibility to the nation's ruling elite after a series of corruption scandals' (Keeley, 2011).

Third, in the state of the nation debate on 28 June 2011, the Spanish prime minister announced measures to help those people affected by negative equity who end up losing their homes while still in debt to the banks (Congreso de los Diputados, 2011). This was seen as an effort to appease the movement whose support base includes movements against evictions, such as the Plataforma de Afectados por la Hipoteca (Platform for those Affected by Mortgages – PAH). Continued pressure from the PAH and the 15-M movement contributed to making the reform of the current mortgage law a key theme in the electoral campaign prior to the 20 November 2011 general election and obliged all the parties to position themselves with regard to this issue (Blanchar, 2011).

Problems of democracy

The 15-M movement highlights a number of problems of democracy from the point of view of the participants. The first is one of misinformation about the movement and the difficulties the movement experiences in getting its messages across accurately faced with hegemonic discourses which prescribe what can be talked about, the terms in which things can be talked about and even what can be imagined. As Fraser argues (1992: 139), 'The public sphere produces consent via circulation of discourses that construct the common sense of the day and present the existing order as natural and/or just, but not simply as a ruse that is imposed.' For movements like the 15-M, it is important to challenge the prevailing 'common sense' which, in their case, means not accepting as given the hegemonic neo-liberal discourse that there is no alternative to the current economic crisis but to institute austerity measures that hit the most vulnerable the hardest. By refusing to accept this premise as given, however, it is all too easy for detractors to portray the movement as simply youthful optimism. Niall Ferguson labelled the spread of demonstrations often, but not solely, by young people across various parts of the world as a 'global temper tantrum' (Ferguson, 2011). An alternative strategy of the right wing in Spain is to portray the movement as part of a left-wing conspiracy to pervert the electoral process. According to Esperanza Aguirre, the right-wing Popular Party's President of the Autonomous Community of Madrid, the Left is trying to 'manipulate this movement against the PP' (Cué, 2011). What both of these critiques evidence is the paternalism displayed towards movements organised predominantly, but by no means exclusively, by young people. They also miss the fact that, though young people have been the protagonists of the 15-M demonstrations and subsequent camps, they receive broad popular support, not just in the opinion polls, as mentioned above, but through the various sympathetic movements such as the PAH which represent many different age groups. DRY is successful precisely because it combines over two hundred different organisations (http://www.democraciarealya.es/adhesiones/2011). Many older people, from fifty upwards, joined the Sol occupation, not least because those with children want their offspring to have a better future (Junquera, 2011).

Another common strategy is to accuse the movement of failing to come up with concrete proposals or to portray the movement as simply 'anti-system', implying that it is a negative rather than constructive movement. On the one hand, this is erroneous. Though heterogeneous in nature, the movement has some common themes and demands as well as concrete proposals. Three demands have gained consensus from all of the assemblies throughout Spain: a more participatory democracy, political transparency and reform of the electoral law (*15M News* 2, 2011b; author's translation). Other common demands include: greater control over the banks, quality public services, sustainability and accessible housing. They propose the nationalisation of financial systems, higher taxes on the wealthy, the control of tax evasion and fraud, investment in social services, education and the environment in order to create jobs, and the guarantee of a minimum income and an increase in the minimum wage (Limón, 2011). As Artal (2011) argues, 'The manifesto of the 15-M movement doesn't demand much more than what is laid down as rights in the Spanish constitution.' On the other hand, accusing the movement of failing to come up with concrete proposals is to miss the point that 'One of the activists' goals is to make us wonder about what we are doing, to rupture a stream of thought, rather than to weave an argument' (Young, 2001: 687). The irony of this accusation is also not lost on the movement which questioned why 'Those who have never asked us anything now ask us for proposals' (*15M News* 1, 2011a; author's translation).

A second problem of democracy which arises from the experience of the 15-M movement is the difficulty, not just of getting their demands heard but of getting their demands represented accurately. One of the responses of the Socialist Party to the movement, 'Seat 351' discussed earlier, highlights the gap between the movement and the political class. In response to the movement's demand for a more participatory democracy, the Socialist Party candidate for the general election in November 2011, Alfredo Pérez Rubalcaba wanted the PSOE electoral programme to include methods to improve citizen participation in politics. To do this, his team worked on the idea of 'Seat 351' which would allow citizens to intervene in the Congress plenary as representatives of those signing popular legislative initiatives (Garea, 2011a). This rather misses the point. An additional seat within an institution that the 15-M movement feels does not represent them at all is not what the movement means by a more participatory democracy. One of the key slogans of the movement is 'no, no, no they don't represent us' in protest against a Spanish political system which they feel is corrupt and dominated by two parties with no room for alternative ideas. An additional seat in Congress for citizen representatives will not solve the wider political problems identified by the 15-M movement and ignores their sugges- tions on electoral reform, for example, which would have a far greater impact on the nature of democracy in Spain.

The future of the 15-M movement

At the time of writing (May 2012), the 15-M movement was planning to celebrate its first-year anniversary with a march on Madrid and a temporary camp in the emblematic Plaza de Sol. It is the case, however, that the move- ment has declined in visibility a year after its explosion into Spain's public sphere. Those who attend the weekly assemblies in the Plaza de Sol now number in their hundreds rather than their thousands but the 15-M movement continues to work at the level of the neighbourhood and with other collectives to address contemporary problems. The San Blas assembly in Madrid, for example, has created a 'Time Bank' called the *Sinergías Cooperativa San Blas* which allows neighbours to exchange services among themselves without money; the Concepción neighbourhood in Madrid organises an exchange market every Sunday while a debtors' co-operative in Catalonia (*Cooperativas de Autofinanciación Social en Red*) brings together debtors to respond collectively to creditors. All of these co-operatives are the result of initiatives from the 15-M neighbourhood assemblies (Elola, 2012b). Other *indignados*, for example, now work with the PAH to stop people being evicted from their homes; others are involved in forming new movements to help people who can no longer pay their increas- ingly expensive rents (Saleh, 2011) or in the Oficina Precaria to help people in precarious employment situations (Alvarez, 2012). Some of *los indignados* argue that 'the 15-M cannot disappear because it's not an organization but a politicisation of daily life' and that 'We are going slowly because we're going far' (Suleng, 2012). It can be argued that the strength of the 15-M movement is in the visibility which it has given to other long-standing organisations, such as the PAH, whose spokesperson argued that 'the support of the 15-M changed everything overnight. We saw how a river of people signed up to our cause' (Elola, 2012b). Others within the 15-M movement lament its horizontal nature which they regard as a block on the movement's capacity for action. Some of those originally behind the 15-M, for example, have constituted DRY as a not-for-profit organisation to 'exercise co-ordinated pressure on the institutions' in recognition of the need for a more traditional form of organisation to realise their aim of 'transforming [last year's] indignation into a constructive energy capable of generating real changes' (EFE, 2012). The widely predicted victory of the right-wing Popular Party in the November 2011 general election could also be interpreted as a sign of the weak impact of the 15-M movement on Spanish politics. A high 73 per cent of those consulted in a Metroscopia opinion poll in October 2001 said that the 15-M protests would not influence their vote in the November general election (El País, 2011c). Yet another interpretation is possible. Abstention increased by 3 per cent. The reform of the electoral law has been one of the most oft-repeated demands of the 15-M movement. Any of their proposals for reform, such as an alternative to the D'Hondt method of distributing seats, a larger Congress, the use of the autonomous community, rather than the province, as electoral district, would have meant that the PP would not have obtained an absolute majority and the configuration of the parliament after the 20 November elections would have been very different (El País, 2011d). Moreover, the movement continues to chime with public opinion. In a poll conducted for the BBC World Service on economic fairness, there has been a dramatic worsening of views in Spain. In 2009, 66 per cent felt that economic benefits and burdens have not been fairly shared but this figure had increased to 92 per cent by 2012 (Globescan, 2012). In a Metroscopia poll in October 2011, 73 per cent of Spaniards consulted considered that *los indignados* are right. Among socialist voters, this figure was 79 per cent while it was 55 per cent among right-wing PP voters. Eighty-one per cent of Spaniards in the same poll believe that it is markets not states that really wield power. Though only 20 per cent of those consulted had participated in a protest organised by the 15-M movement and only 8 per cent had participated in one of its assemblies, 63 per cent still felt the movement should continue (El País, 2011c).

Lessons from the 15-M movement

The problems of democracy in practice encountered by the 15-M movement bring to our attention two areas that are not accorded sufficient attention by theorists of deliberative democracy. The first difficulty of challenging hegemonic discourses in the public sphere reminds us that, in addition to attempting to bridge the gap between ideal and practice, we would do well to question the ideal of deliberation itself. The second difficulty encountered by the 15-M movement of getting their voices heard and getting them heard accurately reminds us that often much has to occur before deliberation can even begin. This is the questioning of the practice of deliberation as a means of enacting democracy.

The centrality of both the ideal and the practice of deliberation in theorising about democracy is inadequately questioned because insufficient attention is paid to the ineradicability of conflict in liberal democracies. Conflict is inherent in liberal democratic life not just because of the plurality of ideas of the common good to which Rawls's public reason and Habermas's communicative action are posited as the solution. Conflict is inherent because 'liberal democracy is not democracy per se but is a historically specific form of democracy which capitalism has both facilitated and constrained' (Blakeley, 2005: 192). It is the tension between the formal political equality of the public sphere and the inequalities within the private sphere arising from the exploitative relations between capital and labour which both enabled the unique formula of liberal democracy while demarcating its limits (Wood, 1995). This tension makes conflict the defining feature of liberal democratic politics (Blakeley, 2005: 192–3) and questions the centrality of deliberation as both ideal and practice. Deliberative theorists, however, tend to dismiss conflict too readily or try to adapt deliberative democracy better to accommodate or resolve it. According to Mouffe (2000: 93), this is because deliberative theorists, including both Rawls and Habermas, aim to secure a stronger link between democracy and liberalism and, by so doing, deny 'the fundamental tension between the logic of democracy and the logic of liberalism'.

It is surprising that more work has not been done to question the primacy of the ideal of deliberation, given that we know from Foucault (1990: 92–3), for example, that there is no such thing as a neutral discourse and that power relations of some kind are constitutive of all discourses. Thus, the charge is not just that deliberative democracy falters because of the gap between the ideal and the reality of functioning democracies but that the ideal itself is flawed. Kohn argues that there is no reason why we should view deliberation as the normative basis of democratic theory because, even under ideal conditions, language is not fully transparent in the way that Habermas argues. For Kohn, (2000: 408–9) 'Discursive democracy's emphasis on communication as the universal basis of democratic politics … hides the fact that even linguistic competence is hierarchically distributed and implicated in the reproduction of dominant exclusions.' It is worth remembering that deliberation was core to the exclusionary democratic politics practised in Athens, and that Aristotle ([350 BC] 1962: 28) used 'the power of reasoned speech' as a way of marking off man as a political animal from other non-political animals which, at the time, included women, foreigners and slaves.

In an imaginary dialogue between an activist and a deliberativist, Young (2001: 683–5) argues that advocates of deliberative democracy have no satisfactory answer to the criticism that the starting premises for deliberation are often *Of course!* unacceptable because they accept as given existing structural constraints. For movements like 15-M, one of the hardest struggles is challenging the hegemonic neo-liberal discourse which accepts as given existing structural constraints that are construed as 'common-sense'. One can argue that the circularity of Rawls's and Habermas's form of argumentation helps to construct this 'common sense': arguing that political liberal principles would be chosen by rational individuals, in idealised conditions like Rawls's veil of ignorance or Habermas's ideal speech situation, presupposes that such rational individuals are by definition those who would accept the principles of political liberalism (Rawls, 1997: 775–7; Mouffe, 2000: 26, 64). This makes imagining, let alone questioning, 'unreasonable' alternatives difficult.

What the 15-M movement also shows us is the range of political tools needed to challenge entrenched power and this casts doubt on the centrality of deliberation as practice. The 15-M movement engaged in and fostered deliberation in the public sphere in Spain but it also engaged in mobilisation and collective action. In Habermasian terms, the 15-M movement draws not only on communicative rationality but also on instrumental and strategic rationalities. Both Kohn (2000: 425) and Bohman (1994: 927) remark that empirical studies show that a great deal of collective organisation and mobilisation usually occurs prior to success in gaining public attention and being able to influence the behaviour of formal institutions. In short, 'Deliberation by itself is not enough' (Kohn, 2000: 425).

Walzer and Kohn argue for an approach to democratic theory and practice which reserves an important place for deliberation but does not place it at the centre of either theory or practice. Kohn (2000: 424) argues that 'we must evaluate deliberation as one of a variety of possible procedures of interpreting and realizing the normative core of democracy' but we should also acknowledge that 'building the material and ideological resources to challenge existing exclusions demands the whole repertoire of tactics – from canvassing to consciousness raising, fundraising to festivals – developed by contemporary social movements'. Walzer (1999: 67) includes deliberation on his list of activities that a democratic political process requires but argues that it doesn't have an 'independent place' because 'deliberation's proper place is dependent on other activities that it doesn't constitute or control'.

Both Kohn and Walzer question the centrality of deliberation because politics is inherently conflictual. Kohn (2000: 425) argues that advocates of deliberative democracy tend to ignore the 'crucial dimensions of mobilization and power' and Walzer (1999: 66) argues that 'political life is not merely adversarial but inherently and permanently conflictual'. For Walzer, therefore, deliberation is insufficient to deal with the 'permanence of conflict' and the 'prevalence of inequalities' in political life: 'popular organizations and mobilizations' are the only way to continue to fight and to oppose entrenched inequalities.

Even allowing for theories of deliberative democracy which have moved away from the ideal of reaching consensus, such as that propounded by Mansbridge et al., (2010), conflict still tends to be played down because insufficient attention is paid to the tension inherent in the unique formula of liberalism and democracy. This is not just the tension, which Mouffe (2000) identifies, between liberalism's stress on individual liberties and democracy's emphasis on equality. It is the 'endemic conflict between capitalist markets and democratic politics' (Streeck, 2011: 6). Marx celebrated the partial 'political emancipation' of liberal democracy and recognised that the democratic vote was of real value to the working class, but he also recognised that 'the freedom and equality won in the political sphere were limited by the fact that they left untouched the lack of freedom and equality in the economic and social spheres' (Blakeley, 2005: 198). Thus, for Marx, 'the social antagonisms that survive political emancipation cannot be resolved by *pure reason* or the vote of representatives within this particular emancipated sphere' (Marx, 1973: 13; my italics added). Faced with this conflictual nature of politics, one is left wondering what deliberation can offer us which other, more collective, modes of acting politically cannot.

Herein lies the rub. As Walzer (1999: 68–9) argues 'Deliberation is not an activity for the demos.' His argument is not that ordinary men and women lack the capacity to reason but rather that they are unable to deliberate together in great numbers. Yet it is precisely this collective dimension that is crucial in challenging entrenched power. It is worth remembering in this regard Therborn's (1977: 29) analysis of the establishment of bourgeois democracy which showed that the democratic element of the liberal democratic equation was achieved long after the gains of liberalism and only following 'mass struggles of varying degrees of violence and protractedness'. Therborn (1977: 29) highlighted the vital role of the labour movement in the struggle for democracy and thus urged a focus on 'the conditions favouring popular struggle'. This focus is missing from accounts of deliberative democracy. Calhoun highlights Habermas's neglect of social movements and argues 'the absence of social movements from Habermas' account ... reflects an inattention to agency, to the struggles by which both the public sphere and its participants are actively made and remade' (Calhoun, 1996: 37). It is not just an inattention to agency per se, however, which is critical: more specifically, the absence of social movements from Habermas's account is indicative of a loss of faith in *collective* agency whereby any earlier notion of a 'macrosocial subject' is supplemented with the idea of 'subjectless communications' (Leet, 1998: 91).

Without an attention to collective agency, however, we do not know how, in what conditions and in what ways civil society can develop 'impulses with enough vitality to bring conflict from the periphery into the centre of the political system' (Habermas, 1996: 330). This is the problem of transmission. Deliberative theorists trying to flesh out Habermas's conceptualisation of the move from opinion formation to will formation are vague in how this can occur. Mansbridge (1999: 212), for example, uses an expansive concept of a deliberative system which pays 'as much attention to citizens' everyday talk as to formal deliberation in public arenas'. The relationship between the two, however, depends on the vague concept of 'influence' whereby 'the different parts of the deliberative system mutually influence one another in ways that are not easy to parse out' (1999: 213). Hendriks (2006: 499-500), on the other hand, proposes an 'integrated deliberative system' which would 'celebrate the multiplicity of deliberative venues' and, importantly, would 'foster the connections between these venues'. The micro (formal modes of deliberation) is connected with the macro (informal modes of deliberation) through what she terms 'mixed discursive spheres that combine formal and informal modes of deliberation'. Quite how these mixed spheres serve to connect the micro and macro deliberative worlds, however, seems as vague as the modes of influence in Mansbridge's continuum.

Deliberative theory is not able to tell us much about how, when and under what circumstances the public sphere is capable of detecting social problems, sharpening them into a 'consciousness of crisis', and introducing them into the parliamentary context 'in a way that *disrupts* the latter's routines' (Habermas, 1996: 357–8; italics in the original). It is not enough to rely on Habermas's claim that 'in a perceived crisis situation, the *actors in civil society* thus far neglected in our scenario *can* assume a surprisingly active and momentous role' (Habermas, 1996: 380; italics in the original). To explain how this can happen we need to look to beyond the ideal and practice of deliberative democracy, to other ways of doing democratic politics. In particular, we need to turn to social movement theory and concepts like Tarrow's (1994) political opportunity structure to understand how, in certain circumstances, the kind of move from opinion formation to will formation can take place.

Questioning the centrality of the norm and practice of deliberation also points towards 'a way of thinking about democracy' which is 'reflexive' and 'open-ended'. Moves towards sequencing or combining, by some theorists of deliberative democracy, are steps in the right direction away from discrete 'models of deliberative democracy' but such approaches still leave unquestioned the primacy of deliberative democracy. (See also Chapter 4, '"Scaling up" deliberation', by André Bächtiger and Alda Wegmann.) Saward's (2003) approach goes further. His 'reflexive' approach, which consists of combinations of principles of democracy, devices which enact these principles, and stages of democratic decision-making, does not prejudge which principles, devices and institutions should receive priority at any given stage of the democratic decision-making process. Instead, he urges theorists to 'be content with the contingency and dynamism of meaning and reference' that a reflexive approach requires (Saward, 2003: 162). This means that we should not give priority to deliberative or aggregative mechanisms but, rather, we should see 'principles, mechanisms and institutions' as open to constant change and adjustment of their meaning and importance' (Saward, 2003: 161). Such reflexivity and eschewal of prioritising is borne out by contemporary political struggles such as the 15-M movement

in Spain. The obstacles they face in challenging hegemonic discourses, which make envisaging any alternative to current political and economic models difficult, show that such struggles require all of the principles, devices and institutions of democratic politics they can lay their hands on, and there is no reason to accord normative priority to any particular one. At a time when politics seems to be in retreat as national governments respond to the imperatives of the global financial markets rather than voters, Streeck (2011: 28) provides a powerful reminder that 'street riots and popular insurrection may be the last remaining mode of political expression for those devoid of market power'.

Conclusion

Conflict is constitutive of politics because of the tension inherent in the relationship between democracy and capitalism. The struggles of the 15-M movement in Spain are testament to this 'permanence of conflict' and 'prevalence of inequalities' (Walzer, 1999). The 15-M movement highlights the need to be open and reflexive about which principles, devices and institutions to prioritise at any given moment. Reflexivity allows the strategic selection of those devices that might advance particular causes in a given context, perhaps by prompting or forcing deliberation on a hidden or suppressed issue where the political system seems sclerotic or stagnant with respect to new needs and claims. This is true for all political struggles but it is particularly true for those that question the very relationship between political forms of democracy and economic forms of capitalism and question the 'common-sense' view that 'this is as good as it gets'. Democratic theory should be concerned with the democratic process as a whole and, therefore, with the relationship of its parts to the whole. There is no reason why deliberation cannot be one of these parts and a valued one at that but it is not the whole.

Notes

1. Private e-mail communication with the author.
2. Private e-mail communication with the author.

[handwritten margin notes:] Assumes an ongoing capitalist context.

☆ Two levels of deliberation
✗ Both constrained/repressed by a capitalist economy and resulting society.

CHAPTER 2

Inequality and deliberative democracy

Peter McLaverty

As is clear from the Introduction and other chapters in this book, the meaning of deliberative democracy has been debated, deliberated over and contested over the years. Debates about the meaning of the concept continue. I shall not consider the arguments in this chapter, however. Instead, I shall summarise what I think are the core features of deliberative democracy and the areas where I think there continue to be debates and differences among scholars of deliberative democracy. This will establish the background for a consideration of the relationship between deliberative democracy and (in)equality.

It is probably fair to say that there is much agreement among writers that deliberative democracy represents a situation where participants can be swayed by the reasons, arguments and justifications of others, and participants give reasons, arguments or justifications in support of their positions in a reciprocal manner. There are debates, however, about the role that 'non-cognitive' reasons and emotions should play within deliberative democracy. Deliberation, as opposed to democratic deliberation, does not necessitate inclusion of all opinions on the subject under deliberation and groups who will be affected. With deliberative democracy, however, the inclusion of all interests and opinions is generally seen as essential. Debates continue about whether deliberative democracy is compatible with self-interest and whether deliberative democracy demands consensus between participants, though most writers on deliberative democracy today would not regard consensus as an essential element of deliberative democracy (for a consideration of these issues see, for example, Mansbridge et al., 2010 and Thompson, 2008). There is another approach to deliberative democracy, based around the contestation of discourses. I shall look at this approach later in the chapter.

If core features of deliberative democracy include the giving of reasons, arguments and justifications for their opinions by participants in a 'political' interaction, in a reciprocal way, and a willingness to be swayed by the strength of the arguments presented by other participants; and if it is also based on the inclusion of all opinions and interests relevant to the subject, how does deliberative democracy relate to questions of inequality? To address this general issue, I shall consider a number of related questions. Can deliberative democracy hope to achieve the inclusiveness that it is seen as demanding, given that participation in political activities, such as voting to elect political representatives, in many countries, achieves figures far short of 100 per cent (IDEA International, 2009) and voting turnout often reflects major social differences between those who do and those who do not participate? This raises important issues of motivation. Why should those who currently benefit from 'non-deliberative' processes, in terms of the exercise of power and material advantage, agree to participate in processes of deliberative democracy that might threaten their exercise of power and the benefits that accrue from it? This raises questions about whether deliberative democracy can be institutionalised. If deliberative democracy is institutionalised, what guarantees can there be that the powerful in society will abide by the requirements of deliberative democracy in practice? Will deliberative democracy always work in favour of the educated and the articulate, those who know how to operate within the 'rules of the game', and against the interest of the less well educated, the inarticulate and those who feel uncomfortable with the deliberative democracy rules of the game? Would deliberative democracy, if fully instituted, demand too much of some social groups: for example, those in paid employment who also have caring responsibilities? Can deliberative democracy only be achieved if social justice and social equality exist? In the rest of this chapter, I shall consider these questions.

Can deliberative democracy achieve inclusivity?

Deliberative democracy is generally seen as demanding that all interests which will be affected by an issue and all opinions on the issue should be included. This is in line with the 'all-affected principle' which is seen by some as an essential element of democracy (cf. Fraser, 2005). It is argued, however, that this will never be achieved as some social groups will always participate more in politics than others. Turnout in 'political elections' can be used to support this contention. Let us take as an example the turnout in general elections in the United Kingdom. Based on a survey of citizen participation in Britain, Pattie, Seyd and Whiteley (2003: 632–3) argue that the 'well-resourced' (those with good educational qualifications and high incomes) participate more in formal politics (including in elections) and civil society activity than those who are 'less well resourced' (lack educational qualifications and have low incomes). Britain is not unusual in experiencing such outcomes. Similar outcomes occur in a number of other countries (see Dalton, 2006; Hay, 2007: 19–20). Pattie, Seyd and Whiteley (2004: 282) end their consideration of the conditions under which active citizenship can thrive by warning of the dangers extreme inequality presents to this. They argue:

> Civic values are best protected by an egalitarian ethic which emphasises social inclusion. The fact that everyone's vote counts the same in a democracy provides legitimacy to governance. If individuals are marginalised in a system that depends increasingly on financial power in the marketplace rather than voting

power in the *polis*, then citizenship will be fatally weakened. In an extreme case government itself will be seen as irrelevant in such a system, as the well resourced attempt to buy their way out of the insecurities produced by extreme inequality and social exclusion, and the excluded fight back against the injustices resulting from these developments.

This argument has relevance beyond voting in political elections and is potentially an important obstacle to the achievement of deliberative democracy. Inequality has grown around the world in recent years and, in some cases, considerably (cf. Therborn, 2006). Such a climate is hardly ideal for the advancement of deliberative democracy.

One possible way around the problem of the underrepresentation of individuals from certain social groups is to ensure that all affected interests and social groups, if not individuals, are represented. This is what citizens' juries and some other deliberative mechanisms try to achieve, in respect of social group representation, through the use of stratified random sampling. Ensuring that all opinions on a subject are represented is much more difficult, as people are not included because of their opinions but because of their social position. It might be argued that the use of experts and specialists to give information and opinions to jurors who can question the experts and specialists can ensure that all opinions on the subject are considered. This does not ensure, however, that, in their deliberations, jurors will give the same importance to all the views they hear. If none of the jurors initially supported an opinion, that opinion might not get much of a hearing in their subsequent deliberations even if the facilitator tried to ensure that this happened.

Why should the powerful support deliberative democracy?

If deliberative democracy is to mean more than the ad hoc use of citizens' juries, consensus conferences and citizens' assemblies to contribute to policy development on specific issues, then non-deliberative mechanisms in the public policy process will either have to be adapted, replaced or integrated into a system that is dominated overall by mechanisms that promote deliberative democracy. This raises issues about how this can be achieved in a society where there are substantial inequalities of power. Cohen and Rogers (2003) address this issue in their response to the case studies on Empowered Participatory Governance contained in Fung and Wright's book *Deepening Democracy*. They argue that, if power imbalances exist between participants, those with the greater power will be able to pressurise others to accept their view of the world (or the subject under discussion). Deliberation, where the views of all participants count equally, may not require complete equality of power between participants but large-scale inequalities of power may inevitably distort such deliberation. Political equality is widely seen as a crucial element of democracy. While there have been debates about whether political equality requires social equality, it has generally been accepted by scholars that liberal democracy can exist without social equality and that political equality can be divorced from wider social inequality. The work of Pattie et al. outlined above, however, and the arguments of Phillips (1999) give cause to question this. More specifically, the argument of Cohen and Rogers raises strong questions about whether deliberative democracy is achievable where there is large-scale social inequality. As Cohen and Rogers (2003: 248) put it, the powerful are unlikely to engage in deliberation:

> They will recognize, to paraphrase Hobbs, that reasons without the sword are just words with no force to tie anyone's hands. So actors with sufficient power to advance their aims without deliberating will not bother to deliberate. Or if for some reason they formally agree to deliberation, we can expect them only to offer 'reasons' for action that in fact are purely self-serving proposals.

Fung and Wright (2003a: 259–60) accept the force of the argument of Cohen and Rogers. They recognise that power inequalities can undermine deliberation. They, therefore, argue that for Empowered Participatory Governance (which can be seen as in line with deliberative democracy) to be successfully implemented, countervailing power needs to be in evidence. They say 'the key question, then, is whether or not it is plausible that the required kind of countervailing power can emerge in the contexts of EPG [Empowered Participatory Governance] institutions to enable them to function in a robust, sustainable manner'. They raise the question of whether the idea of countervailing power is compatible with ideas of deliberative democracy, as it is usually seen as based around the issuing of threats and the mobilisation of people in opposition, rather than the use of reason. They conclude, however, that countervailing power is compatible with ideas of deliberative democracy and that, indeed, EPG depends on it. They argue that achieving collaborative countervailing power is very difficult in many cases. I shall not consider their specific arguments on this subject but will stress that the question of inequalities of power, and that countervailing power may be needed to overcome the distorting impact of power inequalities, makes the development of successful deliberative institutional designs even more difficult. This is particularly the case if Fung and Wright (2003a: 267) are correct that, generally, even the most robust rules and procedures will not on their own ensure the inclusion of collaborative countervailing power: 'Appropriate institutional design can facilitate the rise and entry of countervailing voices. However, explanations of their presence and strength are separate from, though linked to, questions about the shape of collaborative institutions themselves.'

Przeworski (1998) has argued that, where interactions are about the means to achieve certain ends, rather than the determination of ends, the less powerful can be ideologically dominated by the more powerful, as well as by the organised and the articulate. In such cases, Przeworski (1998: 141) argues, decisions are generally on technical matters where some will be able to give the impression that they are more knowledgeable than others. The less powerful may end up supporting positions that do not reflect their interests. (For a consideration of the role of experts in deliberative democracy see Chapter 3, 'Expertise and deliberative democracy', by Mark Brown.)

Can deliberative democracy be institutionalised?

The questions surrounding whether the powerful will engage in deliberation with the less powerful feed into issues surrounding the institutionalisation of deliberative democracy. There are debates between scholars about what the institutionalisation of deliberative democracy would involve. Some, like Dryzek (2000, 2010), support the development of a system dominated by discourses. In this view, the aim should be to produce a political system where different discourses are considered and compete for influence. It is the access to different discourses that is crucial in this approach. For Dryzek (2000: 18):

> A discourse is a shared means of making sense of the world embedded in language. Any discourse will always be grounded in assumptions, judgement, contentions, dispositions, and capabilities. These shared terms of reference enable those who subscribe to a particular discourse to perceive and compile bits of sensory information into coherent stories or accounts that can be communicated in intersubjectively meaningful ways. Thus a discourse will generally revolve around a central storyline, containing opinions about both facts and values.

This approach rests on 'a conception of democracy that emphasizes the construction of public opinion through the contestation of discourses and its transmission to the state via communicative means, including rhetoric' (2000: 4). How this transmission takes place, or might take place, is not completely clear. (In recent work, Dryzek and Niemeyer (2010: 42–65) have proposed the establishment of a chamber of discourses but questions about the accountability of the chamber to 'the people' and its role in the public policy process remain.) In so far as Dryzek's approach may be lacking in a completely clear and entirely convincing picture of how the contestation of discourses will link into a democratic public policy process, it can be subjected to the same criticisms as the two-track approach of Habermas (1996) where public opinion is constructed through deliberation in the informal public sphere and is taken up, in a largely unspecified way, by the people's elected political representatives. This approach can also be criticised from a Marxist perspective for failing sufficiently to recognise that, in a capitalist society, the discourses that oppose, or are critical of the workings of, capitalism will find it very difficult to get the same hearing as pro-capitalist discourses (cf. Miliband, 1973: 196–213). Moreover, in a society with widespread inequality, what can be termed for short 'anti-capitalist' discourses will struggle to be accepted by public policy-makers, given the imperatives of the state to maintain capital accumulation and the conditions for the successful operation of private businesses – a point that Dryzek himself has, at least in part, accepted (Dryzek, 1996). (For further consideration of this issue, see Chapter 1, 'Conflict and deliberation', by Georgina Blakeley.)

This discourse view, however, is only one wing of the 'deliberative democracy school' and not the most popular. Other approaches are more concerned with how the type of principles associated with deliberative democracy, and set out at the beginning of this chapter, might inform the whole political system. This is not necessarily incompatible with some element of democratically elected representation. The aim is to produce a system where the interactions between participants in the making and implementation of public policy are dominated by the reciprocal giving of reasons, arguments or justifications in support of positions, where people are swayed by the force of the arguments they hear and willing to change their positions on the basis of strong arguments and where all interests and opinions are included in the deliberation. Developing institutions that reflect these principles is an important part of this commitment. A number of writers in recent years have argued that 'institutionalising deliberative democracy' is the major task ahead for academic supporters of deliberative democracy (Elster, 1998; Fung and Wright, 2003b; Smith, 2003; Warren, 2007; Thompson, 2008 and Elstub, 2010a). Given large-scale social inequalities, however, it might be asked whether this is possible. If one of the reasons for supporting deliberative democracy is that it is likely to produce more just policies, then there are reasons to believe that deliberative democracy may not be universally popular. The socially powerful, whose power tends to be connected to their wealth, their sex (men are more likely to be socially powerful than women) and their ethnic origin, and who are gaining from the existing non-deliberative democracy are, as Cohen and Rogers argue, likely to oppose the development of deliberative democracy, especially if they see it as potentially threatening their power, their wealth and their other privileges. There is no intrinsic reason to believe that the opposition of the powerful cannot be overcome in liberal democracies but there is also no reason to believe that doing so will be easy.

If, for the sake of argument, we assume that deliberative democracy can be institutionalised, that does not mean that deliberative democracy will automatically follow. Establishing the right institutions may be a necessary condition for deliberative democracy but it is not a sufficient condition. As Shapiro (2003: 48) has argued:

> It is doubtful … that government can ever really insist that people deliberate. Government can try to structure things so as to make deliberation more or less likely, but ultimately deliberation depends on individual commitment. By its terms, deliberation requires solicitous goodwill, creative ingenuity, and a desire to get the best answer. These cannot be mandated.

From the concerns of this chapter, the question is whether large-scale inequality will prevent the powerful from having the motivation to deliberate. As has been shown, Cohen and Rogers are doubtful that the powerful will have the right motivation. If they are correct, the point becomes whether they can be made to participate in a deliberative fashion. A number of writers on deliberation have argued that the motivations of participants are not crucial in determining whether deliberative democracy occurs. Habermas (2006b: 419–20), for example, has argued that, if the institutions are right, then deliberation will follow. He argues:

> Players on the virtual stage of the public sphere can be classified in terms of the power or 'capital' they have at their disposal. The stratification of opportunities to transform power into public influence through the channels of mediated communication thus reveals a power structure. This power is constrained, however, by the peculiar reflexivity of a public sphere that allows all participants to reconsider what they receive as public opinion. The common construct of public opinion certainly invites actors to intervene strategically in the public sphere. However, the unequal distribution of the means for such interventions does not necessarily distort the formation of considered public opinions. Strategic interventions in the public sphere must, unless they run the risk of inefficiency, play by the rules of the game. *And once the established rules constitute the right game – one that promises the generation of considered public opinions – then even the powerful actors will only contribute to the mobilization of relevant issues, facts, and arguments.* [emphasis added]

From a slightly different angle, Thompson (2008) also argues that the motivations of participants in deliberative democracy are not crucial. For him, if a participant gives reasons for his or her opinions that other participants can engage with in a reciprocal manner, the motives of the person for giving those reasons do not matter.

Theory alone will never determine which of the arguments is correct. It seems justified to say, however, that some institutions, where the initial differences between the participants are great, the participants are expected and encouraged to engage in strategic bargaining, participants have much to gain or loose, and the powerful participants have an effective veto, can make deliberation almost impossible. Institutions do matter. But it has not been shown that institutions are *all* that matter.

Another argument that suggests that getting the right institutions may not ensure deliberative democracy is provided by writers who argue that societies should not make too many demands on people to engage in politics. This type of argument is put forward by Weale (1999: 54–102) who maintains that, while politics is an important aspect of life, it is not the only commitment that people have, and it is unreasonable to expect people to prioritise political activity over all other activities. It is extremely likely that a system of deliberative democracy would expect people to participate more in politics than is generally the case in liberal democracies where the hope is that people will vote periodically in political elections and little more is expected. It can be questioned, however, whether deliberative democracy would demand so much participation from individuals that it interfered with other social or personal commitments. At present, in most liberal democracies, people's engagement in politics is small, and in some cases non-existent. There is surely space for most adults to participate more in politics. Occasionally participating on a citizens' jury or its equivalent would not seem an unreasonable expectation and surely would not have fatal results for the economy or for people's lives more generally.

That said, one aspect of social inequality may well have an impact on this issue. It is common in advanced capitalist societies for women to have greater domestic and caring responsibilities than men. It may, therefore, be much easier for most men to find the time to engage more fully in politics than most women. And it may be easier for middle-class women, who can afford to pay for care while they take part in political activities, than it is for working-class women who may well lack the resources to buy help with their caring responsibilities. There are two possible ways round this: the caring responsibilities could be shared more equally between women and men and people could be paid to engage in political activities. Whether the state is willing to pay people to engage in politics would probably depend on the general importance that political activity was seen as playing in the society, and that cannot be determined in the abstract. It should be noted that, in some cases in some countries, people are paid for participating in deliberative events.

Will deliberative democracy mean the rule of the articulate and the highly educated?

It has long been recognised that those with good educational qualifications have a strong tendency to participate more fully in politics in liberal democracies than those who have few educational qualifications (Dalton, 2006; Hay, 2007). The well educated are seen as having largely unintended political advantages in these societies. It is argued that promoting deliberative democracy would only increase the advantages of the educated 'middle-class', even further. This is because those who have had a university education have gained the skills on which deliberative democracy thrived. In other words, they are articulate, tend to be unafraid of speaking in public and expressing their views, and understand the 'rules of the game' that are associated with deliberative democracy or find it easy to accommodate to the rules. Perhaps the most consistent critic who argued in this style was Iris Marion Young. Young did not criticise deliberative democracy because she thought it was, in principle, undesirable but because she thought it would not be sufficiently democratic and would not help to empower or improve the position of the most disadvantaged in advanced capitalist societies. In a series of works, Young (1996: 129–32; 2000: 57–77) argued that people from minority ethnic groups, women, and working-class men would be disadvantaged under deliberative democracy as it was generally proposed. She did not suggest that the traditional institutions of liberal democracy were a satisfactory alternative to deliberative democracy. Instead, she argued that the processes of deliberative democracy should be amended so that people from disadvantaged social groups could participate more easily and play a bigger part.

For her, it was crucial to recognise how socially and politically disadvantaged groups communicated. She, therefore, called for greeting, storytelling and rhetoric to become an accepted part of deliberative democracy. Without a change in the rules of the deliberative democracy game, Young argued, deliberative democracy would prove unacceptable. Her work in this area produced a wide-ranging debate. Miller (2000), for example, denied the distinction, made by Young, between reason and emotion. For Miller (2000: 153) 'all political speech and argument must convey the feelings and commitments of the speaker, but must also give reasons either positively for some proposal or negatively against some alternative (which might just be the status quo)'. He argued that rhetoric is more likely to benefit the advantaged, rather than the disadvantaged, and 'because rhetoric conceals rather than reveals the grounds on which decisions are taken, it is less likely than reasoned argument to produce socially just policies' (Miller, 2000: 156). For Miller (2000: 155–6), testimony has two drawbacks: it is often very difficult to know if the testimony of one person is reflective of the experience of others; and adding together individual testimonies is unlikely to provide a solution to problems the testimonies are expressing. Others, however, have taken on board Young's arguments, and now see storytelling and emotional justifications as, in principle, compatible with deliberative democracy (cf. Mansbridge et al., 2010).

Some argue, however, that, even if the definition of deliberative democracy is extended, it is still likely that it will favour some and not others. One writer who takes this approach is Hooghe (1999). He makes a number of points against the practicality of deliberative democracy. One of these is the importance of cultural hegemony. If the term is used as it was originally developed by Gramsci, he argues, then we have to accept that the rules of the game operate in the interests of the advantaged elite. He writes that:

> It is not possible to think of a speech situation in which literally everybody has an equal chance to get his or her voice heard. Even in our efforts to conceive such an ideal speech situation we will always be influenced by our own class, gender and culture. (Hooghe 1999: 292)

As a supporter of Walzer's theory of complex equality, he argues that deliberative democracy could only possibly work in a society that is egalitarian to an extent which has never been seen, certainly in the modern world. His criticism of the practical impact of trying to achieve deliberative democracy goes even further. He argues that deliberative democracy goes against the insights developed by Walzer (1983) in his idea of complex equality, where those who benefit in one area of social life cannot use those benefits to gain advantage in other areas of social life and, therefore, different people will benefit in different areas or spheres. For Walzer there is no single unifying principle that determines how benefits and burdens will be distributed across society. Each sphere of society should have its own defining principle of distribution. For Hooghe (1999: 293–4), deliberative democracy falls foul of this understanding. It privileges the articulate middle class, and would continue to do so, in Hooghe's view, even if greeting, storytelling and rhetoric were included, when the skill of being able to argue most convincingly is more appropriate in the scientific or educational spheres. In other words, members of the educated middle class are able to take skills developed in the educational sphere and apply them to the political arena where they are inappropriate. This would undermine the equality of the vote in electing political representatives and represents, in Hooghe's argument, a retrograde step.

A number of criticisms has been made of Walzer's approach to justice (cf. Miller and Walzer, 1995). Whether or not this is an attractive theory of justice, however, will not be considered here; it will simply be accepted that it is. Instead, the focus will be on whether deliberative democracy is compatible with the theory. Does deliberative democracy really favour the well-educated, articulate members of society, who are relaxed about speaking in public, at the expense of the less well educated, the inarticulate and those who are not so happy about speaking in public?

In response to this criticism, it might be pointed out that liberal democracies tend to be dominated by the economically successful, the well educated and the articulate who are happy speaking in public. Taking Britain as an example, the overwhelming majority of MPs in the House of Commons have degrees and/or occupied professional or managerial positions before they entered Parliament (cf. Hackett and Hunter, 2011). Critics might reasonably reply, however, that deliberative democracy claims to overcome the weaknesses of liberal democracy by promoting a more inclusive form of democracy which strengthens ideas of political equality. Moreover, this is irrelevant, it can be argued, to a discussion of whether deliberative democracy is compatible with Walzer's theory of complex equality. In reply, it might be argued that some deliberative mechanisms, such as citizens' juries, consensus conferences and planning cells, make use of facilitators or moderators to try to ensure that participants do deliberate and that some participants do not dominate the discussion at the expense of others. (See Chapter 10, 'Mini-publics', by Stephen Elstub for a full discussion of the role of facilitators and moderators.) Provided, therefore, that the membership of deliberative democracy institutions is representative of the major social groups, and assuming facilitators and moderators perform their roles successfully, in principle, there is no reason why at least some deliberative democracy mechanisms should be dominated by a particular section of society. Admittedly these are big assumptions as has been shown earlier. It would be foolish, however, to deny that any activity where the giving of reasons, the construction of convincing arguments, the uncovering of flaws in arguments, and the presentation of opinions in public will favour those who have had a training in those activities. As those skills will always be crucial elements of democratic politics, and especially deliberative democracy, and they are generally developed through a good formal education, the case for improving the formal education of the most educationally disadvantaged would seem to be important even if some degree of educational inequality continues. This may be a case where improving the position of the least advantaged may be more important then trying to achieve substantive equality.

It can be questioned, however, whether the articulate having an influence over decisions, which is disproportionate to their numbers, is really a problem for deliberative democracy. If the articulate have 'better' arguments than others, arguments that make it easier to achieve agreed goals, that incorporate all interests or reduce the chances of some people feeling that their interests have been ignored or excluded, why should not their arguments win out? It also seems patronising to suggest that people who have few educational qualifications and who are materially poor are unable to distinguish between 'good' and 'bad' arguments if given the chance to do so. Problems occur, of course, when the articulate use their speaking and arguing skills to silence or marginalise the less articulate in the group, whether consciously or unconsciously. If the less articulate feel unable to express their views, then, the principles of deliberative democracy will be undermined. In reviewing the results of empirical studies on deliberative democratic events, Thompson (2008: 499) concludes 'the empirical findings are mixed or inconclusive' in showing whether the aims of deliberative democracy theorists are achieved in such events, including inclusive, egalitarian decision-making. He argues that results of deliberative events are contingent. For him, this means that theorists can use the negative findings from empirical studies to concentrate on reducing the flaws that are exposed. Yet Thompson (2008: 500) also argues: 'Theorists should not take too much comfort from the mixed or contingent character of the empirical conclusions. The conditions under which deliberative democracy thrives may be quite rare and difficult to achieve.'

Do globalisation and international inequalities make deliberative democracy less likely?

So far, the arguments in this chapter have looked at the relationship between deliberative democracy and inequality within nation states. In the world today, however, it is argued that an increasing number of issues are decided on an international or a global level. International bodies such as the European Union, and global organisations, such as the World Trade Organisation, the International Monetary Fund, the United Nations, the G8 and the G20, are seen as increasingly important political players. There are, of course, debates about how far these bodies have undermined the power of national governments and the extent to which they extend the power of nation states (or, at least, some of the richer and more powerful nation states) (cf. Scholte, 2005). Developments in this area are also relevant to a consideration of deliberative democracy and inequality.

It is not impossible to imagine situations where people from different countries take part on a face-to-face basis in deliberative events. This would, however, require major organising and would almost certainly be made harder by large-scale international social inequalities. If it is difficult to get poorer people and those with few educational qualifications to engage in political activities, such as political voting, in rich, advanced, capitalist societies, it is easy to see how the problems of ensuring that the poorest and the least qualified participate in international face-to-face events would be compounded. One possible way around this problem is the use of computer technology and other information and communication technologies to bring people together. Experiments in using computers to run deliberative mechanisms have been conducted (cf. Smith, 2009: 142–60). These experiments have been held in rich countries, however, and have not included any of the poorest people in the world. Even in rich, advanced, capitalist societies, access to computers tends to be unevenly distributed, with the poorer members of society and those with a limited education, as well as older people, having less access than others. These sorts of problems are, of course, made even worse if the position of people in the poorer and poorest societies in the world is taken into account. The United Nations has defined Internet use as a human right but the situation where all people have access seems a long way off. This has major implications if we see deliberative democracy as a way of creating democratic inclusiveness and ensuring that all relevant interests and opinions are included. One possible way of addressing the problem is to let people from the rich world speak for the people in the poor world or to let global international non-governmental organisations (such as Oxfam, Amnesty International and Friends of the Earth) represent the interests of people in the poor world. Without in any way wanting to disparage the work of INGOs, such as those mentioned, this seems a less than acceptable solution from a deliberative democracy perspective. (For further considerations on the issues around the 'scaling-up' of deliberative democracy, see Chapter 7, '"Scaling up" deliberation', by André Bächtiger and Alda Wegmann.)

Does deliberative democracy necessarily involve an unachievable level of equality?

As has been shown, Hooghe (1999) argues that deliberative democracy can be hoped to be achieved only if a level of substantive equality is achieved that is unknown in human history and that is unachievable. If correct, his argument is condemning. To consider the strength of the criticism, however, it is important to try to clarify what deliberative democracy does and does not involve. Some have argued that deliberative democracy means the replacement of aggregative voting, as applied in liberal democracies, with decision-making that results from deliberation between participants (cf. Squires, 2002: 133). Deliberative democracy is seen as the opposite of 'aggregative models of democracy'. Squires (2002: 133), however, goes on to write:

> [C]onsideration of most arguments in favour of deliberation reveals that what is being proposed is an augmentation of aggregative democracy with deliberation. In other words, the deliberative democracy literature does not represent a direct refutation of the liberal democratic commitment to representative democracy. Rather it suggests that we could usefully supplement this practice with others, which encourage interactive debate and the transformation of preferences.

While written a decade ago, and despite the developments in the theory and practice of deliberative democracy over the last ten years, Squires's argument can be seen as still generally correct. The extent to which deliberative democracy wants to augment liberal representative democracy, however, remains open, together with the implications of that augmentation.

As is well known, what might be called 'deliberative democracy mechanisms' have been applied by different levels of government and other organisations engaged in the public policy process in a number of countries for a number of years (cf. Fung, 2003; Smith, 2009). These mechanisms include citizens' juries, consensus conferences, planning cells, citizens' assemblies, and deliberative opinion polls. The application of such mechanisms is limited. The decisions reached by the participants are generally consultative and feed into other areas of the public policy process. (An exception to this is citizens' assemblies but, even here, the decisions of an assembly are put to the people in a referendum which either accepts or rejects the assembly recommendations.) The impact of the decisions of such initiatives on public policy is often unclear (cf. Smith, 2009; Hendriks, 2005), and the role the initiatives play in the public policy process is sometimes very limited (cf. McLaverty, 2009). The current use of such mechanisms would not generally be seen as the end point that advocates of deliberative democracy would like to reach.

Most writers on deliberative democracy are not concerned with drawing blueprints of what deliberative democracy might ultimately look like. It is argued, and I think correctly, however, that deliberative democracy, if it is to be true to its democratic tag, must involve more of the people in democratic deliberation than is mostly the case around the world today, and it must have processes whereby the outcomes of people's deliberations are directly related to public policy decision-making (cf. Chambers, 2009). For some writers, an emphasis is placed on civil society and the extent to which it promotes deliberation and the ways in which the public opinion that is developed in civil society feeds into the formal political system (cf. Habermas, 1996 and 2006b; Chambers, 2009; Dryzek, 2000). In terms of this chapter, a crucial point in relation to this approach is the extent to which social inequalities will 'distort' communication in civil society. In a society with large-scale social inequalities, it is not unreasonable to argue that the opinions of the rich and the powerful will carry more weight than those of other people. From a Marxist perspective, it would also be argued that, in capitalist society, given the imperatives of the capitalist system, the mass media are extremely likely to give more importance to the opinions of the rich and powerful and, given the importance of the mass media, this is likely to undermine open, egalitarian deliberation in the public sphere of civil society. Moreover, there are debates about whether, in capitalist societies such as the United States, people with different political opinions are in the sort of contact that will allow deliberation to take place in civil society (cf. Mutz, 2006), and whether people want to deliberate (cf. Hibbing and Theiss-Morse, 2002) – an issue that is discussed in Chapter 9, 'The public sphere as a site of deliberation: an analysis of problems of inclusion', by Maija Setälä .

Some writers have suggested ways in which liberal democracy can be transformed to incorporate at least some direct elements of deliberative democracy (cf., for example, Parkinson, 2006a; Saward, 2003; Mansbridge et al., 2011). The proposals developed will not be considered in any detail. The idea of 'the deliberative system' has gained interest. The basic idea is that deliberative events or elements should be seen as part of a democratic system, not all of whose elements will be deliberative or comply with the principles of deliberative democracy. The overall system will, however, be deliberative. As Mansbridge et al. (2011: 35) argue, however, one of five pathologies that can infect a deliberative system is social domination. 'This arises when a particular social interest or social class controls or exerts undue influence over many parts of the deliberative system.' I think this is a major potential problem for the practical achievement of a deliberative system, in many present-day societies. The danger, in a society of large-scale inequality, is that the rich and the powerful will be able to use their positions in society to dominate a deliberative system and prevent it achieving the three functions Mansbridge et al. (2011) see as connected to a deliberative system – truth-seeking, establishing mutual respect, and inclusive, egalitarian decision-making.

In the 1970s, C. B. Macpherson (1977: 100–8) argued that, in western capitalist societies, a vicious circle restricted the development of participatory democracy. For him, for greater democratic participation to be possible there had to be greater equality but, for greater equality to be achieved, there had to be more democratic participation. He suggested that there were some loop-holes in the circle but he viewed them as no more than cracks in the edifice. Some, like Elstub (2008: 200–4), argue that a possible way out of this circle is to expand socially inclusive deliberative mechanisms into more areas of society. (He supports the development of a social system dominated by associations, run on deliberative lines.) The argument, which connects with that of Habermas above, is that, if more and more decisions are taken using deliberative processes, the rich and the powerful will have to accept this or lose influence over the decisions. If truly inclusive, the use of deliberative mechanisms will involve the poorer and less affluent members of the population. In this way, the vicious circle can be broken.

I think this view is over-optimistic. While I would not suggest that the rich and the powerful in capitalist liberal democracies will always get what they want, I do think that their power in the society, especially if it is based on ownership of the means of production, will make it difficult for governments and others to introduce decision-making processes that they think will, or even might, undermine the interests of the rich and powerful. I am not suggesting that this is impossible but it would probably need a change in social thinking among most of the population so that they explicitly supported such developments.

Conclusion

So, in conclusion, what is the relationship between deliberative democracy and inequality? There seem to be convincing reasons to believe that the achievement of a political system that might be called a deliberative democracy will be made very difficult in any society where large-scale inequalities exist. Where inequali-ties give political power, and where deliberative democracy is a threat to existing inequalities of power, it is likely that the powerful will oppose efforts to develop deliberative democracy. There have to be doubts, therefore, about the extent to which deliberative democracy can be instituted without much greater social equality than exists in most societies. Even if deliberative democracy could be institutionalised on a far wider scale than it is anywhere in the world, there are strong reasons to believe that the powerful would at best be wary about engag-ing in deliberation and would at worst refuse to do so. It is the case that those who can put forward arguments in an articulate and convincing way, uncover flaws in arguments and feel happy expressing opinions in public, whether in face-to-face settings or on the Internet, will have an advantage where principles associated with deliberative democracy are applied. The use of facilitators and moderators can help to reduce those advantages but is unlikely ever to remove them entirely. Within civil society, it seems reasonable to question whether, without limiting inequalities, open deliberation will be the means by which 'public opinion' is established.

Does this mean that it would be sensible to abandon deliberative democracy? I do not think so. Efforts to extend any type of democracy will be hindered by large-scale social inequality. In recent years, the trend has been towards greater inequality in most parts of the world but this is not inevitable. Many countries became more equal in the years between 1945 and the 1970s. In Britain, for example, financial inequality declined from 1918 to 1980 (cf. Dorling, 2010). And there is research that suggests that more equal societies have big advantages over less equal ones (Wilkinson and Pickett, 2009). Such research may have political impact in the future. Moreover, elements of deliberative democracy have been implemented even in very unequal societies. My final point, however, is that substantial moves towards greater deliberative democracy will need to go hand in hand with moves to greater social equality.

CHAPTER 3

Expertise and deliberative democracy

Mark B. Brown

Introduction

Expertise plays an ambiguous role in the theory and practice of deliberative democracy. By involving lay citizens in reasonable discussion on complex topics, deliberative democracy aims to bridge the gap between populist and elitist forms of democracy. Deliberative democracy provides an alternative to both ignorant mob rule and technocratic rule by experts. When lay citizens have real opportunities publicly to discuss their interests, opinions, and experiences, they are more likely to reach reasonable decisions. Lay deliberation enhances the epistemic quality of political decisions and, in this respect, deliberation might be seen as a substitute for both technical and ethical expertise. Deliberative democrats thus often reference Aristotle's notion that, because different people know different things, when they put their knowledge together, they collectively know more than the experts. Nonetheless, most deliberative democrats also recognise the value of lending greater credence to those with specialised knowledge about a particular topic with regard to questions about that topic (Goodin, 2008: 93–7). Nearly all public problems today involve technical knowledge of one kind or another, so effective public deliberation inevitably relies to some extent on expertise. Lay citizens would not even be aware of problems such as climate change or toxic pollution without the studies produced by scientific experts. And expert knowledge has the potential to improve efforts to design, implement, and evaluate public policies on a wide range of contemporary issues. Though policy-relevant expertise is often uncertain and controversial, it is an important resource for effectively addressing public problems.

Most lay citizens seem to know very little about science, leading to much hand wringing over the dismal state of 'science literacy' in advanced democratic societies (Mooney and Kirschenbaum, 2009). Indeed, standard surveys of public knowledge of basic scientific facts and processes reveal much room for improvement (National Science Board, 2012). More contextual studies of science literacy, however, suggest that, when faced with a particular sociotechnical controversy, citizens are usually capable of acquiring the expertise they need to clarify and articulate their interests (Bauer, 2008). But how can citizens best make use of the expertise they acquire? How can they determine which experts are reliable? Which questions should citizens delegate to experts and which should they reserve for lay deliberation? What should citizens do when experts disagree? Should experts always play the same role in lay deliberation, or does it depend on the specific issue or the specific social context, and who decides?

With a few notable exceptions, deliberative democratic theorists have rarely devoted much attention to such questions. In fact, they have often defined lay deliberation in explicit opposition to technical expertise (Manin, 1987: 355; Fung, 2003: 343). Practitioners, in contrast, have increasingly sought to increase the public legitimacy of technically complex policy decisions by instituting various forms of deliberative governance (Bäckstrand et al., 2010; Renn et al., 1995). This chapter first examines how several leading deliberative democratic theorists view the role of expertise in public deliberation. John Rawls and the co-authored studies by Amy Gutmann and Dennis Thompson rarely mention expertise but what they do say is revealing. More extensive discussions of expertise appear in the work of Jürgen Habermas, James Bohman, Mark Warren, and like-minded thinkers. For these authors, expert authority supports deliberative democracy when it is embedded within an institutionalised culture of public scrutiny. These authors say little, however, about questions regarding expert credibility, uncertainty, and disagreement. The second part of the chapter takes up these issues, arguing that the proper role of expertise in public deliberation depends on the specific features of the issue at hand, especially with regard to the degree of scientific certainty and political disagreement. Seen in this light, the proper role of expertise in deliberative democracy often becomes a political question, which is shaped by various social and cultural factors, the interpretation of which should also be subject to lay deliberation.

Deliberative democrats on the role of experts

A search through the indexes of books on deliberative democracy for terms such as 'science' and 'expertise' usually produces few, if any, results. Indeed, as various commentators have pointed out (Turner, 2003: 2–5; Baber and Bartlett, 2005: 188), most contemporary political theorists have devoted little attention to the politics of expertise. Nonetheless, deliberative democrats occasionally remark on the role of expertise in public deliberation, and it is worth seeing what a few of the most influential authors have to say.

John Rawls notes that citizens who reason about justice 'reason only from general beliefs shared by citizens generally, as part of their public knowledge' (Rawls, 1993: 70). In this respect, he suggests, citizens engaged in public reason do not require technical expertise. Another key requirement of public reason, however, is to accept what Rawls calls the 'burdens of judgment', the sources of disagreement between reasonable people in pluralist societies. Some disagreements, of course, result from irrationality, ignorance, egoism, and other threats to reasonableness. But Rawls argues that, even if such factors could be eliminated and people would conscientiously attempt to reach agreement on basic moral questions, the burdens of judgement would ensure that people in contemporary pluralist societies would continue to disagree on many fundamental questions. The burdens of judgement include ambiguous and indeterminate normative claims that people weigh and interpret differently, owing in part to different life experiences. They also include uncertain technical expertise – that is, situations in which the 'evidence – empirical and scientific – bearing on the case is conflicting and complex, and thus hard to assess and evaluate' (Rawls, 1993: 56). When the technical expertise relevant to basic moral questions is uncertain, Rawls rightly argues, people will probably disagree about its implications for those questions. Rawls, however, does not discuss how lay deliberators might best assess such conflicting and complex empirical evidence. Indeed, he later suggests that public reason can usually rely on scientific consensus when he writes that the values of public reason include 'accepting the methods and conclusions of science when not controversial' (1993: 139; see also 224). Rawls does not seem to recognise how rarely policy-relevant science remains uncontroversial. Moreover, Rawls does not discuss any special role for technical experts in public deliberation. For Rawls, write Baber and Bartlett (2005: 57; see also 188–9), scientists 'produce the information necessary to trigger the precommitments that have been arrived at by rational decision makers in the original position and thus set these in motion'. But scientists apparently do not play any particular role in shaping those precommitments or deliberations about them.[1]

Critics have often argued that Rawls's theory of justice itself amounts to a form of expertise because his approach seems to reduce public debate on questions of justice to the hypothetical deliberations of philosophers (Habermas, 1990: 66; Dryzek, 2000: 15–16). Rawls rejects this critique, explaining that wide-ranging discussions in civil society do not recognise epistemic distinctions among participants. 'The point of view of civil society includes all citizens … There are no experts: a philosopher has no more authority than other citizens' (Rawls, 1995: 140–1). And he applies the same point to more structured deliberations on constitutional essentials which follow the requirements of public reason and lead to Rawls's notion of justice as fairness. 'In justice as fairness there are no philosophical experts. Heaven forbid!' (Rawls, 1995: 174; see Baber and Bartlett, 2005: 52–3). All citizens, Rawls argues, can adopt the presuppositions of the 'original position' and arrive at Rawls's principles of justice for themselves. Whether or not Rawls's theory of justice supports some sort of rule by philosophical experts, Rawls says nothing about how disagreements among either ethical or technical experts should be addressed by lay citizens.

Moreover, Rawls restricts the requirements of public reason to deliberation on constitutional essentials, which seems to exclude most expert deliberation. All corporate bodies and associations, Rawls writes, including 'churches and universities, scientific societies and professional groups', engage in a form of reasoning that is public with regard to their members but non-public with regard to citizens generally (Rawls, 1993: 220). Rawls rightly notes that each kind of association has its own rules of evidence and criteria of justification, and he acknowledges that associations must respect their members' basic liberties. But Rawls does not discuss whether citizens might sometimes be justified in calling for reforms within scientific associations, especially those that address questions of social and political relevance.

Like Rawls, Amy Gutmann and Dennis Thompson (1996; 2004) say little about expertise but they occasionally note that lay deliberation needs to be informed by appropriate empirical evidence. Indeed, they conceive empirical claims as an important component of the key deliberative virtue of reciprocity.[2]

> Reciprocity asks that our empirical claims in political argument be consistent with reliable methods of inquiry, as these methods are available to us here and now, not for all times and places. Neither relativity nor uncertainty is grounds for abandoning the most reliable methods of inquiry at our collective disposal. By using the most reliable methods of inquiry, we demonstrate our mutual commitment to reach deliberative agreement in the empirical realms that are relevant to moral argument. (1996: 15; see also 56)

Despite this acknowledgment that lay deliberation depends on expertise, Gutmann and Thompson devote most of their other comments on expertise to emphasising its limits within public deliberation. With regard to the US abortion debate, for example, they note that the two sides each relies on different kinds of expertise: pro-life advocates emphasise medical knowledge about embryonic development; while pro-choice advocates reference social scientific studies on the societal effects of unwanted pregnancies. Gutmann and Thompson reasonably conclude that the constitutional status of the foetus is not likely to be settled by further scientific research (1996: 74). Similarly, when discussing public deliberation on health care priorities, Gutmann and Thompson rightly argue that, even if 'legislators could show that the most significant issues on the dispute over health care funding were technical', the relevant 'medical and scientific information, though important, could not determine the choices that affect basic opportunities' (1996: 226). Like Rawls, Gutmann and Thompson argue that expertise can never answer basic moral and political questions. This point is certainly correct but it offers little guidance for how expertise might best inform lay deliberation on such questions.

Gutmann and Thompson do mention that, for experts to inform deliberation, they must translate their expert knowledge into ordinary language. 'Citizens are justified in relying on experts if they describe the basis for their conclusions in ways that citizens can understand; and if the citizens have some independent basis for believing the experts to be trustworthy', such as a record of past reliability, as well as an institutional system that fosters critical scrutiny by other experts (Gutmann and Thompson, 2004: 5). Put differently, the role of expertise in deliberative democracy – like all other institutional arrangements – should itself be subject to deliberative scrutiny. These points seem correct, as far as they go, but Gutmann and Thompson say nothing about different possible roles that experts might adopt. Nor do they consider how the content of expertise itself – as opposed to its political role – might be shaped by lay deliberation.

In contrast to these brief comments on expertise by Rawls and Gutmann and Thompson, Habermas offers a more detailed account of how the politics of expertise might shape deliberative politics. Building on the Frankfurt School tradition, including concerns about the technical 'rationalization' of politics voiced by Weber and Horkheimer and Adorno, Habermas took an early interest in the relation of science and politics. In *Toward a Rational Society* (1970: 66–80), Habermas draws on John Dewey to argue for a pragmatist view of expertise based on the mutual shaping of scientific knowledge and political decisions. Habermas draws a now familiar distinction between the instrumental orientation of 'work', associated with science and technology, and the communicative orientation of 'interaction', associated with public deliberation. By reducing political questions to technical questions, he argues, elites expand the legitimate human interest in the instrumental control of nature into an ideological programme for defending elite privilege. But Habermas also criticises the Weberian insistence on insulating science and politics from each other. Social values and interests can be realised only through appropriate technical means, and emerging technologies foster the generation of new values and interests. Democratic politics should direct technical progress towards self-conscious practical needs, Habermas argues, rather than towards the assumed needs generated by consumer capitalism. And these practical needs should be assessed in the light of the technical possibilities for realising them.

Habermas recognises that intelligent communication between experts and politicians faces many practical obstacles, and he warns against subjecting scientific discussion to the whims of mass opinion (1970: 69). But he also criticises the positivist rejection of dialogue between lay people and experts. Such scepticism about lay competence 'confuses the actual difficulty of effecting permanent communication between science and public opinion with the violation of logical and methodological rules' (70). The communicative barriers between lay people and experts result from practical institutional constraints rather than from an essential epistemic divide. Habermas goes on to advocate building an interactive 'net of rational discussion stretching between practice and science' (71).

Technical expertise also plays a key role in Habermas's theory of discourse ethics, which rests on three kinds of validity claims that together render statements normatively valid: factual truth, normative rightness, and subjective truthfulness or sincerity (Habermas, 1984: 273 ff.; 1990: 58; 1996: 164; Warren, 2002: 192). The empirical facts determined by scientific experts are thus integral to the normative validity of claims made in public deliberation. But Habermas also makes clear that normative claims are only 'analogous' to scientific claims of factual truth.[3] Whereas the meaning of norms depends on 'legitimately ordered interpersonal relationships', the empirical states of affairs assessed by science 'must be assumed to exist independently of whether we formulate them by means of true propositions or not'. Language and the social world are mutually dependent in a way that language and the natural world are not (Habermas, 1990: 56, 61). Habermas, in short, adopts a constructivist view of moral rightness and a realist view of factual truth. Constructivist research in the social studies of science, in contrast, while not denying that nature exists prior to science, emphasises the social structures and practices that shape scientific claims (Jasanoff et al., 1995).

Habermas's more recent work integrates his theory of discourse ethics with a deliberative theory of law and democracy. He emphasises the need for a functional division of labour between expert administration and political deliberation. But Habermas also warns that the 'specialized and competent fulfillment of tasks by experts is no protection against a *paternalistic* self-empowerment' by administrative agencies (1996: 188). He insists that 'the administration be empowered to carry out its tasks as professionally as possible, yet only under normative premises not at its disposal: the executive branch is to be limited to *employing* administrative power according to the law' (1996: 188). That is, experts alone should not determine the purposes for which their expertise is used.

The key to limiting administrative power lies in Habermas's 'dual track' model of deliberative democracy which locates deliberation in formal state institutions (especially parliaments but also administrative agencies) and in the informal public sphere. The latter is constituted by a wide range of different types of organisational settings, including civil society organisations, the news media, and conversations at work or across the garden fence. Expertise potentially enters the process of public opinion and will formation at any of these multiple sites. Experts may shape decision-making in state institutions but they may also influence opinion formation in the informal public sphere. The public sphere includes a jumble of diverse participants – religious leaders, literary figures, sports heroes, and film stars, as well as scientific experts (Habermas, 1996: 363) – with various kinds of reputation and authority. Unlike the equal power guaranteed by the formal sovereignty expressed through voting, the informal sovereignty of public opinion ensures unequal power. That is, those with more deliberative resources – including time, attention, information, ability, reputation, and authority – may legitimately become more persuasive than others (325).

But the political influence that the actors gain through public communication must *ultimately* rest on the resonance and indeed the approval of a lay public whose composition is egalitarian. The public of citizens must be *convinced* by comprehensible and broadly interesting contributions to issues it finds relevant. (364)

Whichever arguments end up convincing this 'public of citizens', it retains the task of influencing and monitoring the exercise of formally authorised political power by the state (300, 351). So, like Rawls and Gutmann and Thompson, Habermas argues that the influence of experts on public deliberation ultimately depends on their power to persuade the public. (For more discussion of the public sphere see Chapter 8, 'The public sphere as a site of deliberation: an analysis of problems of inclusion', by Maija Setälä).

More than these other authors, however, Habermas recognises how easily expertise becomes politicised. 'As soon as specialized knowledge is brought to politically relevant problems, its unavoidably normative character becomes apparent, setting off controversies that polarize the experts themselves' (Habermas, 1996: 351). The politicisation of expertise cannot always be avoided, Habermas notes, but expert controversies can be integrated into deliberative politics, and thereby, 'shaped by the publicly organized contest of opinions between experts and counterexperts and monitored by public opinion' (351). Habermas thus suggests that we respond to politicised expertise not by invoking the ideal of value-free science but by democratising expert controversies.

Similarly, Habermas argues that the technocratic image of administrative expertise has never matched reality, and the increasing need for administrators to weigh competing normative values 'can be treated rationally only in discourses of justification and application that cannot be contained within the professional confines of a normatively neutral task fulfillment' (440). Habermas thus sees a need for 'a "democratization" of the administration that … would supplement parliamentary and judicial controls on administration from within' (440). For Habermas, public deliberation needs both to constrain and to direct the power of administrative experts.[4]

Building on these considerations, James Bohman and Mark Warren offer more extensive discussions of technical expertise in deliberative democracy.[5] Given the unequal distribution of knowledge in society, Bohman writes, citizens are often forced to 'surrender their autonomy to experts, delegates, and other forms of division of labor' (Bohman, 1996: 168). Bohman notes that expert authority rests not simply on knowledge but also on trust – both the trust of other experts and, when it comes to policy-relevant expertise, the trust of affected publics (168). Like Habermas, Bohman argues that 'expertise must be publicly convincing to be effective, and it can be lost through abuse and disuse' (169; see also 46). Public trust in experts can be enhanced by public challenge insofar as such challenges receive a response that citizens deem adequate. Just as elected representatives seek to maintain the support of multiple constituencies, 'experts, too, have to enlist the ongoing cooperation of the public to keep their enterprises functioning' (Bohman, 1996: 192; Warren, 2002: 193; Baber and Bartlett, 2005: 104–5). Mark Warren makes a similar point when he argues that expert authority is constituted in part by the existence and vitality of 'institutionalized opportunities for discursive challenge' and a 'critical political culture' that enable experts and laypeople publicly to challenge expert claims whenever the need arises (Warren, 1996: 49, 55–6). Bohman and Warren thus offer a democratised version of the epistemic division of labour envisioned by Rawls and Gutmann and Thompson. As Bohman puts it,

> The division of labour can be democratic so long as it fulfills two conditions: It must establish free and open interchange between experts and the lay public and discover ways of resolving recurrent cooperative conflicts about the nature and distribution of knowledge. (Bohman, 1999: 592; see also Bohman, 2000)

Though lay citizens must trust experts, their trust need not be blind. When technical uncertainty or public controversy raises justifiable doubts about expert claims, lay citizens and their representatives need effective opportunities to hold experts publicly accountable.

In a more detailed treatment of the same idea, Warren (2002: 194–5) discusses several ways in which deliberative democracy helps to improve the role of experts in politics. By encouraging flat organisational structures and limiting hierarchies, deliberative democracy improves information flows and increases the pool of socially available knowledge. By equalising opportunities for public discussion, deliberative democracy encourages the expression of diverse types of expertise, especially non-professional, experiential expertise that otherwise has difficulty being heard. And, by limiting the influence of money and power, deliberative democracy helps to ensure that citizens can assess expert claims on their merits. Under such conditions, Warren writes, 'experts are left to establish their authority – as they should – on *epistemic* grounds, on the basis of which warranted trust in expertise can develop' (Warren, 2002: 195).

But what does it mean to establish authority on epistemic grounds? Does it exclude social considerations? Warren's formulation suggests what sociologists of science call 'asymmetry' in the assessment of scientific claims: relying on social factors such as money and power to explain the production of false knowledge claims while explaining the production of true knowledge claims solely on epistemic grounds. A symmetrical approach, in contrast, shows how social values and political interests (as well as non-human forces) shape both the acceptance and rejection of scientific claims (Bloor, [1976] 1991).[6] This becomes important for deliberative democracy once one realises, as I discuss below, that lay judgements of expert authority need to employ both epistemic and social criteria.

The notion that experts must translate their claims into ordinary language so that lay people can understand them – as Gutmann and Thompson, Bohman, and Warren all argue – makes a good deal of sense but it raises some difficult questions. First, emphasising popular translation efforts by experts easily suggests that lay people remain passive with respect to expert claims: either experts speak their esoteric language and lay people cannot understand anything or experts translate their claims into ordinary language that lay people automatically understand. What capacities and concerns do lay people bring to their interactions with experts? How can lay people best judge among competing expert claims? The next section takes up these questions.

Second, the authors discussed here say little about cases in which experts consistently fail to persuade large segments of the general public. How should deliberative democrats respond to many lay people's rejection of the scientific consensus on climate change and biological evolution? This problem is less pressing than many assume. As I discuss in the next section, public support for effective public policies rarely depends on public support for the expert knowledge relevant to those policies. Those concerned about public rejection of expertise often exaggerate the role in politics of experts. Moreover, to the extent that experts disagree among themselves, it is neither likely nor desirable that any single group of experts persuades the entire public to adopt its position. Experts working in policy-relevant areas have often sought to increase their policy influence by concealing their disagreements (Beatty, 2006), and public scrutiny helps keep experts honest. Nonetheless, widespread public rejection of mainstream scientific knowledge in certain areas remains disconcerting. With regard to climate change, for example, experts have sometimes played down their disagreements about various details but many people reject even the robust expert consensus on the basic notion that anthropogenic climate change is occurring. How to respond? Some call for environmental authoritarianism but much evidence suggests that, on the whole, democracies produce better environmental policies than authoritarian regimes (Bättig and Bernauer, 2009; Held and Hervey, 2009). A better response, therefore, is to attempt to improve democracy rather than abandon it in the face of excessive public scepticism toward experts. The institutions and practices advocated by deliberative democrats increase the likelihood that lay citizens will respond to expert consensus with critical trust rather than with outright rejection or blind acceptance.

Lay evaluation of expert claims

As the preceding discussion indicates, several leading democratic theorists argue that expertise can inform lay deliberation only to the extent that experts translate their claims into ordinary language. It is certainly true that much of what citizens know about science depends on the popularisation efforts of working scientists and, more commonly, science journalists, science educators, and science museums. But an emphasis on popularisation can be misleading in at least two ways. First, popularisation is not a specific feature of lay-expert relations but also part of communication among experts. As many commentators have noted, expert discourses are closed not only to non-experts but also to experts from other disciplines. Experts communicating with experts from other fields need to translate their language into something close to everyday language (Turner, 2003: 66). Similarly, the notion that experts need to persuade lay people by translating expertise into ordinary language should not be taken to mean that authority can be eliminated from lay-expert communication. Regardless of what experts might say, lay people can always request further evidence, and then more evidence to support the previous evidence, leading to an infinite regress (Latour, 1987: Chapter 1). At some point, expertise inevitably depends not on persuasion but on authority. Authority need not be conceived as unquestioning acceptance, as noted previously, but it cannot be eliminated from lay-expert relationships.

Second, by emphasising the need for experts to translate their claims into ordinary language, commentators cast lay-expert relations in terms of the public's lack of knowledge. This neglects the many experience-based cognitive resources that lay people bring to deliberative settings. It also suggests a 'deficit model' of science communication which emphasises the lay public's knowledge deficit and gives scientists the task of rectifying it (Irwin and Wynne, 1996).[7] Similarly, emphasising translation or popularisation suggests a one-way, transmission-belt image of lay-expert communication. In practice, however, lay people often attempt to evaluate expert claims for themselves.

Some argue that, because lay people lack the time and competence to understand the basis for expert claims, they have no choice but blind trust in experts (Hardwig, 1985). But, even if lay people cannot evaluate the *esoteric* claims specific to a particular discipline, they can use social indicators, heuristics or other cognitive shortcuts to assess *exoteric* claims that go beyond a particular field of expertise (Goldman, 2001: 94). The use of social criteria to assess expert credibility is also common among experts themselves – not only among experts from different fields, as with the translation efforts discussed previously, but also among experts from the same field. Empirical studies of scientific practice show that experts assess other experts according to their apparent skill, honesty, personality, professional affiliation and nationality, among other factors (Collins and Evans, 2007: 50, n. 10). Indeed, according to Collins and Evans (2007: 45–6), lay people's capacity to identify trustworthy experts is merely a special case of the judgements that we all make every day about friends, acquaintances, salespeople, politicians and others we encounter in daily life. As members of advanced industrial societies, most people have developed a tacit sense of who properly counts as a scientific expert and who does not.[8] Beyond such tacit judgements, however, scholars have specified various metacriteria, some more effective than others, that lay people use to evaluate expert claims to authority.

Elizabeth Anderson (2011) suggests three criteria that lay people might use to assess the relative credibility of experts in public discourse: expertise, honesty, and epistemic responsibility. For assessing a person's *expertise*, Anderson (2011: 146–7) outlines a 'hierarchy of expertise': those at the bottom lack any academic credentials; those at the next few levels have increasingly rigorous academic credentials in fields of increasing relevance to the issue in question; experts at the top levels supplement their academic credentials with relevant professional experience and recognition. Anderson argues that lay people should weigh experts' testimony in proportion to their place on the hierarchy. She fails to note that many people who lack academic credentials – environmental justice activists, for example, or farmers or factory workers – may have relevant knowledge and experience (Collins and Evans, 2007: 67).[9] Moreover, those with academic credentials may offer partial, and thus misleading, testimony without violating professional standards insofar as their thinking is confined within a disciplinary framework.

Anderson also offers several criteria for assessing the *honesty* of experts. Financial conflicts of interest or a record of fraud and deception are reasonable grounds for being sceptical about expert claims. But some of Anderson's other examples of dishonesty – 'cherry picking data or other misleading use of statistics', 'misrepresenting the arguments and claims of scientific opponents' (Anderson, 2011: 147) – are inevitable features of the politics of expertise. When taken to an extreme, of course, misrepresenting data amounts to dishonesty. But in the rough-and-tumble world of everyday politics, what one person calls 'cherry-picking' another might call 'popularization' (Sarewitz 2004). Moreover, what some might call expert biases are actually incorporated into the basic assumptions of entire disciplines. Epidemiology and toxicology, for example, typically focus on different explanations of disease. Rather than relying on professional honesty, lay people may be better served by more broadly assessing the general character of experts who testify in public, using the same everyday cues they use to form opinions about politicians and other public figures (Dryzek, 2000: 53–4).

Finally, Anderson's criteria for judging *epistemic responsibility* include various standard features of scientific practice, such as sharing data with colleagues and facilitating the replication of one's experiments. But they also include epistemic responsibility towards the public, expressed by refraining from mass-media publication of one's results until they are peer reviewed, and avoiding 'dialogic irrationality' which involves 'continuing to repeat claims after they have been publicly refuted by others, without responding to the refutations', as well as avoiding association with 'crackpots' (Anderson, 2011: 147–8). Other things being equal, lay people should lend greater credence to experts who exhibit various deliberative virtues: inviting opponents to express disagreement; offering patient and charitable responses; showing interest in possible counter-evidence; and readily admitting mistakes (Dryzek, 2000: 165; Goldman, 2001;

Matheson, 2005: 151–5). Of course, experts may adopt deliberative virtues that lend their testimony a reasonable form even while the content is false or misleading (Anderson, 2011: 148). In such cases, lay people probably have little recourse but to rely on additional experts to expose expert irresponsibility.

These various cognitive shortcuts may help lay people assess the credibility of expert testimony but they also raise several problems. First, cognitive shortcuts allow lay people to make intelligent judgements with limited information but that does not eliminate the need for at least some information (Delli Carpini and Keeter, 1996: 52–3). Though Anderson says that her indicators of expert credibility can be assessed by anyone with an Internet connection, many of them seem to require significant time and effort. Indeed, in some cases – such as misleading use of statistics or misrepresenting claims of opponents – assessing the indicators requires knowledge and experience similar to that of the experts themselves. It may even require what Collins and Evans (2007) call 'interactional expertise' which involves the ability intelligently to discuss technical matters with leading scientists in the field without being able to contribute to the science itself.

Additionally, finding ways for lay people to assess competing experts still frames expert advice in the linear terms of the deficit model mentioned previously. It suggests that effective public deliberation on complex problems depends on lay people first getting the science right and then choosing policies supposedly implied by the science. Anderson repeatedly suggests, for example, that a key obstacle to effective American climate policy lies in widespread public ignorance about climate science and, more specifically, in the American public's failure properly to assess the relative credibility of duelling climate experts. But, despite more than twenty years of trying, no major industrial country has used climate policy significantly to reduce greenhouse gases, including countries such as Denmark and the Netherlands that enjoy broad societal acceptance of mainstream climate science. Conversely, the United States government has frequently implemented major policies without scientific consensus on relevant factual matters, including ozone depletion and, more recently, health care and financial reform (Sarewitz, 2011). As Roger Pielke puts it, 'disagreement about science does not preclude consensus on action, and general agreement about science does not preclude opposing views on action' (Pielke, 2007: 128). These points suggest that there is less need for lay people to judge which experts are most credible than to determine whether sufficient evidence exists for no-regrets policies – that is, policies that remain defensible regardless of which experts end up having more truth on their side.

Finally, most efforts to devise criteria for assessing expert credibility, including Anderson's (2011), do not distinguish different roles for experts depending on the particular issue at hand. The appropriate role of experts can be expected to vary according to any given issue's public salience, degree of public mobilisation, expert credibility, and perceived scientific and political consensus. In a field such as theoretical physics, with low public salience and little controversy among either experts or politicians, the deficit model of science communication may be entirely appropriate. Experts can present the consensus view of their discipline, allowing lay deliberators to incorporate the best available factual information into their political judgements. In fields such as genetic engineering or climate research, in contrast, scientific uncertainty and political controversy render top-down models of science communication obsolete (Bucchi, 2008: 70–1; Ezrahi, 1980; Pielke, 2007).

Put differently, most prominent public issues today involve 'ill-structured' or 'wicked' problems that combine high decision stakes with a lack of societal agreement on both science and values (Ezrahi, 1980; Fischer, 2000: 127–9; Funtowicz and Ravetz, 1993; Turner, 2003: 52–4, 66–9). Effectively address-ing such problems requires the insights of multiple scientific disciplines which employ diverse methods and standards of evidence. Decision-makers must consider not only different possible responses to a problem but also different conceptions of the problem itself. Moreover, the knowledge relevant to such problems often contains irresolvable uncertainties, especially with regard to long-term impacts such as those associated with climate change. This means that technical choices inevitably become intertwined with social values and political interests, and reaching democratically legitimate judgements requires the involvement of lay citizens. Under such conditions, even if experts suc-cessfully translate their claims into ordinary language, and even if lay people correctly identify the most credible experts, many questions remain about how expert advice can best shape lay deliberation.

Alternative roles for experts and expertise

Experts and expert knowledge enter into lay deliberation in various ways. At the most basic level, expertise is always already part of deliberation because it permeates the cultures of modern societies and shapes people's identities and assumptions (Foucault, 1978). Organisers of consensus conferences and citizen panels have often sought to recruit 'blank slate' participants with no prior knowledge of the issue at hand but such efforts are naive because the most inno-cent lay person has inevitably absorbed various cultural messages about science and technology, and they are also self-defeating because informed and opinion-ated participants are likely to devote more effort to deliberation (Kleinman et al., 2011).

Experts and expertise also play a role in framing the topic of deliberation (Parkinson, 2006a: 128–33). How broadly or narrowly is the topic defined? Which aspects of the topic are deemed distinctly political, and hence subject to lay deliberation, and which aspects are considered technical, and hence reserved to experts? Which symbols and metaphors do participants employ to discuss and understand the topic? For example, deliberation about climate change will proceed rather differently depending on whether the issue is conceived as primarily a matter of technological innovation, market regulation, social transformation, global justice, or democratic governance. When organisers of deliberative forums select expert briefing materials and expert witnesses, they inevitably go beyond merely informing the participants and also frame the topic of deliberation (Tucker, 2008: 136).[10] As I discuss below, framing effects do not invalidate lay deliberation but they pose challenges for institutional design and deliberative practice. ✗

Beyond these matters of background assumptions and issue framing, many science policy scholars have argued that the role of expert advisers should vary according to the specific issue at hand (Ezrahi, 1980; Habermas, 1970; Jasanoff, 1990; Weingart, 1999). Pielke (2007) identifies four acceptable roles for expert advisers. When the issue is characterised by widespread consensus on both science and values, experts can play the role of *pure scientist*, limiting themselves to summarising the state of knowledge in their particular field. Or they can adopt the role of a *science arbiter* who responds to lay inquiries about specific technical matters. In situations where both science and values are in dispute, experts might choose to act as *issue advocates* who openly promote a particular political agenda or interest group while being careful to specify that their political arguments do not follow directly from their scientific expertise. Or they might become *honest brokers of policy alternatives* who combine technical and political considerations to clarify existing policy options and identify new options for policy-makers. Given the hybrid nature of their task, honest brokers are usually interdisciplinary advisory committees rather than individual experts (Pielke, 2007: 151, 154–6). The United States's former Office of Technology Assessment, for example, included diverse experts and worked closely with policy-makers to produce reports that identified a range of policy options (17, 95).

Depending on the issue context and the personal preferences of the expert, Pielke argues, any of these four roles may be appropriate. Never acceptable, however, are *stealth issue advocates* who fail to distinguish their scientific claims from their political views, and pretend the former directly entail the latter. Pielke focuses on experts who provide advice to public officials but one might extend his analysis to consider different roles for experts with regard to various kinds of lay deliberation.

In the case of specially designed deliberative forums, such as citizens' juries, consensus conferences, and deliberative polls, organisers usually establish a separate expert panel and then schedule one day on which the lay participants question the experts (Brown 2006). This approach tends to put the experts in Pielke's science arbiter role: the experts provide politically neutral answers to specific technical questions chosen by the lay citizens, and the experts do not become engaged in deliberation about policy alternatives. This approach has much to recommend it. The science arbiter role seems more likely to enrich lay deliberation than asking the experts simply to summarise their areas of expertise (pure scientist) or to advocate specific policies (issue advocate). But Pielke rightly argues that the science arbiter role becomes implausible when the issue involves extensive political controversy and scientific uncertainty. Under such 'wicked' conditions, mentioned previously, it becomes almost impossible for experts to avoid becoming enrolled in political controversies. Partisan activists do not even need to resort to bribery or corruption to garner expert support, insofar as legitimate differences in disciplinary perspective and expert opinion allow all parties to find qualified experts who support their views (Sarewitz, 2004). One might consider, therefore, how the experts involved in citizen panels might adopt the role of honest broker. A step in this direction appears in efforts by organisers to recruit experts and counter-experts with competing political views (Fishkin, 2009: 120).

To develop further the honest broker role, citizen panels could be organised as hybrid deliberative bodies that include experts and lay people (Brown, 2009: 231–7; Turner, 2003: 67–9; Callon et al., 2009). Many government advisory committees and collaborative planning processes take a hybrid form, involving scientific experts and diverse stakeholders in joint deliberation (Brown, 2008). Avoiding an institutional divide between experts and lay people may help participants to avoid exaggerating the impartiality of experts and the ignorance of lay citizens. Most so-called lay people have expertise of one kind or another about one topic or another, and the relevant expertise often becomes apparent only during deliberation itself (Goodin, 2008: 104–7). There is something ironic about deliberative forums that aim to challenge the political dominance of experts but then provide experts with a privileged spot in the programme and reduce lay–expert communication to a staged question-and-answer format.

To be sure, engaging experts and lay people in joint deliberation raises concerns about experts dominating the discussion but similar concerns already exist with regard to the many deliberative inequalities among lay participants. Some people are more talkative than others without necessarily being more thoughtful and informed. The common remedy is to employ a skilled facilitator who ensures that participants are treated with equal respect and have an equal opportunity to make their voices heard (Callon et al., 2009: 162; Smith, 2009: 85–8). A good facilitator ensures that all participants receive equal consideration, and the facilitator's basic task remains the same regardless of whether the participants are experts or lay people. Indeed, even without experts among the deliberators, facilitators need to have enough expertise to ensure that deliberation remains informed by the best available science without undermining the epistemic authority of the deliberators themselves (Moore, 2011). Moreover, it is not obvious that lay deliberators are always susceptible to expert domination, and many empirical studies find little evidence of excessive lay deference towards experts. Studies of consensus conferences and similar deliberative forums have generally found that lay participants were able both to learn from and thoughtfully challenge expert testimony (Chen and Deng, 2007; MacLean and Burgess, 2010). Fishkin notes that 'once participants learn that the experts disagree they feel freer to re-examine the issues for themselves' (Fishkin, 2009: 120).[11] Empirical studies also suggest that 'left to their own devices, groups tend to use information that is already commonly shared, downplaying unique information held by specific individuals', whereas more extensive discussion makes it more likely that deliberators will take up new information (Delli Carpini et al., 2004: 328). In the end, whether experts are relegated to a separate panel or asked to engage in ongoing deliberation with lay people, it is important to remember that effective lay–expert communication does not happen automatically. Some empirical studies thus highlight the need for long-term capacity building among laypeople and experts (Powell and Colin, 2008).

Societal contexts of expert advice

In addition to the factors discussed so far, the role of expertise in public deliberation is also shaped by the broader societal and cultural context. The politics of expertise takes different forms in different cultures, and it is also shaped by internal differences within cultures. Only two societal factors can be briefly considered here. First, in addition to the frames created by the organisers of deliberative forums, science communication research shows that mass-media frames significantly affect how lay people view scientific expertise. In the United States, for example, the media's tendency to adopt a controversy frame with regard to climate change, giving equal weight to mainstream climate scientists and their critics, long contributed to an exaggerated public perception of scientific controversy (Boykoff and Boykoff, 2004; Nisbet, 2009).

Second, research on 'cultural cognition' indicates that people's basic values and assumptions shape their assessments of expert credibility. For example, those who reject mainstream climate science may do so in part because they perceive a conflict between climate science and their cultural values. According to one study, those with hierarchical and individualist values tend to dismiss expert claims about environmental risks because they assume that accepting such risks would lead to government regulation which they reject. Those with egalitarian and communitarian values have the opposite response (Kahan, 2010).

There are at least three different strategies for responding to the effects of both cultural cognition and media frames. The first seeks to reframe expert advice to accommodate people's existing presuppositions. One scholar suggests presenting information in a way that affirms rather than challenges people's values and suggests, too, employing experts with diverse value orientations.

The aim is 'to create an environment for the public's open-minded, unbiased consideration of the best available scientific information' (Kahan, 2010: 297; Anderson, 2010: 156–7). This approach, taken by itself, continues to cast lay citizens as the passive recipients of expert knowledge.

A second and more promising strategy seeks to reframe expert advice to appeal to a broader and more engaged public. The common framing of climate change in terms of 'environmental catastrophe' or 'junk science' suggests a linear model of science advice, polarises public discussion, and leaves unclear how lay people might shape the policy response to climate change. A 'public accountability' or 'economic development' frame, in contrast, highlights opportunities for constructive public engagement that may appeal across ideological lines (Nisbet, 2009).

A third strategy is to subject media frames and cultural values to critical scrutiny through public deliberation. Most research on frames uses surveys or laboratory experiments to assess individual opinions in the absence of social interaction. But empirical research on deliberation shows that cross-cutting conversations that include diverse perspectives tend substantially to reduce framing effects (Druckman and Nelson, 2003). Such studies suggest that neither media frames nor cultural values should be seen as barriers to be eliminated on the royal road to objective expertise but as resources for and objects of collective deliberation. Moreover, not only lay people but also experts are influenced by media frames and culture cognition. Deliberation about expertise, therefore, might best take the hybrid form mentioned previously, including experts and lay people in joint discussion about the various values, interests, and scientific claims that shape their assessments of the issue at hand (Lane, 2011).

Conclusion

Both lay deliberation and expert advice aim to improve the epistemic quality of public decision-making. In this respect, they both contribute to the normative legitimacy of political decisions and they both contain a technocratic potential. For the poorly informed, it probably does not matter much whether policies are justified with reference to lay deliberation or expert advice – in either case, those who lack the relevant epistemic resources may well reject such decisions. The most common response – to attempt to improve science literacy and increase opportunities for lay deliberation – makes sense as far as it goes, but it offers little guidance for coping with the current situation in which so many lack access to both expertise and deliberative opportunities. A complementary response, which has become increasingly common among deliberative democrats, is to emphasise the role of non-deliberative modes of political activity, such as bargaining, voting, advocacy, testimony, and so on. As Dennis Thompson puts it, 'deliberative democracy includes many kinds of political interaction other than deliberation' (Thompson, 2008: 502). Similarly, Mansbridge and colleagues (2010) persuasively argue that deliberation should not exclude expressions of power and interest as long as these are eventually justified in deliberative terms.

This growing interest in non-deliberative modes of politics needs to be matched by increased attention to the role of expertise. With regard to narrowly defined technical questions on which experts agree (such as whether lead in drinking water harms human health), there may be little need for lay deliberation, and lay people would be well advised simply to ask the experts. On broad political questions (such as the relative priority of reducing lead in drinking water compared to other goals), experts should not be asked to provide decisive answers but their expertise is an important resource for public deliberation. But exactly how to make the best use of the available expertise remains a difficult question. It becomes especially difficult when experts disagree and when their disagreements become intertwined with political disagreements. This chapter has outlined a few considerations for coping with such situations. But, like other political questions, the role of experts in deliberative democracy should not be answered by experts alone.

Notes

1. According to Baber and Bartlett (2005: 154) 'in sharp contrast to Habermas, Rawls seeks to incorporate expertise but allows no special role for the individual expert in deliberative democracy'.
2. 'Reciprocity is to justice in political ethics what replication is to truth in science … Just as repeated replication is unnecessary once the truth of a finding (such as the law of gravity) has been amply confirmed, so repeated deliberation is unnecessary once a precept of justice (such as equal protection) has been extensively deliberated' (Gutmann and Thompson, 2004: 133–4).
3. Baber and Bartlett (2005: 88) write that:

   according to Habermas: the same processes of redeeming validity claims through appropriate types of argumentation is [sic] implicit in practical (moral and legal) disputes, as well as disputes about aesthetic judgments and scientific generalizations. All anticipate and, indeed, presuppose noncoercive and nondistoritive communication.

4. On Habermas's view of experts, see also Baber and Bartlett (2005: 189–91).
5. See the discussion of Bohman, Rawls and Habermas in Baber and Bartlett (2005: 49–54). Though he shares much of Habermas's view of expertise, Bohman also argues that Habermas's highly diffuse conception of public deliberation in civil society eviscerates the notion of democratic self-rule, since dispersed public opinion cannot plausibly be said to govern (Bohman, 1996: 179–80).
6. The 'symmetry principle' of the strong programme in the sociology of science is often associated with the notion that science is a 'social construction' that is unconstrained by non-human nature. The symmetry principle is better understood, however, as a methodological principle for studying the production of scientific knowledge. The symmetry principle does not deny that scientific knowledge is shaped in part by

mind-independent reality. It says only that reality alone cannot explain the acceptance or rejection of scientific claims.

7. See Kusch's (2007) discussion of Cass Sunstein's writings on risk assessment.

8. Collins and Evans (2007: 57–60) call this 'ubiquitous discrimination'. A more special case, which they call 'local discrimination', occurs when lay people identify trustworthy experts based on locally acquired experiential knowledge, such as workers' familiarity with the experts at their workplace.

9. Collins and Evans (2007: 67–9) argue that experience alone is the most reliable criterion for evaluating experts, though they acknowledge that it, too, can be misleading.

10. Fishkin (2009: 126), in contrast, argues that the selection of balanced briefing materials and competing experts ensures that competing stakeholders have the opportunity to articulate different frames of the issue.

11. Fishkin also reports that participants in deliberative polls often show large gains in political knowledge (Fishkin, 2009: 121).

CHAPTER 4

Interests, public policy and deliberation

Darren R. Halpin and Juraj Cintula

Introduction

Dedicated scholars of deliberative democracy have focused upon critiquing representative models of democratic decision-making and promoting both the merits and empirical feasibility of institutional design for decision-making procedures consistent with deliberative principles. More recently, a concern with deliberation itself has been taken up by studies exploring the way institutions – or even specific individual 'deliberative events' – can be designed to promote deliberation among stakeholders, citizens or even elites (see Parkinson, 2004; Smith, 2009). Some work has focused on macro-level processes, such as the role of civil society in facilitating broad and open deliberation over key issues of the day. Others emphasised micro processes, discrete decision-making events with a focused agenda and limited participation.

These 'events' – such as citizens' juries and the like – are most often studied bracketed off from the broader 'orthodox' policy process within which they are frequently positioned. As such, the question of how – if at all – they fit with the broader policy process is underexplored: for instance, are they supplementary exercises to the 'orthodox' policy process? Though the actual link such exercises have back to the orthodox policy process have been largely ignored, we can still find that some research has been done in this field – specifically concerning the true nature of deliberative events and initiatives in real life. For example, Magin (2007) offers a complex analysis of the urban planning process in Western Australia and tries to find out whether its major deliberative initiative ('Dialogue with the City') is inconsistent with deliberation ideals. He is pessimistic. The scope of events considered in the literature has recently extended to online consultations by the British central government (see John et al., 2010). Regardless of the scope of the analysis, it has been persuasively argued that a new generation of scholars has pursued 'real world approximations of deliberative democracy' (Elstub 2010a). Our approach taken in this chapter is generally consistent with this noted shift in concern towards what might be called *deliberation in policy practice*. Yet, our point of departure is not the first-generation political philosophy of Habermas or Rawls but, instead, the deployment of deliberation as a part of the repertoire of 'orthodox' public policy. We start with policy practice and work back to make links with the 'core' deliberative literature.

Our focus on the emergence of deliberation outside deliberative events *is* shared by some recent scholarship. More recently, some have started to explore the ways in which deliberation might just emerge within the institutional settings of the orthodox policy process. Indeed, our emphasis finds immediate encouragement in the recent work on deliberation – note, not deliberative democracy – in European legislatures (see Weale et al., 2012; Steiner et al., 2004). Such work provides a prime illustration that the deliberation literature is moving more directly into orthodox representative political settings to seek out deliberation: we follow this thread and try to push it forward.

It is perhaps no surprise, then, that the policy world is engaging with deliberation in a similarly broad manner. The world of public policy tells us – if we are listening – that deliberation is increasingly attractive to practitioners. In this connection we note with interest that many policy actors seem enthusiastically to endorse these types of exercises as providing new and exciting ways to legitimate policy actions (separate from elections and orthodox consultation processes, such as with interest groups). As such, scholars would be well served by reviewing the usage of the concept in popular policy discourse if only to guard against any hollowing out of its use. We shall take up this idea here. Specifically, in this chapter, the aim is to look at the way in which deliberation has been taken up by another set of scholars, namely public policy researchers. The aim is to make apparent their multiple uses of the term and to try to make links to the dedicated deliberative research community. In so doing, we hope to render the discussion of deliberation more accessible to our public policy colleagues and to make it more relevant to the policy work of policy-makers themselves.

This chapter proceeds in several parts. Part one provides an overview of the 'mainstream' public policy and political science literatures' recent deployment of deliberation and how policy elites deploy deliberation. In so doing, we gauge how far it has become a part of public policy frameworks and theories. The second part turns to one of the key challenges facing deliberation in practice, namely the coupling of representative and deliberative modes of politics. We pay particular attention to the way deliberation may emerge in policy processes but, in so doing, present real challenges to 'representative agents', specifically interest groups. Here we outline the way interest groups might be caught between two logics, highlighting one of Mansbridge's key insights into forms of deliberation. The final section develops a call for students of deliberative democracy to engage more directly in the debate about the place of deliberation in orthodox public policy. To focus our argument we set out to enunciate some key research questions that might be fertile themes for future research.

Deployment of the 'deliberation' concept: scholarly and practitioner usage

As discussed at the outset, the term 'deliberation' has generated a normative shine that encourages its appendage to all sorts of initiatives and activities. To 'deliberate' is met with more normative approval than, say, to 'bargain'. But, those with a longstanding engagement with deliberation will appreciate that the term has many nuances and that, to preserve its analytical value, the term must be distinguished from other forms of interaction and 'talk'. In this section we focus on the popularity of the term by two separate constituencies: the broader public policy/political science literature, and policy practitioners/elites.

Scholarly deployment of deliberation

Our basic motivation here is a sense that the literature has become corralled into work on two basic levels which we believe maps well on to Hendriks's distinction between micro and macro deliberation (2006, cited in Elstub, 2010a: 299). This bifurcation has left us with two distinctive literatures: (a) the first debates issues associated with large-scale reforms aimed at realising a deliberative form of democratic governance at national, or post-national scales, while (b) the second analyses the prospects of what we called 'deliberative events' (citizen juries, deliberative polls, and so on). Yet it strikes us that deliberation has also become drawn into debates in political science more generally about the different ways in which actors might form, and perhaps even change, preferences. We suspect this is an area where the deliberation 'specialists' might want to become more directly engaged. But what is the scale of this 'new' broader application?

Counting up the totality of articles in international journals is beyond the scope of this chapter but, to get some flavour of this diversity, we examined how scholars used the term 'deliberation' in the general political science journals. A rudimentary analysis of the content of major American, British and European political science journals reveals three broad categories of article: (a) primarily theoretical or conceptual; (b) focused on a deliberative 'event'; or (c) applied to a public policy context or 'representative' institution (such as a parliament).[1]

For instance, put the term 'deliberation' into a journal such as *Public Administration* and it will return around a hundred articles in the last ten years. Of course, not all articles focus on deliberation but the term is now in very broad use. Many of these articles focus on new policy instruments, forms of governance and co-ordination, modes of participation or consultation and, of course, experiments with deliberative events. Clearly usage is likely severely to lack consistency and coherence but this is itself a reason for some policing from those who see it as a concept worth preserving.

We argue that deliberation *is* an important concept and that it has a high degree of value for public policy scholarship. If, for instance, we take the longstanding policy community literature seriously, then there *must* be a place for learning and norm building among frequently interacting persons and organisational representatives (see discussion in Halpin and Daugbjerg, 2008). This, at least to us, implies a prospect for deliberation to emerge. But this is not the same as placing deliberative events – such as citizens' juries, and so on – within otherwise representative policy settings.

Practitioner usage of deliberation

How do actual policy-makers make use of 'deliberation'? A search for 'deliberation' in American media sites will locate a range of reportage associated with Obama's apparently 'deliberative' style. This seems to be something to do with meeting and talking with stakeholders directly, and being open to new ideas: talking with a blank page in front of him, as it were. This type of discussion of deliberation as a 'policy style' is not so divorced from the public policy scholarship discussed below. While it does not sit easily with the more narrow deliberation literature, it cannot simply be dismissed as literary licence among journalists. Certainly, there is also coverage of deliberative polls and 'deliberative sessions' used by local school boards and the like. As is widely reported in the literature, many national and regional governments are interested in utilising deliberative approaches to decision-making. The Scottish government has provided a guide to deliberative methods for its civil servants (Scottish Government Social Research Group, 2009). But it is a term with increasing currency in more orthodox settings. Perhaps reflecting the fashionable nature of the term, consultations with local communities in Western Australian land-use planning were once referred to as 'community deliberation' even though they did not conform to any of the deliberative methods in the literature. Again, deliberation is an increasingly attractive term for policy-makers but its usage is characterised by its breadth and inconsistency.

Orthodox policy settings: where interest-group representation meets deliberation!

The risk of concept stretching is obvious when 'our' scholarly formulations fall into the hands of 'others' in allied subdisciplines or even practitioners. A less obvious, but not less important, challenge emerges when concepts such as deliberation are deployed in the study of less familiar policy contexts – that is, outside institutional arrangements that might otherwise be considered as 'designed' deliberative. Recent reviews of the deliberative democracy literature suggest that scholarship has proceeded in waves or generations. A salient observation is that the second (and current) generation of work is more empirically minded; probing the ways in which 'empirical approximations' of first-generation normative accounts of deliberation might be applied in policy contexts. Even more notable is the contention that much of this work accepts that a role may be played by a set of organisations variously referred to as interest groups, associations or civil society organisations (Elstub, 2010a). In their assessment of the literature, Bächtiger et al. (2010: 32) further emphasise the 'beginning of an empirical turn'. They also note that such a turn has been accompanied with the increased risk of concept stretching; that 'mere talk' comes to be bracketed as deliberation. Based on our discussion in the previous section, this seems like a justifiable concern. Thus, there is good reason – both on the grounds of generating an empirically rich literature on deliberation and defending against concept stretching – to be clearer as to how deliberation *might* be usefully deployed in empirical analysis.

In this section we take up this task but with specific focus on deliberation *within* what might be called orthodox policy-making. We regard this as a useful enterprise not only because a focus on policy contexts beyond deliberative events is a key facet of the 'new' wave of deliberative studies but also that it will bring into sharper relief the need to be clear on what deliberation means – when we have it and when we do not. Put another way, the risk of deliberation being understood as 'mere talk' is highest in such orthodox contexts.

A key challenge in introducing the concept of deliberation into analysis of 'public policy work' is a long-noted difficulty in distinguishing between deliberation and strategic communication. This distinction is central to (early) Habermasian discussions of deliberative democracy – the necessary and sufficient conditions required for 'talk' to transcend strategic communication and become deliberation were *the* focal point for debate. Yet, in empirical policy contexts, it becomes difficult to discern if conversations are deliberation or not – if they are not, they might be considered to be 'bargaining'. This difficulty is well understood, with Bächtiger et al. (2010: 48) wisely cautioning that, in expanding the scope (what counts for deliberation) and site (where deliberation might be expected to occur) of deliberation, we run the risk that the concept is stretched beyond any analytical use.

This warning has particular resonance for our present discussion, for it acknowledges that deliberation may (a) occur out of the bounds of deliberative institutions and (b), following on from this, that one cannot know – in advance – that (or where) deliberation will occur (at least until 'after' a policy episode is over). In this latter connection, Bächtiger et al. (2010: 56) suggest that a 'sequential' approach might be more plausible. By that they mean that the actual moment of deliberation becomes part of a broader process, and the unit of analysis is the 'deliberative sequence'. This approach might be read as consistent with an earlier observation made by McLaverty and Halpin (2008) that deliberation is more plausibly considered as something that emerges (and then sometimes recedes) as individuals develop patterns of communication (and trust and background framing of key questions to discuss) that might support the type of ideal deliberation discussed in the literature: what they call 'deliberative drift', on which more below.

Recent work by Mansbridge and colleagues (2010) also moves in somewhat similar directions. They acknowledge explicitly that deliberation (a) may encompass what has hitherto been denoted as bargaining, and (b) that deliberation may be viewed as part of a process of communication and decision-making that includes non-deliberative elements. On this latter point, she suggests 'deliberation ideally ends not in consensus but in a clarification of conflict and structuring of disagreement, which sets the stage for a decision by non-deliberative methods, such as aggregation or negotiation among cooperative antagonists' (2010: 68).

This provides us with some background justification for pursuing more explicitly how groups can fit into accounts of deliberation. Our starting point, however, is *not* deliberation scholarship. Rather, we start from the public policy literature – noting the ways in which deliberation is (increasingly) deployed and how groups feature in such accounts – and work our way back to the specific concerns of deliberative scholars.

The public policy connection
As set out in the introduction, for some time deliberation has been the preoccupation of a small – yet growing – community of scholars concerned with theoretical possibilities, and then increasingly with empirical possibilities and experiments (see review by Elstub, 2010a). It was part of an enterprise that sought to sketch out an alternative – read 'better' – manner of doing politics. More recently, what could be called mainstream public administration and public policy researchers (and even civil servants and politicians) have found it a useful concept. While much separates these literatures, we argue that there is at least some level of agreement on the critical role played by interest groups (aka civil society organisations or voluntary associations) in fostering deliberation. But precisely how can groups engage or be discussed in terms of deliberation?

One way to unpack this basic – but, we suggest, important – insight is to connect it up with the well-known distinction made by Mansbridge (1992) between qualitative types of policy deliberation involving groups. To refresh the memory, she distinguished among:

- *Competitive deliberation:* groups offer up their fixed position to the public and policy elites for them to judge the value of the better argument. Here, there is no direct engagement among groups and thus no reason or mechanism to enable groups to moderate or vary their starting positions. In this model the type of dialogue among groups, at least to our ears, seems hardly to deserve the label deliberation.
- *Collaborative deliberation:* by contrast, group elites engaged with policy elites in ongoing, sustained and repeated engagement which, by itself, might

transform *their* preferences. This is, in fact, the general insight from the policy community literature that emphasised governance through 'communities' of stakeholders engaged in getting some of what they wanted most of the time as part of the 'orthodox policy process' (Grant, 2001). Of course, a key dilemma in such processes is in actually bringing along members with elites. It is a major weakness of such processes that group elites will have trouble legitimating compromises made away from members' gaze, in which case there are strong functional incentives for groups to seek autonomy from members (often through membership recruitment practices that emphasise weak supportership style attachments prompted by selective material incentives) (see Halpin, 2010; Jordan and Halpin, 2004).

- *Corporatist deliberation* focuses on direct engagement among individuals with a willingness to change opening preferences and, as such, find solutions that reflect a shared (Mansbridge herself says public) interest. Mansbridge distinguishes between two levels of preference change. The first is agreements or compromises made *between groups*, and the second is deliberation *within groups* to find or discover common interest (against the notion that groups simply aggregate pre-existing interests of members).

In what follows, we focus on the two aspects of corporatist deliberation identified by Mansbridge (with some attention to overlaps and transitions with other 'types'). And, we identify how the public policy literature treats these.

Policy deliberation among groups?

Like Mansbridge (1992: 32), we also detect an oversimplification in the notion that groups engage in politics to pursue established (self-) interests, the results of which can be evaluated in zero-sum terms. While such characterisations *are* rife in the group literature – especially that concerned with detecting influence (see review by Dür, 2008) – much public policy work sketches in a role for groups in ways more amenable to a deliberative 'interpretation'.

This broad approach is evident in the general public policy literature that sees 'associative' capacities as critical to generating state 'governing', 'policy' or 'transformative' capacity (see Atkinson and Coleman, 1989; Peters, 2005: 80; Painter and Pierre, 2005: 11; Weiss, 1998). The central point here is that the relations between groups and the state are not zero-sum interactions: capable groups are a necessary, but insufficient, condition for governing or policy capacity. This thread in the literature has been particularly interested in explaining the ability of some nation states to better their national industries in the face of increasingly competitive globalised trade: the role of capable interest groups in governance arrangements has been implicated as a key explanatory variable. For instance, Peters (2005: 80) talks of the 'capacities of society' as being crucial to a 'capacity to govern'. Peters (2005: 80) identifies '. . . the capacity to deliver the commitment of its members and/or other actors in the policy sector' – that groups having been involved in decision-making will go along with the decision. He also identifies 'information about the wants, needs and demands of their constituents'. Painter and Pierre (2005: 11) suggest that groups help the state 'acquire essential knowledge, while cooperative relations with them also ensure compliance'. In a similar vein, Bell and Hindmoor (2009: 163) talk of the 'capacities of associations' as crucial factors in the success, or otherwise, of 'governance through associations'. Such capacities include, '… high membership density or coverage, effective internal procedures for mediating member interests, and selective incentives to help mobilise members in collective action …' (Bell and Hindmoor, 2009: 163).

The last capacity, to mobilise collective action among members, can be reinterpreted as resting on dialogue, even deliberation, among members. For instance, in the highly influential *Varieties of Capitalism* genre, Hall and Soskice (2001: 11) suggest that a cornerstone of the competitiveness among co-ordinated market economies (CMEs) is the capacity – achieved mostly via capable peak interest groups – to catalyse 'deliberation' among parties (mostly firms) where new information and discussion lead to better policy outcomes. Others refer to the importance of deliberative networking between groups and the state (see Halpin and Daugbjerg, 2008). Even in the context of the United States, deliberation is deemed relevant. For instance, McFarland (1993) argues that *co-operative pluralism* (a form of elite deliberation) can be developed, *without* specific deliberative events. His study of the engagement between senior management in a coal company and an environmental interest group showed that repeated interactions generated trust and mutual understanding. He notes that both sides shifted positions upon making new understandings, albeit that the respective constituencies revolted against the 'enlightened' consensus of the leaders involved directly in discussion (we come back to this dilemma below).

The risks inherent in balancing representation and deliberation – which arguably McFarland alluded to – were elaborated further by McLaverty and Halpin (2008). Their broad argument is that group involvement in 'orthodox' public policy *can* develop into deliberation – so called 'deliberative drift' – owing to the repeated interaction of policy-making elites with group elites within often closed, or at least 'private', venues. The value of such drift, however – that it might allow for groups to share and shift preferences, to educate one another, to stand outside their own interests, to think from the other's perspective, etc – can be easily and readily undone by virtue of the fact that such 'opportunities' for deliberation must be legitimated within a broader representative process. The chief problem raised was simply that group leaders might find it hard to legitimate deliberative outcomes to their members given the members had not been on the same 'journey'.

This above discussion highlights a broader tension in making deliberation work among groups in public policy settings; namely, there are two audiences. In his work on the role of transparency in policy deliberation, Daniel Naurin (2007) has drawn attention to the fact that it becomes harder for stakeholder representatives engaged in 'lobbying' to conduct the type of free dialogue that might facilitate something like deliberative drift. Thus, in practice, deliberative drift, while possible, seems to demand some tricky 'juggling' between private and public debate – a juggling act that some may see as offending key tenets of deliberative democracy, especially free and open public debate.

Does this have any relevance for Mansbridge's analytical categories discussed in the preceding section? We think so. The notion of drift discussed here might be reframed, in Mansbridge's terms, as a shift from collaborative deliberation to corporative deliberation, and then back again. Namely, groups come to the table with set preferences that may shift and contribute to 'new' interests and preferences but that ultimately need to be accepted or 'sold' to group members as their interests.

Policy deliberation within groups?

Consistent with Mansbridge's second type of deliberation, recent work in comparative public policy has focused on the capacities of groups themselves to foster deliberation among their membership. Of course, this broad concern with internal group dynamics has a long history: the literature on Scandinavian (neo)corporatism suggests that the survival of corporatist intermediation is – in part – reliant on groups possessing the requisite 'properties' which include group capacity to deliver their members' support (Öberg et al., 2011). Here, however, we believe the work of Culpepper (2001; 2003) is particularly worth dwelling on. His work on efforts to implement industry training in several sectors of German industry finds that the capacity of business associations was the crucial independent variable. Capable associations were those that could facilitate non-market co-ordination among member firms but, among other things, circulate information, *deliberate* and mobilise members (2001, italics added).

Culpepper (2001: esp. Chapter 1) thus distinguishes between strong and weak levels of co-ordination. According to Culpepper, the success of implementing industrial change rests largely on how firms respond to policy initiatives that try to stimulate a new (and often higher-cost) equilibrium. This hinges on levels of co-ordination: high levels of information circulation and 'dialogic' capacity lead to strong levels of firm co-ordination (2001: 190). Weak levels of co-ordination reflect a scenario where market players engage in co-ordination with others to meet their individual pre-existing interests. Information circulation alone might be an example of this, as it may make individual firms better placed to execute their individual market strategies. High levels of co-ordination, by contrast, involve market actors not just sharing information but deliberating with one another in such a manner as to provide the possibility that initial prescriptions of prevailing interests might change, and hence raise the prospects of a better overall outcome (for all participants). Such discussions seem crucial in convincing market actors that the up-front cost of engaging in a new market will pay off where the success of the new market relies on buy-in from several independent actors. Thus, in policy-outcome terms, strong levels of firm co-ordination might be expected to generate new and more optimal outcomes while weak co-ordination might lead to sustained levels around an existing, but sub-optimal, outcome.

What is salient here is that Culpepper suggests that the core of associative capacity lies in the ability to foster 'deliberation' among member firms. This is not an unthinking application: Culpepper (2003: 17) makes a distinction between 'deliberation' which is about changing preferences by weight of the better argument, on the one hand, and 'deliberation' which involves discussion that helps agents 'develop collectively solutions they might not have conceived on their own' (21). At least part of the distinction lies in the 'rules' that bring parties to the table in the first instance. In the former, it is a background willingness to abide by fair rules of debate and to cast aside extant interests; in the latter it is precisely the extant interests that bring parties to the table, and it is sharing these interests – and learning about others' interests and intended actions – that Culpepper suggests *can* lead to deliberation. Put bluntly, agents come to be in a position where deliberation *might emerge* – they enter into dialogue – precisely because they have clear existing interests and that these are at stake or may be threatened by the actions of others. But dialogue can deal with problems of bounded rationality and informational deficits, and out of that may emerge new *and shared* problem definition and above zero-sum outcomes. This style of argument has some similarities with McLaverty and Halpin's (2008) idea of deliberative drift, and the Bächtiger et al. (2010) processual approach.

The 'why' of deliberation in this literature is straightforward: it reduces transaction costs for actors associated with attaining win–win solutions to common (and often expensive) dilemmas. Culpepper shows that associations can potentially play an important role in enacting industry policy by organising decentralised co-operation among firms. His key insight is that co-operation is often necessary to achieve implementation (especially in attaining high-equilibrium outcomes) because individual market actors will act (for example, by investing or accepting high start-up costs) and react (for example, to state subsidies or other inducements) with reference to what other relevant actors are likely to do (rather than how state agencies will react). The work of Culpepper is insightful, not least because it reminds us that deliberation is not just important when we consider 'decision making' but also further downstream in terms of implementation. Much deliberative democracy work focuses upon processes that make decisions or set agendas (see Elstub, 2010: 303). Yet, as the public policy literature suggests, there is much work to be done in turning these plans into action.

Summary

In sum, we have a movement by deliberation scholars to look beyond deliberative events, and public policy scholars eager to attach policy success to mechanisms like deliberation. In all this, one might reasonably be concerned with conceptual stretching: are we all talking about the same phenomenon when we say 'deliberation'? This is not something we can answer in generality but at least we can note that there is a hint that *even* the non-committed can find deliberation within orthodox policy settings. While the risks of deliberation being all things to all people is no doubt there, ample evidence exists that, in the hands of public policy scholars, it is being nuanced in relatively useful and thoughtful ways. We suggest that this nuanced application beyond deliberative scholars will preserve the concept and not define it into elegant irrelevance.

Critical research questions

While we have touched on some specific issues facing the involvement of groups in deliberation, many remain outstanding. We review just two here.

There is the question of the limits of deliberative forms of governance, especially inattention to agenda-setting phases of the policy process. Parkinson (2006a) and Maginn (2007), among others, argue that one of the biggest problems of various deliberative events they investigated is the undemocratic feature of the agenda setting by elites which leads to doubts about the limitations and legitimacy of this kind of process. On the one hand, it is clear that especially micro-deliberative forms need narrowly focused discussion about smaller amount of issues but, on the other hand, citizens should not get the impression that they are restricted in their possibilities to influence decision-making (Parkinson, 2006a: 132). From Maginn's example of Perth's Dialogue with the City Initiative, we can deduce it is necessary that stakeholders should be given enough space and time 'to engage in ... meaningful inclusionary argumentation and thus develop a mutual understanding of the needs and wants of other stakeholders' (2007: 348). Otherwise the deliberative event risks ending up as a combination of different (not purely deliberative) approaches 'where the agenda is essentially owned and controlled by policy-makers' (Maginn, 2007: 348). Moreover, Parkinson claims that participants will often defend their initial positions and therefore will not conduct themselves in compliance with the principles of deliberative democracy which can result in a biased form of deliberative democracy.

> The potential social and cultural bias of deliberative democracy is one of the aspects that Parkinson identifies as exacerbating, and even causing, motivation problems among potential actors in deliberatively democratic decision making, encouraging some social groups to exclude themselves from biased deliberative processes. (Elstub, 2010a: 297)

Concerning the issue of non-democratic agenda setting, Parkinson (2006a: 170) suggests that specific bodies (such as a parliamentary committee) should accept proposals and submissions from activists and experts which, combined with large-scale online deliberation (for example, Electronic Town Hall), should eliminate or, at least, significantly lower the rate of discrepancy with the principles of deliberative democracy, and therefore make the process of agenda setting more equal.

An additional point that has received insufficient attention concerns the interconnection between orthodox and deliberative events. As discussed above, in public policy it is usual for interest groups or stakeholder groups to be the participants in deliberative exercises or in processes that drift into deliberation. This deliberatively derived outcome, however, then needs to be legitimated more broadly with the constituencies these groups represent. Herein one can identify a key point of friction. How is it that stakeholder representatives, having deliberated, can defend and justify the collective outcome to rank-and-file members or constituencies that have themselves not participated in the process directly? This is not simply a theoretical or logical possibility. Elsewhere it has been shown that just this problem emerged in the context of environmental planning in rural Australia (McLaverty and Halpin 2008). More work needs to be directed at understanding the interface between orthodox and deliberative styles of working in public policy settings. How can representatives legitimate deliberatively derived outcomes? Are any claimed benefits of deliberative working retained once outcomes are made subject to the forces of representative legitimacy? And, more broadly, does deliberation then signify a normatively 'better' style of working if its outcomes simply alienate the broader – non-participant – community? It strikes us that these types of questions – and related empirical research – deserve a priority among scholars of deliberation concerned with public policy work.

Conclusions

In his study on 'Double Devolution' processes in the United Kingdom, Jordan (2007) raises questions of the desirability and feasibility of deliberation, mainly because of the deficit of critical assessment of this concept. According to him, the 'place of deliberation in political theory is so special that it seems to have power to suspend critical analysis ...' (Jordan, 2007: 53). In his perspective we should rethink if deliberation is really what we want, especially if it has power not only to generate consensus but to 'promote disagreement and enhance conflict' (Shapiro, 1999: 31) as well. If so, the results of deliberation would endorse not only full consensus (as described by Habermas) or moderate agreement but also some more 'extreme alternatives' which, in the end, would not be very effective and/or desirable in the public policy sphere (Jordan, 2007: 59). While sharing this caution over the rush to be seen to be 'doing deliberation', we also see much 'sensible' deployment of the term in public policy circles.

We believe that one lesson for those engaged in the normative 'project' of extending deliberation is that active engagement with more applied fields is necessary to protect the 'brand'. Politicians, think tanks and civil servants are quick to spot a new frame with which to re-legitimise old practices. And, in this regard, it is perhaps unsurprising that yesterday's 'stakeholder meeting' becomes today's 'policy deliberation'. When it cannot be bad to be said to deliberate, there is no incentive to do anything else. This is not an argument for dropping the concept or the project; quite the opposite. The instinct we seek to instil in the research area is of further engagement with the world of application. Elstub suggests that the third generation of work on deliberative democracy had a broad focus of 'deliberation in practice' (2010: 292). This is, indeed, true. But it still revolves around deliberative events – institutional designs that will deliver deliberation as imagined (but not well specified) by earlier waves of theorists. Our suggestion here is that advancements can be made by engaging fully with public policy colleagues for whom the idea of finding a consensus will not seem as foreign as one may expect. Of course, many models of politics emphasise bargaining and instrumental rationality but there is a very broad tradition that finds the practice of politics to be more multidimensional.

Note

1. We examined the following journals in late 2011: *Public Administration*; *Journal of Public Policy*; *Journal of European Public Policy*; *Political Studies*; *European Journal of Political Research*; *British Journal of Political Science*; *American Political Science Review*; and the *American Journal of Political Science*.

CHAPTER 5

Pluralism and deliberative democracy

Manlio Cinalli and Ian O'Flynn

The term 'pluralism' features prominently in many accounts of deliberative democracy. Usually, it is taken to describe the fact that people hold different values and beliefs, and hence arrive at different conclusions about how we ought to live. Accordingly, a central question in the theory of deliberative democracy is how we should respond to the fact that people not only differ but also disagree. As one might expect, deliberative democrats have offered a range of different answers to this fundamental question. We begin this chapter by discussing one such answer. As John Rawls argues, in seeking to resolve disagreements about the basic structure of a democratic society, the members of that society should appeal not to their own beliefs and values but to the sorts of political value that one might naturally expect to find inherent in the public political culture of any democratic society – equality, freedom, fairness, toleration, the rule of law, and so on (Rawls, 1996; 1997). As such, Rawls does not try to deal with the fact of pluralism directly through democratic deliberation. Rather, he seeks to deal with it by excluding it from the political domain. For Rawls, deliberation need not go all the way down.

While Rawls thinks that we should respond to the fact of pluralism by requiring people to couch their political arguments in terms of general political values, critics argue that his approach is too restrictive. In their view, Rawls is insufficiently sensitive to the fact that some people – for example, those with little formal education or the members of some minority ethnic, linguistic or religious groups – may struggle to express themselves in such terms (Sanders, 1997; Young, 2000). Rather than privileging any one mode of political argument, the critics think that the theory of deliberative democracy should incorporate a plurality of modes of political communication, including storytelling and singing. Our sense is that many deliberative democrats think that the critics are broadly right (for example, Bächtiger et al., 2010). Yet the claim that some people may struggle to couch their arguments in terms of general political values is an empirical claim that has yet to be properly tested.

In the second section of this chapter, we offer a quantitative analysis of data on ethnic relations in Britain retrieved from two quality British broadsheets, *The Guardian* and *The Times*, during the course of 2007.[1] Following Koopmans and Statham (1999), the coding scheme that we employ allows us to analyse the claims actors make in terms of their 'linguistic grammar' (for a more detailed discussion, see Cinalli and O'Flynn, 2013). Among other attributes, we check to see whether a given claim includes a general political value and, if so, which one. While ethnic groups are precisely the sorts of actor that one might expect to struggle on this measure, our data suggest that the case against Rawls's approach is far from decisive.

'Pluralism' can also be used to refer to 'value pluralism' which is a (meta-ethical) theory about the nature of value itself. According to this theory, values are irreducibly plural and, in significant measure, uncombinable and incommensurable.[2] Value pluralists therefore stand opposed to the view that conflicts between values can be resolved by tracing those values back to an underlying master value such as utility or by ranking them hierarchically along a single scale. Value pluralists are not relativists. On the contrary, they insist that there is a world of objective values (Berlin, 1991: 11). They also insist, however, that there is no 'perfect whole' or 'ultimate solution' in which all the different values might be reconciled (Berlin, 1991: 13).

It is surprising that deliberative democrats have not spent more time considering the challenge that value pluralism poses to deliberative democracy. As we explain in the third section of this chapter, the truth of value pluralism would render deliberative democracy redundant in the face of value conflict. If values (democratic or otherwise) cannot be rationally compared, we might bargain or vote, or perhaps just resort to power. But what we cannot do is seek to convince or persuade others that our preferred values are superior to theirs.

Rather than persisting with deliberative democracy, some radical democrats think we should instead seek to cultivate a political sensibility that is capable of transforming 'antagonism' into 'agonism' (Connolly, 2005; Mouffe, 2002). Yet, as we argue in the fourth section, before rushing to embrace radical proposals of this sort, we should first check whether the empirical evidence actually supports the truth of value pluralism. Once again, we draw on data from our research into ethnic relations in Britain. Yet, this time, instead of merely coding values, we draw on network analysis to see how different values and actors relate to one another.[3] As we suggest, the variable relational patterns that emerge allow us to test the combinability and commensurability of different values, and hence to assess the extent to which the empirical evidence confirms or disconfirms the truth of value pluralism.

The fact of pluralism

According to Rawls, the fact that people hold different beliefs and values is not merely a contingent and unfortunate fact about the world. Rather, it is a natural consequence of our use of reason in circumstances of freedom, particularly given the burdens of judgement (the burdens of reasoning under conditions of incomplete information, moral uncertainty and so forth). Yet, because reasonable people will recognise that everyone is subject to the same burdens of judgement, Rawls thinks it is important to distinguish the mere fact of pluralism from the fact of *reasonable* pluralism (Rawls, 1996: 37, 54–6, 61 and *passim*).

Two points should be noted here. First, the distinction between the mere fact of pluralism and the fact of *reasonable* pluralism enables us to see why Rawls is not a value pluralist – or, perhaps more accurately, to see why value pluralism does not figure in his account. For Rawls, value pluralism is (what he terms) a 'comprehensive doctrine'. That is, it is precisely the sort of ethical doctrine about which people can reasonably disagree and it cannot therefore provide a foundation for a just and stable democratic society. Admittedly, some commentators have not read Rawls in this way. For example, George Crowder argues that Rawls's acknowledgement of the burdens of judgement amounts to a commitment to value pluralism (Crowder, 2002: 165–72; but see Jones, 2006: 197–8). Yet Rawls himself did not think so – and we think he is right not to think so because there is no logical link between the two. Rawls seeks to explain why people disagree and does not root his explanation in any theory about the nature of value. Nor need he do so because the burdens-of-judgement idea is independent of the truth or otherwise of value pluralism (see Jones, 2006: 197–8).[4]

Secondly, the reasonableness for which Rawls argues is not part of some larger epistemological theory; though it has epistemological elements, it is not about defining the content of reasonableness per se. Rather, it is part of a broader normative understanding of what the political equality of democracy demands (Rawls, 1996: 49–50, 62). On that understanding, recognising others as equals in political argument means recognising that those others can have reasons to hold their views as firmly as we hold ours. Accordingly, if we do not make a serious effort to deliberate with them and try to find reasons that they can freely accept, we fail to treat them as political equals. This does not mean that we have to become milk-and-watery in the way in which we hold our views; Rawls never intended his argument for deliberative democracy to be interpreted in that way (Rawls, 1996: 62–3; Jones, 2003: 104–6). But it does mean that, when it comes to deciding important matters of law and policy, we should not simply insist on the truth of our own values and beliefs (though we may well believe them to be true).

Thus, on this view, arguments that people would be able to accept only if they were to become the adherents of some particular religious doctrine have no place in democratic deliberation – they have no place because they will not be generally accessible and acceptable (Rawls, 1996: 62; Barry, 2006: 23–4). When we make no effort to couch our arguments in terms that other people could in principle accept, or to develop our own views in ways that makes them responsive to theirs, we do not treat those with whom we disagree as equal partners in a common democratic enterprise – at best we treat them as an obstacle to be overcome (Dworkin, 2006b: 132–3).

To understand why Rawls thinks that the members of a democratic society should couch their political arguments in terms of general political values, one therefore needs to understand the account of political equality with which it is bound up (Rawls, 1996: 100–1; 1997: 770). (For further discussion of the relationship between deliberative democracy and equality see Chapter 2, 'Inequality and democracy', by Peter McLaverty.) On that account, democratic deliberation should proceed from common ground, and Rawls thinks that that ground can be found in democratic values. For example, different religious groups might be able to share the same principle of fairness, even though each conceives of that principle as grounded in its own faith (Rawls, 1996: 147).[5]

Of course, the fact that people share the same political values does not mean that political agreement will inevitably follow. Rawls accepts this much (Rawls, 1996: 240). In particular, he accepts that a point may be reached when political values no longer help and we can no longer keep comprehensive doctrines out of political decision-making (Rawls, 1996: 247–54; cf. Rawls, 1997: 797–9). Yet, while some matters will have to be resolved through the ordinary democratic process (that is., through bargaining or logrolling or voting), he nevertheless thinks that political values can have a vital role to play, particularly in decisions about the basic structure of society, including, for example, constitutional matters, family law or economic regulation.

Still, as we pointed out in our introductory remarks, Rawls's approach has come in for considerable criticism. One criticism that comes up repeatedly in the broader deliberative democracy literature is that, in seeking to constrain what people can and cannot say, Rawls's approach is insufficiently sensitive to the very fact of (reasonable) pluralism to which it is meant to respond. We offer an empirical assessment of that criticism in the next section.

Who appeals to general political values?

Rawls's approach is exclusive rather than inclusive. It does not try to deal with the fact of pluralism directly through democratic deliberation but, instead, leaves that fact in place and provides political arrangements that are independent of it. Those who criticise Rawls for 'taking the politics out of politics' are therefore broadly right: for the most part, he seeks to deal with the fact of pluralism constitutionally rather than democratically (for example, Habermas, 1998: 58). Yet the reason why he insists that people couch their arguments in terms of general political values is to ensure that political power is not used to impose, promote, impede, or disadvantage any part of reasonable pluralism (Rawls, 1996: 217, 243). In other words, the point is to ensure that democratic deliberation will be fair, or proceed on fair terms, given the fact of pluralism.

Against this approach, critics, such as Lynn Sanders and Iris Marion Young, argue that what Rawls fails to see is that, through no fault of their own, some people may struggle to couch their arguments in terms of general political values (Sanders, 1997: 352–3, 361; Young, 2000: 56). For example, those with little formal education or those belonging to a new immigrant group may simply lack the requisite vocabulary; in the case of some linguistic minorities, the point here may be doubly true. As a result, their views may be excluded from serious consideration, not necessarily because of what they say but because of how they say it.

Neither Sanders nor Young is hostile to deliberative democracy per se. But each thinks that it needs to be expanded or enlarged so as to take alternative forms of political expression into account (see also Bohman, 1995). Young, for example, argues that narrative or storytelling should be included because it can provide crucial insights into people's fears and aspirations, the motivations they attribute to others, and their willingness to act in some ways but not in others. Indeed, she claims that narrative 'is often the only vehicle for understanding the particular experiences of those in particular social situations, experiences not shared by those situated differently, but which they must understand in order to do justice' (Young, 2000: 73–4).

Recently, some scholars have suggested that the sort of 'type I' approach that Rawls advocates and the sort of 'type II' approach that Sanders and Young advocate 'might be integrated in such a way as to complement each other' (Bächtiger et al., 2010: 34). In fact, Rawls allows that, on the 'wide view of public reason', people may appeal to their own beliefs and values but only on the condition that, in due course, political values are presented to support their case (Rawls, 1996: li–lii; 1997: 783–7). Narratives can enable groups to present a unified front which may help them to get their views and concerns across to the wider public. But decisions about the basic structure of society cannot simply be based on narratives, not least because different narratives can conflict. When they do conflict, we must seek to deliberate from common ground or risk one group imposing its way of life on others (see Dryzek, 2000: 68–9).

Nevertheless, while there are good reasons for privileging general political values, one might still worry that some people will struggle to couch their arguments in such terms. As we pointed out in our introductory remarks, however, the issue here is ultimately an empirical one: does who we are make a difference to our ability to deliberate in the way that Rawls suggests?

Table 5.1 below is based on our analysis of claims or (what we term) 'deliberative interventions' made in the field of ethnic relations in Britain, as reported in the pages of *The Guardian* and *The Times*. Formally, we define a deliberative intervention as a verbal statement made by an actor in the public sphere that rests upon a variable articulation of an argument in relation to the argument of another actor. More prosaically, an intervention usually takes the form of a direct quote and usually supports or opposes the views of some other actor. For example, defending his view that imams should be trained at British universities

Table 5.1 Actors and values

	Institutional actors %	Intermediate actors %	Minority actors %	Civil society actors %	All actors %
No value	12.6 (33)	14.7 (10)	10.0 (11)	9.0 (16)	11.3 (70)
Civil and political liberties	13.0 (34)	10.3 (7)	15.5 (17)	12.4 (22)	12.9 (80)
Justice	15.6 (41)	13.2 (9)	13.6 (15)	17.4 (31)	15.5 (96)
Safety, security and prosperity	17.9 (47)	7.4 (5)	7.3 (8)	6.7 (12)	11.7 (72)
Respect for difference	19.5 (51)	23.5 (16)	20.9 (23)	29.2 (52)	23.0 (142)
Social cohesion	10.3 (27)	10.3 (7)	10.0 (11)	7.3 (13)	9.4 (58)
Other values	11.1 (29)	20.6 (14)	22.7 (25)	18.0 (32)	16.2 (100)
Total	100.0 (262)	100.0 (68)	100.0 (110)	100.0 (178)	100.0 (618)

N between parentheses
Cramer's V = ns

to help Muslims integrate into mainstream society, the then prime minister, Tony Blair, argued that 'The voices of extremism are no more representative of Islam than the use in times gone by of torture to force conversion to Christianity represented the teachings of Christ'. In response, Mazin Younis, a volunteer imam at Leeds University, argued that 'Extremism is not created from abroad, it is coming from within. Blair's plans could have the opposite effect.'[6] The coding of support and opposition allows us to map relations between actors, and between actors and the values to which they appeal (which is central to the relational analysis that we present later).

Data are aggregated according to a number of broad categories of actor: for example, 'institutional actors' includes government, parliament and the judiciary, 'intermediate actors' includes political parties, trade unions and the media, 'minority actors' includes ethnic as well as various religious minorities such as Muslims, Jews and Sikhs, and 'civil society' includes NGO movements and general professional organisations. Data are also aggregated according to a number of broad categories of value: thus, 'civil and political liberties' includes human rights, freedom of religion and the good of democracy itself, 'justice' includes the right to a fair trial, fairness and equal treatment, 'safety, security and prosperity' includes peace, personal well-being and economic growth, 'respect for difference' includes empathy and mutual understanding, and 'social cohesion' includes inclusion, toleration and community.

The first point to note is that this is not a 'top-down' elitist field in which institutional actors account for the vast majority of interventions. 'Bottom-up' intervention is strong and, in particular, minority actors are highly visible. The overall figure of 110 interventions for minorities goes well beyond that of sixty-eight for intermediate actors. And when minorities are taken together with civil society, their visibility is actually higher than that of institutional actors. The second point to note is that minorities do not seem to have any difficulty appealing to the same values as everybody else. A quick glance at the data is sufficient to show that the situation in the field of ethnic relations in Britain is far from fostering 'internal exclusions of style and idiom', as Young suggests.

But what about the distribution of values across actors? The test of significance shows that there are no relevant differences in terms of the distribution of values between different categories of actor. Put simply, one can say that variations of value are not significantly linked to variations of actor. That said, disaggregating data does allow for some more specific remarks.

Take, for example, Muslims – a minority actor whose speech is supposedly particular rather than general. Our findings show that Muslims chiefly appeal to the value of social cohesion. But they also frequently appeal to 'other values', that is, to values that do not feature strongly in public political debate – for example, the need to increase moral standards, the importance of reputation and respect for animals. This last characteristic, however, is not all that unusual because it is also shared with civil society actors.

While we recognise the provisional nature of these findings, and hence the need for further research in this area (for relevant contributions, see Wessler, 2008; Dolezal et al., 2010), overall our data suggest that minorities do not struggle to couch their arguments in terms of general political values, or in terms of the sorts of value one might expect to find inherent in the public political culture of a modern democratic society. On the contrary, they seem to have relatively little trouble doing so.

The challenge of value pluralism

In our introductory remarks, we said that, to date, deliberative democrats have not had much to say about value pluralism. That may be because they have yet to see that value pluralism is potentially a problem or it may be because abstract theories are hard to translate into concrete empirical studies (if, indeed, they can sensibly be translated at all). But whatever the case, the truth of value pluralism would seriously impair the case for deliberative democracy. According to value pluralism, we can all agree that justice, equality, generosity, freedom, community, and so forth are genuinely valuable. Yet the trouble is that there is no uniquely right way of putting them together or of ranking them on a single scale (but see Dworkin, 2006a). We are always having to make trade-offs and sacrifices, and people make these in different ways.

If there is no uniquely right way of putting values together, there is little point in thinking that deliberative democracy might serve as a solution to value conflict. I might be able to appreciate your values and you might be able to appreciate mine. But should our values conflict, and should they also turn out to be uncombinable and incommensurable, there is no basis on which we might reason our way to a solution (cf. Bohman, 1995: 254). Of course, not all conflicts are conflicts of value. Some are conflicts of interest which might still be resolved through deliberation. But, unfortunately, some of the most pressing problems that we face today do involve conflicts of value which is why the challenge here is so great.

Obviously, the truth of value pluralism would undermine Rawls's approach: though Rawls thinks that we should couch our arguments in terms of general political values, those values might well be uncombinable and incommensurable. But the truth of value pluralism would also undermine attempts to include narrative and other forms of political communication: the values which different narratives seek to express might be subject to the same problems as the values Rawls extols. (Naturally, the truth of value pluralism would also undermine attempts to integrate 'type I' and 'type II' approaches.)

Thus, in the somewhat dystopian words of John Finnis, 'if worldviews are incommensurable, we have no reason to accept a scheme of social decision making, a constitution, a Rule of Law. For each person, then, the challenge is simply to become and remain one of those who are in charge' (Finnis, 1997: 217). Rather than accept such a conclusion, radical democrats, such as William Connolly (2005), Chantal Mouffe (2002) and Glen Newey (2001), advocate a less overtly rational, more immanent, approach to dealing with conflicts of value. There are important differences between each of these thinkers but, for purposes of illustration, we can focus on the arguments of Connolly.

For Connolly, a 'pluralist' is someone who has his own beliefs and values but who also strives to accept, value and respect the positions of others. Thus, 'a pluralistic society inculcates the virtues of relational modesty between proponents of different faiths and creeds, and it seeks to limit the power of those who would overthrow diversity in the name of religious unitarianism' (Connolly, 2005: 40–1). That view is similar to Rawls's idea of the good citizen who adheres to his own comprehensive doctrine but who, as a citizen, is also committed to others, with their different comprehensive doctrines, having the same part as himself in the political process. The difference is that Connolly thinks that pluralism will apply to all matters including people's notion of the just or fair society. It is, therefore, a comprehensive doctrine of the sort that Rawls thinks should not be used to justify important decisions of law and policy.

The pluralism that Connolly adheres to is also different from 'value pluralism' as we find it in the works of, for example, Isaiah Berlin or John Gray. His pluralism is not simply a theory of value but is also about recognising, embracing, valuing and providing for a world that is pluralist in nature. (That is, it is not just a meta-ethical theory but it is also an ethical theory about how we ought to live.) It is not about overcoming conflict but about 'transmuting' 'antagonism' into 'agonism'. In particular, it is about generating 'agonistic respect' among people who hold different beliefs and values (Connolly, 2005: 47–8).

Thus, Connolly not only accepts but positively celebrates (or would have us celebrate) the uncombinability and incommensurability of values. 'Agonistic respect' emerges not through democratic deliberation but through the development of a 'relational sensibility'. That sensibility does not seek to place deliberative democracy 'above faith' but, instead, seeks 'to forge a positive ethos of public engagement between alternative faiths' (Connolly, 2005: 49, 60). Agonistic respect works from within rather than from without.

Connolly advances a positive agenda – he thinks that uncombinability and incommensurability can be addressed through the cultivation of appropriate dispositions. Yet uncombinability and incommensurability are not themselves interrogated. By this we do not mean to suggest that they remain undefined. Rather, the problem is that Connolly simply assumes that different values are frequently incommensurable without every really testing that assumption.

As we have said, the truth of value pluralism would be extremely damaging for deliberative democracy: if value pluralism were true, conflicts of value could not be rationally arbitrated. But is it so?

Assessing the truth of value pluralism

One way in which we might proceed is to ask about value pluralism's explanatory power as a theory. The theory of gravity seems to do a pretty good job of explaining why things fall down. But does the theory of value pluralism do a good job of explaining value conflict – for example, a conflict between groups belonging to different religious faiths? According to Berlin, we 'are doomed to choose, and every choice may entail an irreparable loss' (Berlin, 1991: 13). But is that really how religious believers see things? Do they really think of themselves simply as having made different trade-offs and sacrifices? As Peter Jones argues, someone who is genuinely committed to a particular religious faith would be unlikely to accept that other faiths are no less valuable than his own. But if religious faiths really are incommensurable, that is indeed what he should accept (Jones, 2006: 194). Because that seems implausible, it raises questions about the truth of value pluralism.

Rather than continue on this conceptual tack, let us instead proceed by considering whether the empirical evidence actually confirms or disconfirms the truth of value pluralism. In just a moment we shall introduce our own data but first we want to highlight some existing empirical research that bears on this question.

Evidence from deliberative polls shows that deliberation consistently brings political preferences closer to 'single-peakedness' (Farrar et al., 2010).[7] Simon Niemeyer and John Dryzek arrive at similar conclusions based on deliberative experiments using Q methodology (Niemeyer and Dryzek, 2007). These findings are important because they suggest that deliberative democracy can bring people to understand an issue in the same way or along the same dimension. When there is more than one issue dimension, there is more than one social choice. But when there is only one issue dimension, decision-making is much less arbitrary.[8]

This body of evidence does *not* show (nor does it claim to show) that deliberative democracy leads people to agree, only that they see what they disagree about so that there is an underlying dimension for their disagreement. In other words, it shows that deliberative democracy enables people to arrive at a meta-agreement on what the issues really are and what shared dimension underlies their differences (Fishkin, 2009: 103–4). So it seems that deliberative democracy is not powerless in the face of value conflict: people may disagree but deliberative democracy can at least bring them to understand the choice before them in the same way – including the values that ought to underpin their collective choice.[9]

The problem, however, is that this evidence does not refute the truth of value pluralism altogether. Deliberative democracy may lead people to agree that the policy options represent a choice between two values. For example, immigration policy, which might conceivably bring any number of values into play, might universally come to be seen as a choice between equal treatment and security. But those two values might still turn out to be uncombinable and incommensurable. At that point, deliberation might have run its course; there might be no possibility of reasoning with one another beyond that point (see Gray, 1995b: 71).

We accept that this may happen but the vital question is to what degree? To get a handle on this question, we think that a relational analysis across actors and values is potentially a worthwhile research strategy.[10] More specifically, a relational analysis allows us to do two things. First, it allows us to consider how different values are connected through the actors that make use of them. In this way, we can tackle the question of combinability; the higher the number of actors that appeal to a given pair of values, the more those values are combinable. Secondly, it allows us to compare patterns of exchanges that actors forge when referring to different values. In this way, we can tackle the question of commensurability: the more that values are rooted in similar relational patterns, the more they are commensurable. In both cases, we again draw on our data on ethnic relations in Britain.

Starting with combinability, Table 5.2 presents a matrix of values by actors. Because the question we seek to answer is whether individual values are combinable, Table 5.2 does not use aggregate categories of value as in Table 5.1 but, instead, focuses on four specific political values – empathy, justice, equal opportunity and well-being – that minorities use extensively.[11] The number at

Table 5.2 Combinability: values by actors

	Empathy	Justice	Equal opportunity	Well-being	Total
Empathy	x	10	2	15	27
Justice	10	x	4	8	22
Equal opportunity	2	4	x	2	8
Well-being	15	8	2	x	25
Total	27	22	8	25	

the crossing of any two values indicates exactly how many different actors make use of the two values. The higher the number, the more likely it is that actors think of these values as being combinable.

Scores show that values are combinable because each possible pair is connected. Some values are more combinable than others, however: in terms of the numbers of actors who appeal to them, empathy and well-being are the most combinable whereas empathy and equal opportunity and well-being and equal opportunity are the least combinable. The other three possible pairs of values are somewhere between.

Empathy is the most combinable overall, scoring a total of twenty-seven links with all other values. By comparison, justice is less combinable than empathy, yet combines better with equal opportunity. Equal opportunity is the least combinable of the four but is combinable nonetheless. So, while there is variation, scores do not confirm the truth of value pluralism. Actors appeal to many different values and many different pairs of values.

Turning to the question of incommensurability, what needs to be considered is the extent to which values are too different to compare. We treat the degree to which values perform differently to one another as a valid indicator, with 'performance' defined in terms of the relational patterns that are built upon them. Hence, we ask: do values display the same relational pattern or do they display different relational patterns? The more that relational patterns differ, the more it may be that we are dealing with values that cannot be ranked along a single scale. In what follows, we analyse relational information for the same four political values as above. Because, however, we are interested in the patterns of exchanges that actors forge when referring to a given value, we are more explicit about the actors involved.[12] In particular, because much of the ethnic relations debate in Britain focuses on Muslim actors (Muslims), we have treated these actors separately from other ethnic minority actors.

Figure 5.1 deals with the relational patterns that have been built upon the value of empathy. While the central position of governmental actors (Gov) is not a surprise, it is interesting to note that ethnic minority actors (EM) also have a fairly central position in the field. Although Muslim actors do not occupy a central position, they are directly linked to government and hence, via govern-

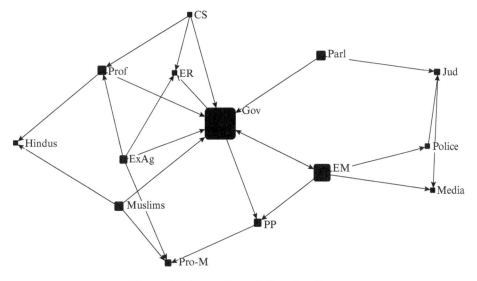

Figure 5.1 Empathy: relational patterns

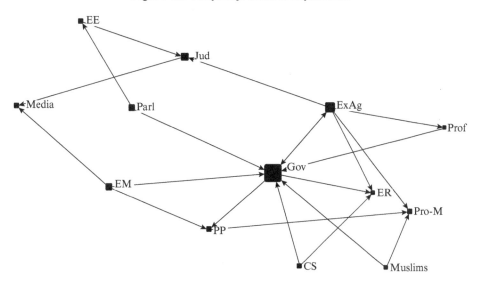

Figure 5.2 Well-being: relational patterns

ment, are well networked. Muslims are also closely linked to Hindus (Hindus) and, perhaps less surprisingly, to pro-minority organisations (Pro-M). More precisely, they act as a bridge between Hindus and government and pro-minority organisations and government.

Figure 5.2 deals with relational patterns that have been built upon the value of 'well-being'. In this case, ethnic minorities occupy a more peripheral position.

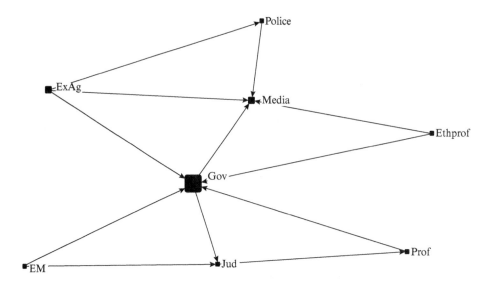

Figure 5.3 Justice: relational patterns

While Muslims have forged ties with far fewer actors, they are once again closely linked to government and, as a consequence, enjoy an indirect link with every other actor in the field. In this respect, we can say that empathy and well-being perform similarly in relational terms.

Moving to the analysis of 'justice' in Figure 5.3, it is noticeable how this value performs similarly to empathy and well-being in terms of the concrete use that ethnic minorities make of it. Though quite peripheral, ethnic minorities are also present in the form of ethnic professional organisations (Ethprof) such as the National Black Police Association. Muslims do not feature in this relational field, however, appealing too rarely to the value of justice to be included in our analysis. To this extent, justice performs differently in relational terms to empathy and well-being.

Figure 5.4 deals with our final value, 'equal opportunities'. Once again, Muslim actors have no role to play in this relation field. Yet, unlike our other three values, ethnic professional organisations are highly central and are directly linked to three of the four actors of the relational field. Interestingly, this inverts the more usual pattern – unlike the other three values, government is peripheral rather than central and ethnic minorities are central rather than peripheral. Accordingly, this value performs very differently in relational terms to the other values we have examined.

In sum, this evidence is fairly mixed. There is evidence of low levels of incommensurability – for example: the fact that government and executive agencies (ExAg) tend to offer a privileged axis of value discussion; the fact that Muslims are usually close to pro-minorities; and the consistent position of the

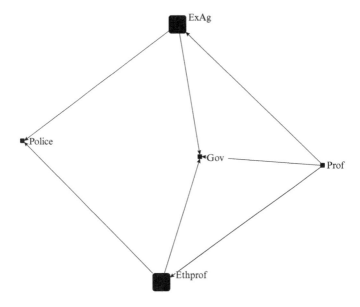

Figure 5.4 Equal opportunities: relational patterns

police (Police). But there is also evidence of incommensurability – most obviously, equal opportunities seems to perform very differently, because it inverts the more usual pattern. Added to that, Muslims feature in only two of four relational fields while the position of ethnic minorities is also variable (at times, they are present in their own right and, at times, present only through the specific role of ethnic professionals).

It is hard to know what to say at this point. Part of the difficulty here is due to the fact that value pluralists themselves are undecided about just how much incommensurability value pluralism entails. So, whereas our evidence might conceivably count against the more extreme position held by John Gray, it might not count much against the more moderate position held by Isaiah Berlin. So, really, a lot depends on where one stands on the theoretical issues. That said, deliberative democrats need to spend time thinking not just about the philosophical issues but also about questions of measurement. We have suggested that the extent to which actors fail to forge similar relational patterns upon different values might serve as an indicator of the incommensurability of those values. Yet we are happy to admit that there might be better, more telling indictors to hand.

Conclusion

It is probably fair to say that, when deliberative democrats think about pluralism, they are thinking about the fact of pluralism. That fact is bound up with the question of how to respond to the fact that people not only differ but also disagree. We based our treatment of that question around a defence of Rawls's claim that arguments about important decisions of law and policy should be couched in terms of general political values – or the sorts of value that one might expect to find inherent in the public political culture of a modern democratic society. While that claim has come in for considerable criticism, we think that many of the criticisms are misplaced. General political values serve to ensure that one way of life cannot simply impose its beliefs and preferences on other ways of life. And, while many deliberative democrats worry that the language of political values can itself have exclusionary effects, our empirical evidence does not support that worry.

The second half of this chapter considered the challenge that value pluralism poses to deliberative democracy. That challenge is bound up with a very different question: if values are uncombinable and incommensurable, is deliberative democracy powerless in the face of value conflict? Our evidence suggests that different values are, in fact, combinable which gives the lie to value pluralism. We accept, though, that incommensurability is a harder nut to crack. We have tried to assess empirically how different values perform in terms of the different relational structures that are built upon them. The guiding thought here was that, insofar as values perform very differently, they are not comparable; they look different because they are different and, hence, it makes little sense to say that they can be ranked along a single scale. Here, the evidence neither confirms nor disconfirms the truth of value pluralism. What it does confirm, however, is the need for further research.

Acknowledgement

The authors are grateful to Peter Jones for extremely helpful comments on an earlier draft of this chapter.

Notes

1. We accept that newspapers are always subject to problems of selection bias and hence to the risk of portraying a distorted deliberative reality (for example, McQuail, 1992: 193–5). Yet the fact remains that newspaper reporting plays its part in constituting the world in which we live and, in effect, determining and delimiting the scope for deliberative democracy. In short, one 'does not need to adhere to the fashion for radical constructivism and post-modernism to recognise that the mass media contribute to the symbolic construction of realities' (Peters et al., 2008: 139).
2. See, for example, Berlin, 1969, 1991; Gray, 1995a, 1995b, 2000; but see Dworkin, 2006a; Jones, 2006.
3. On network analysis, see Wasserman and Faust, 1994; Knoke and Kuklinsky, 1982; Scott, 2000.

4. In *Political Liberalism* (1996: 57), Rawls does make a favourable comment in relation to Isaiah Berlin. In particular, he accepts Berlin's point that hard choices sometimes need to be made between values. Yet that does not commit him to value pluralism. On the contrary, he explicitly dissociates himself from that theory (1996: 57, n. 10). As far as we know, Rawls never makes any use of, or even refers to, uncombinability or incommensurability.

5. In a similar vein, Ronald Dworkin has recently argued that, despite appearances to the contrary, most Americans, whether 'red' or 'blue' in ideological conviction, share a basic commitment to the values of intrinsic equality and personal autonomy (Dworkin 2006b). He then goes on to show how those values can serve as common ground on which to deliberate about some of the most divisive issues in American public policy (abortion, health care. etc.).

6. In our analysis, actors deliberate (or are classed as deliberating) with one another only when they argue back and forth over a repeated number of instances (a single deliberative intervention would not capture the dynamic nature of deliberation as we understand it). We take three such exchanges as the minimum required for there to be deliberation. In the example cited in the text, Blair was coded as 'government' and Younis as 'Muslim'.

7. 'A combination of preferences is single-peaked across individuals if the alternatives can be aligned on some "structuring" dimension, say from left to right, such that every individual has a most preferred alternative and a decreasing preference for other alternatives as they get more distant in either direction from it' (Farrar et al., 2010: 337–8).

8. For an early formulation, see Miller, 1992. For a more extensive study of this and related issues, see Mackie, 2003. For a summary of the social choice critique of deliberative democracy, see van Mill 1996: 740–3.

9. To date, the mechanisms by which all this works are open to debate. How exactly is it that deliberation leads people in the direction of unidimensionality? Miller argues that having to deliberate in public will automatically exclude certain sorts of argument and preference, specifically those that appeal to, or reflect, purely private interests (Miller, 1992: 61–2). Fishkin points to the effects of balanced argument and good information on the preferences people hold (Fishkin, 2009: 34). Niemeyer and Dryzek stress the importance of logical consistency or what they term 'inter-subjective rationality' (Niemeyer and Dryzek, 2007: 50).

10. Methodologically, we draw on network analysis. See note 3 above.

11. The thought here is that values that are notable for the fact that they are used extensively by minority actors will be less combinable overall than values notable for the fact that they are extensively used by majority actors. In other words, the thought is that they provide a sterner test. Whether this is actually the case is in need of further testing.

12. In Figures 1–4, actors are as follows: CS = civil society organisations; EE = ethnic extremists; EM = ethnic minorities; ER = extreme right; Ethprof = ethnic professional organisations; ExAg = executive agencies; Gov = government; Hindus = Hindus; Jud = the judiciary; Media = media; Muslims = Muslims; Police = police; Parl = parliament; PP = political parties; Prof = professional bodies; Pro-M = pro-minority organisations.

CHAPTER 6

Citizen competence and the psychology of deliberation

Shawn W. Rosenberg

Advocates argue that deliberative democracy offers a more normatively appropriate form of democratic governance than mere representative democracy. It provides the opportunity for meaningful political participation that also engenders mutual recognition and is more likely to lead to just outcomes. Deliberative democracy is also viewed as a more practical form of governance, one that is better suited to the multicultural societies of the twenty-first century. By participating in deliberations, citizens with different cultural backgrounds better understand one another and, therefore, are more able to work together to mitigate conflict between them. They will also recognise their interdependence and thus develop a sense of community.

While I agree that a more deliberative form of democracy has the potential to redress some of the normative and practical limitations of representative democracy, I believe that the realisation of this potential requires a realistic understanding of the nature of citizen deliberators and the likely quality of their deliberative practices. Most current theorising fails in this regard. Oriented by its roots in classical liberalism, deliberative democratic theory is premised on felicitous but unrealistic assumptions regarding the capacities of individual citizens and their communicative competence. Consequently, that theory suggests guidelines for designing political institutions that are unlikely to yield the expected deliberative practices or the desired outcomes those practices are intended to produce.

In this chapter, I speak to this issue by addressing four questions: (1) What exactly does deliberation demand of its citizen participants? (2) Are individuals able to meet those demands? (3) To the extent that individuals are unable to do so, what effect will this have on deliberation and its ability to deliver on its promise of conflict resolution, community building and more profound democratic participation? (4) What can be done to improve the skills and capacities of individual citizens and the quality of their deliberations?

What is required of the democratic deliberator?

To function as theorised, democratic deliberation requires citizens who have the capacity to deliberate appropriately. In theories of deliberative democracy, this simple but crucial fact is often dealt with in passing, as a matter of assumption and minimal specification. Individuals are assumed to have the capacities to be logical, rational and communicative in the ways that deliberation requires. Consequently, there is little need to consider carefully what deliberation demands of its citizen deliberators. The concern is typically addressed with a brief comment on the need to give reasons when expressing one's own point of view and to be civil in dealing with the others. In this light, the consideration of dangers to deliberation focuses only on the exogenous factors (for example, status and power) that may interfere with what would otherwise be desirable deliberative practices (for example, Cohen, 1996; Guttman and Thompson, 2004). Here I question the easy assumption that individuals have the capacities to be competent citizen deliberators. In so doing, I problematise these capacities, making them the object of critical consideration rather than foundational assumption.

To begin, it is necessary to be clear about what deliberation requires of its participants. Deliberations are typically organised to consider a community problem (for example, the delivery of education or zoning regulation). These problems typically involve a number of social, economic and political factors. This complexity imposes a considerable cognitive burden on the individuals asked to address them. To begin, relevant evidence must be collected. This requires that the individual deliberator understand how evidence should be collected and appreciate the distorting effects of using substandard methods. Once collected, evidence must be integrated. This demands logical inferences leading to the construction of a systematic, coherent understanding of the players, forces and resources currently and potentially involved. Throughout the individual must guard against her/his prejudices by clearly distinguishing between her/his personal or cultural beliefs on the one hand and the evidence and its logical implications on the other. Finally and with all this in mind, the individual must generate a variety of hypothetical solutions and assess their probable consequences.

Deciding on public policy also requires judging the means and ends of different courses of action. To come to a rational judgement, the individual must go beyond his/her immediate feelings, a response that may be coloured by the circumstances of the moment. Making judgements on such narrow grounds is likely to lead to preferences that are volatile and choices that may subsequently be regarded as undesirable. To avoid this, initial preferences should be considered relative to other preferences or feelings one might have and with regard to one's more long-term goals and moral principles. Only then will judgement best reflect the individual's values and thus be rational.

Though logical analysis and rational reflection are essential aspects of deliberative competence, citizen deliberation is a collective activity, not simply a personal cognitive one. As such, it requires the ability to use talk to work collaboratively with people who have differing points of view to come to a common understanding of a problem and how to address it. This requires a certain communicative competence. Participants must understand the value of talk as a means both for enhancing one's personal understanding of a problem and for co-operating with others in coming to mutually satisfying decisions. Only then will they be willing to suspend action in favour of deliberation.

Democratic deliberation not only requires that participants be willing to talk but that they do so in a way that is conditioned by a respect for the integrity of all involved. People should not be regarded simply as sources of information or as necessary partners in effective action and thus as means to an end. Rather they must be treated as ends in themselves and thus as autonomous agents whose beliefs and preferences, even when different from one's own, are worthy of recognition and respect. In my view, effective deliberation not only requires acknowledging the integrity of others in this way but also caring for them and their concerns (Rosenberg, 2007b). This may be necessary to motivate the individual deliberator to orient to others with the respect, the energy and the possible self-sacrifice that deliberation requires.

A third requisite is that the individual deliberator recognises his/her own subjectivity and its limits. He or she must be aware that he/she comes to a deliberation with a personal perspective. In this light, she/he must recognise that she/he does not necessarily know the truth of the situation but, rather, has beliefs about it, beliefs that may be more or less correct or comprehensive. Similarly he/she must recognise that he/she does not know what is absolutely good or right but, rather, has preferences and values which may or may not be appropriate or moral. The resulting tentativeness about one's own views and the consequent openness to the views of others are critical if deliberations are to go beyond mere strategic negotiation to more co-operative collaboration (Stone et al., 1999).

The individual should also be aware that he/she may reason in a distinctive way. His/her analyses of social problems depend on certain fundamental assumptions regarding people and the world that others may not share. His/her inferences and evaluations also reflect a quality of reasoning (its complexity, abstractness, etc.) that may differ from the reasoning used by others. Oriented accordingly, deliberators are less likely to 'talk past' one another. Instead they will try to communicate in terms that others can comprehend and potentially accept. This is critical if deliberation is to yield commonly understood and mutually acceptable outcomes.

Effective participation in deliberation also requires that individuals be aware that they are not only 'talking heads' but that they are also motivated social actors. Individuals have personalities. Consequently they deliberate not only to resolve problems but also to satisfy emotional and social needs. The attempt to satisfy these needs may inappropriately affect both their judgement of the problem and their interaction with fellow deliberators. Individuals are also socialised members of a structured community. Their participation in a deliberation is regulated accordingly, quite possibly in ways that significantly delimit the contributions they can make. To be a fully competent deliberator, the individual should be aware of how his or her personal needs and social norms may interfere with their ability to express their views or to respond the views of others. The individual must be similarly aware of the subjectivity and motivations of their fellow deliberators. Effective communication – that is speaking to others in a way they can comprehend and listening to them in their terms – depends on this sensitivity to their perspectives, needs and constraints.

To be productive, deliberation also requires the communicative ability to bridge the differences between perspectives. In part, this involves persuasion by argument. This involves the presentation and interrogation of claims of fact or value. This necessarily entails recognising that the validity of any claim depends on reasons that ground them in supporting claims of fact or value. Argument bridges differences insofar as one person's claim is accepted by others because that claim is linked to justifications that they accept. It may transform perspectives insofar as the argument extends to the premises upon which those justifications are based. Perhaps more fundamentally, productive communication also requires establishing a shared understanding of claims. People may understand and judge the same claims quite differently. To bridge these differences, speakers have to elaborate the meaning of their statements with reference to its place both in their own system of beliefs and that of their listeners. Listeners must then respond in kind. In this way, different perspectives are related to one another, creating the requisite common ground for interpreting meanings and making arguments. Some deliberative theorists (for example, Habermas, 1984, 1988; Benhabib, 1996, 2002) suggest that this communicative activity not only bridges differences but also can transform the way individuals think and the terms whereby they engage one another.

Do citizens have the capacities democratic deliberation requires?

To answer, I briefly review some of the relevant empirical research in social, developmental and political psychology.

Basic analytical capacity

A great deal of social psychological research has examined people's social reasoning or cognition. One approach has been to view social cognition as an attribute of mind and, thus, a reflection of basic human capacities. A good example is the research on causal attribution. The focus here is on how people explain past events and predict future ones. In his seminal work, Kelley constructs a normative model of logical processing and integration information.

He and those following him examine if individuals' thinking conforms to this standard (for example, Kelley, 1973; McArthur, 1972). The results indicate that people's causal reasoning is seriously flawed in a number of ways. Oriented by their field of vision or their perceptual biases, people tend to see some features of events more readily than others (for example, the more visually distinctive actors in a group) and thus tend to attribute those features more causal influence (for example, Taylor and Fiske, 1978; McArthur, 1981). People also have trouble utilising more abstract forms of evidence (for example, statistical information) and therefore are overly influenced by the concrete particulars of their experience (Hamil et al., 1980; Kahneman, 2010). In general, there is a tendency to over-attribute causal influence to particular actors and commensurately underestimate the impact of circumstances or context (Ross, 1977). Other research directly examines the cognitive shortcuts or 'heuristics' people use to process information. These simplifying techniques enable them to come to conclusions, albeit often incorrect ones, regarding causal or categorical relationships without having to address or integrate all the relevant information (for example, Tversky and Kahneman, 1982; Kahneman, 2010). Overall, the research suggests that people's analytical capacities are very limited and that they consequently process information in substandard ways often leading to deeply flawed conclusions. There is ample evidence that this extends to people's causal analysis of political phenomena (for example, Rosenberg and Wolfsfeld, 1977; Heradsvcit, 1996; Quattrone and Tversky, 1984).

An alternative approach views social cognition not as a process of calculation but rather as one of applying available mental templates or models to assimilate new information. An early example of this is so-called schema theory (for a review, Fiske and Taylor, 1991). A cognitive schema is defined as a set of elemental factors (for example, particular objects, individuals or actions) which are linked together across time (a causal script) or space (a categorical group). The linkages are learned either through direct experience or as a product of social learning. The latter may include the learning of completely incorrect representations of one's own past, producing what Loftus (1997) has referred to as 'false memories'. Once learned, these schemata then guide the individual's exploration of a situation (Snyder and Swann, 1978), their interpretation of the pieces of evidence gathered (Chapman and Chapman, 1969), their integration of that evidence and subsequent memory of it (Bartlett, 1932; Loftus, 1996). Throughout, the analysis of the situation tends to be biased in a way that reflects, validates and reinforces the schemata being deployed to understand it. A good example of how schemata bias people's political cognition is provided by the work on stereotypical thinking and racism (Mendelberg, 2001; Junn et al., 2011).

The research on schemata not only suggests that thinking is prejudicial but also that, in its prejudice, it tends to be conventional. As the product of learning derived from recurring personal experience, schemata reflect the societal structuring of social interactions. As a product of direct socialisation, they also reflect cultural norms and dictates. Recent research in 'narrative psychology' demonstrates how prevailing social narratives of a group shape its individual members' interpretation and explanation of social events in a way this is consistent with, and typically supportive of, the dominant culture and the distribution of power (for example, Hammack, 2008).

Other research on social cognition adopts a more developmental approach. Here, an attempt is made to go beyond the examination of specific cognitive processing mechanisms and to discover their common underlying logic or structure. Translated into the language of social psychology, the goal is to identify the common structural qualities of the various attribution errors an individual makes, the different cognitive heuristics he or she uses, or the kinds of schemata he/she can readily deploy. In this view, reasoning is assumed to have the potential to develop. This development begins with the concrete and egocentric thinking of the young child and continues through several intermediary steps, ending in the more abstract and sociocentric thinking of a fully developed adult. This last step enables the kind of logical, integrative and coherent thinking typically assumed by deliberative democrats.

While cognitive developmental theory posits that all normal adults begin childhood with the same potential, it recognises that the developmental progress is an interactive product of innate potential and environmental forces. Consequently, what individuals actually achieve depends on their circumstances (Vygotsky, 1978; Luria, 1978; Kegan, 1994; Griffin, 2011). The empirical research suggests that most adults do not achieve the highest levels of development. For example, my own research on social and political reasoning indicates that most adults reason in a way that is piecemeal rather than integrative. They are unable to consider multiple relationships, dimensions or factors. They therefore do not consider the complexity of social phenomena or how they are embedded in broader contexts. In a related way, most people are concrete in their thinking and therefore their judgements do not incorporate more abstract, formal considerations. This result complements the social psychological research. It suggests that the thinking of people in the middle stages of development (that would be most literate adults in developed industrial societies) is structured in such a way that produces the various information-processing deficiencies and mechanisms observed in the research on causal attribution and heuristics (Rosenberg, 2002).

To conclude, the several central strands of social psychological research on causal attribution, heuristics, schemata and narratives suggest that the participants in a deliberation do not think in the logical, integrative coherent, critical, and possibly creative ways required to address complex problems. The developmental research leads to a similar conclusion regarding how most people think.

Considered with regard to the demands of deliberation on public policy problems, the various strands of research converge to suggest that people do not have the basic cognitive ability to analyse social problems. *Importantly, this lack of ability is not regarded to be circumstantial and thus a matter of inadequate information or motivation. Therefore the research suggests that the discovered deficiencies are unlikely to be readily remedied by the social conditions or pressures of a group deliberation.*

For deliberative theory and practice, the negative implications of this conclusion are mitigated somewhat when considering an important distinction between social and developmental psychological research. The social psychological research assumes that it is addressing the inherent, fundamental, and hence universal, qualities of thinking. Thinking may vary quantitatively in its content or complexity but not in its basic quality. In contrast, the cognitive developmental research suggests that the quality of thinking develops. Therefore, though the research indicates that most people currently do not reason in the way deliberation requires, the theory suggests that, if the social conditions of childhood and adult development were more favourable, many more people could develop the requisite capacities for analytical thought. As such, the developmental research offers a less pessimistic prognosis for deliberation than its social psychological counterpart.

Capacities for rational evaluation and self-reflection

Like the studies of people's analytical capacities, the psychological research suggests that people lack the requisite capacities for self-reflection and consequently for rational evaluation. As a result, their view of facts is not insulated from their preferences and is thus biased accordingly. A good example is the evidence of cognitive consistency and dissonance. Following the theorising of Fritz Heider (1958) and Leon Festinger (1957), a large body of research in the 1960s and 1970s demonstrated that people's preferences are intimately intertwined with their processing of information in a way that distorts the assessment of that information (for a review, see Abelson et al., 1968). For example, people tend to make evaluations categorically. Thus, when a person or group has been valued (positively or negatively), there is a tendency to ascribe a similar value to the various attributes or actions of the person or group in question. Reciprocally, the value of an observed action or attribute will be generalised and determine the value of the person or group in question. In general, there is a need to maintain consistency within categories. Thus, when confronted with evidence that carries value implications that are inconsistent with existing evaluations, there is a tendency to disregard, devalue or reinterpret evidence so as to maintain one's prior judgements. More recent work on motivated cognition continues and reaffirms this earlier work. Summarising this research, Peter Ditto and his colleagues (Uhlmann et al., 2009) conclude that people reason not like judges but like attorneys. Thus, rather than first assessing the evidence and then drawing a conclusion, they begin with a conclusion and then work backwards seeking evidence and interpreting it accordingly. In so doing, people do not attend to how they make judgements and thus do not guard against the biases that are introduced.

To be rational, evaluation also requires reflection on the preferences that are evoked in a particular situation at a given moment in time and then considering them in some broader context. This may involve a consideration of other circumstances and the preferences and desires associated with them. The result will be more complex, variegated evaluations. The empirical research suggests that people do not reflect on their preferences in this way. The aforementioned motivated cognition, with its attendant pressure for cognitive consistency, militates against such complex assessments. Instead, it leads to exclusionary and prejudicial considerations of possibly relevant evidence that produce simple black or white judgements of persons, groups, issues and events.

The reflective integration of preferences can also be accomplished by considering them relative to one's life goals or higher-order principles. Here again, the psychological research indicates that people do not evaluate in this way. Jonathan Haidt's work on moral judgement suggests that people's judgements are more a matter of sentiment or intuition than principled reflection (Haidt, 2001, 2007). Drawing on Haidt's work and the research on motivated cognition, Peter Ditto and his colleagues provide evidence that, when making moral judgements, people do not draw on principle to guide their evaluations but rather they first make spontaneous evaluations and then select a moral principle which rationalises their judgement (Uhlmann et al., 2009).

This social psychological research is complemented by work on cognitive development. Unlike Haidt and Ditto, developmental theorists claim that moral judgement has a significant reasoning component, one that varies with a person's level of cognitive development. Their empirical research suggests that most Americans reason about moral dilemmas in a 'conventional' way (for example, Kohlberg, 1984/7; Gilligan, 1982; Kegan, 1982). This involves matching the behaviour or outcome being judged to a concrete, readily available (in memory) practice or belief that is conventionally regarded to be moral. This process is much like the spontaneous moral intuition identified by Haidt or the evocation of internalised social values discussed by Ditto. In either case, the ensuing 'conventional' moral judgement entails little active or self-conscious reflection. Typically, the basis of judgement, the normative value, is itself not subject to consideration or evaluation.

Though developmental research thus supports the social psychological studies of evaluation, it also complicates our understanding of the phenomenon. As in the study of analytical abilities, the developmental research suggests that, even though most adults think and judge in an intuitive and conventional way, a significant number of people do not. On the one hand, it appears that a small proportion of the population thinks 'post-conventionally'. They differentiate between first- and second-order values and, in a self-reflective way, draw on the latter to make judgements deductively regarding the former. On the other hand, there is a substantial number of people whose reasoning is 'pre-conventional' and thus not guided by moral intuitions or social norms. Instead, their judgements are the result of present circumstances cueing a learned association between the object being judged and some experience of positive or negative rewards. These judgements are supported by little or no justification.

From the point of view of deliberative democracy, the results of the psychological research are troubling. Insofar as moral judgements are not based on conventional reasoning and thus are more a matter of intuitions and motivated cognition rather than the reasoned appeal to underlying principles, deliberation under conditions of moral disagreement will lack, and be unable to construct, the common ground needed for productive communication. Instead, the likely result will be mutual alienation and the moral condemnation of those with whom one disagrees. As noted earlier, the social and developmental psychological perspectives diverge in their prognosis. In the former case, the observed incompetence is characteristically human. In the latter case, it reflects a stage and further development is possible.

Communicative competence
In addition to requiring considerable analytical and evaluative capacities, effective democratic deliberation also demands a high level of communicative competence. To motivate participation at the outset, deliberation requires an appreciation of the value of talk and its role in collective decision-making. Despite its importance, there is little psychological research on people's understanding of talk and its relation to action. My own unpublished research is relevant here. As part of a larger project on the development of political reasoning (Rosenberg, 2002), I explored people's understanding of political talk and debate as part of an in-depth interview on politics. The subject population was small but was carefully chosen to vary by gender, level of education and income. The results of the research suggest that only a small minority of people understands talk as a vehicle for clarifying meanings and values that can provide a framework for the co-operative planning of action and thus in the terms that deliberation requires. The vast majority of people do not. For some, talk is meaningful only as an accompaniment to action, and hence it does not make sense to suspend action only to talk. Consequently, these people are unwilling to attend deliberations. If shepherded there, they are unlikely to participate. Most people understand talk as a direct cause of action and therefore appreciate the value of suspending current action to deliberate about plans for future action that would lead to desired outcomes. They emphasise, however, that the discussion should eschew ill-understood considerations of meaning, unneces-

sary accepted values or fanciful hypothetical alternatives. Thus, they would be willing to attend a deliberation but would move to constrain discussion in ways that deliberative theorists believe may seriously restrict what might be achieved.

Once in attendance, a democratic deliberation requires that participants show basic respect for one another and their deliberative contributions even, and especially, when the views expressed contradict their own. The research on cognitive dissonance and consistency suggests, however, that this respect is accorded conditionally, not universally. Participants who have an elevated status or who agree with one's point of view are likely to be given greater attention and respect than those who disagree. Similarly, participants who are members of one's own group are also likely to receive preferential treatment (for example, Tajfel, 1981; Brewer, 2001). Here, again, the qualities of citizen deliberators militate against their interacting in the ways that democratic deliberation requires.

Beyond showing basic respect, communicative competence requires recognising that individuals have personalities and ways of thinking that give a potentially distinctive subjective meaning to their beliefs, preferences and conversational initiatives. As a result, different people may understand the same claims or statements in very different ways. To be communicative, interlocutors must orient accordingly. As speakers, they must clarify the meaning of their own statements in terms their listeners can understand. As listeners, they must actively explore the meaning of others' statements to insure that they are interpreting them correctly. This clarification and this exploration are accomplished by explicating the links, causal, categorical or evaluative, between one's claim and other beliefs or values one has. To have the greatest communicative impact, this should be done in a way that illuminates how these links are comparable to, or differ from, those constructed by one's conversational partners.

My research on the quality of the communicative exchanges which occur in a citizen deliberation suggests that most people, even those who are highly educated and wealthy, do not communicate in this way. They assume that statements have a clear objective or shared meaning. Therefore, they feel little need to clarify the obvious meaning of their own statements or to inquire about the equally obvious meaning of the statements made by others. Consequently, rather than beginning with a discussion of definitions and assumptions with the goal of building a common understanding or frame of reference, deliberation tends to move directly to offers of information and assertions of particular belief or preference followed by responses of agreement or disagreement. As a result, whether they finally agree or disagree, people often misunderstand the claims made early in their deliberation as well as the nature of the accord or discord reached at the end (Rosenberg, 2007).

To conclude, our review of the research indicates that, for the most part, people do not have the capacities that deliberative democratic theory requires of them. The social psychological research suggests that these limits are inherent in human functioning and universal. This rather pessimistic view is mitigated by the developmental psychological research that suggests that, whereas most people are limited in the way that the social psychologists describe, some do have the necessary capacities and, given the requisite time and circumstances, others may develop them.

The elevating or 'enlarging' power of deliberation

Many deliberative theorists acknowledge that citizen deliberators may not have the competence that deliberation requires. Unlike the psychological research discussed thus far, however, they suggest the problem is not one of capacity but of skill. Like the riding of a bicycle, skills are readily developed when the circumstances afford the opportunity and create the need. They suggest that deliberation provides the circumstance in which citizens will develop the skills needed to be competent deliberators (thereby realising their inherent capacities). When deliberating, participants are exposed to different views and thus become better informed both about the problem and about the different perspectives that may be adopted to deal with it. Opposing views are personally presented in a civil way and therefore engender greater respect and tolerance. Overall, participants' views are broadened and their thinking is 'enlarged' (for example, Benhabib, 1996). Citizen deliberation also motivates individuals to perform at higher levels. When they express their beliefs and opinions, participants expose their reasoning to the critical examination of others. Consequently, they are likely to think in more careful, complex ways and to argue in a more reasoned logical fashion. In the process, they will become more coherent in their views, more aware of their prejudices, and thus will evaluate matters more rationally (Chambers, 1996; Guttman and Thompson, 1996; Dryzek, 2000). They will also become more sensitive to how others' perspectives may differ from their own and therefore tend to clarify the meaning of their own claims and to offer reasons that are acceptable to their audience.

When considering the empirical research on the possibly salutary effects of deliberation, it is important to consider what citizens actually do when they attend a deliberation. As theorised, deliberation fosters skill development because it provides the opportunity for deliberators to engage one another in reasoned discussion. This engagement demands the clear formulation of ideas, generates the constructive critical feedback on those ideas and creates the social pressures that motivate careful listening. The problem here is that the empirical research indicates that most 'participants' who attend a deliberation do not, in fact, engage in the give and take of the discussion. An example is the annual outdoor assemblies of all citizens in the small Swiss cantons of Glarus and Appenzell Innerrhoden. Though regarded as signature examples of public deliberation, Reinisch and Parkinson (2007) observe that the meetings are so large that only a tiny proportion of those in attendance get a chance to speak. Though size is not an obstacle in the much smaller town hall meetings in New England, most citizens attending the meeting do not talk at all (Mansbridge, 1980). Research on juries provides further evidence that, even if deliberative groups are very small, individuals often do not participate at all or do so only minimally (Hastie et al., 1983; Strodtbeck et al., 1957). This suggests that the supposed beneficial effects of deliberation will be much less pervasive than supposed.

We turn now to the direct evidence on the effects of deliberation. One critical effect hypothesised is the improvement in participant's reasoning about, and understanding of, the social problems being discussed. Unfortunately, rather than examining reasoning and understanding, most of the research on the cognitive impacts of deliberation has focused more narrowly on the more methodologically, more manageable question of the acquisition of knowledge. Not surprisingly, discussing an issue makes citizens more knowledgeable about it (for example, Price and Cappella, 2002; Barabas, 2004; Fishkin and Luskin, 2005). They also become more knowledgeable about opinions on an issue including those opinions associated with their own view and that of their opponents (Price and Cappella, 2002). Being informed about a topic is important; with regard to the question of citizen capacity, however, it is somewhat beside the point. The issue is not whether citizens have information but, rather, how they are able to work with that information once they have it. The critical concern here is not the amount of knowledge but the quality of their reasoning.

There is relatively less research on possible improvements in reasoning and understanding. Gastil and Dillard (1999) address the problem indirectly by examining the coherence of people's thinking on an issue. Coherence is measured by the degree to which an individual expresses opinions that cluster in a culturally appropriate manner (for example, they hold opinions typically identified as conservative and not liberal). Adopting this standard, the research on participants in the National Issues Forums indicates that people did have more integrated views across issues after participating but that the coherence of their view of a single issue did not improve. The problem here is not only this mixed result but how even a more favourable result is to be interpreted. Gastil and Dillard adopt schema theory to orient their study. Thus, they do not suggest that any observed coherence is the result of logical reasoning and reflects some broader understanding. Rather, it is the result of learning. The culture dictates which opinions are positively or negatively associated with one another. The acculturated individual simply learns to organise his or her beliefs accordingly. Viewed in this light, deliberation is seen to provide an unusually good opportunity for participants to learn the conventions regarding the appropriate contents of the alternative baskets of opinions they may espouse. It is not clear, however, that even this effect is produced. A more recent study of deliberative polls, using the same methodology as Gastil and Dillard, found no significant increase in the coherence of participants' beliefs (Sturgis et al., 2005).

The research on the effects of deliberation on the rationality of people's evaluations parallels the work on the logic of their analyses. It, too, has opted for the strategy of studying the supposed outcomes of a cognitive process rather than studying the process itself. In this vein, researchers have frequently focused on opinion change as a key indicator of rationality. The underlying argument here is that, if an individual is attentive to the arguments of other deliberators and draws on them to reflect on her or his own judgement, it is likely that individual's opinions and policy preferences will change. Adopting this approach, the research has compared the opinions and policy preferences of individuals before and after they have participated in a deliberation. The results are somewhat mixed but, in general, suggest that people's attitudes are affected by their deliberations. This appears to be the case for face-to-face deliberations (for example, Barabas, 2004; Fishkin and Luskin, 2005; Muhlberger, 2005; Niemeyer and Dryzek, 2007) and for online deliberations (for example, Price and Cappella, 2002). On this basis, the authors conclude that deliberation does lead people to be more considered, self-reflective and thus rational in the formulation of their preferences.

The problem here is that, because the research does not examine the cognitive process underlying the observed changes, these changes are readily subject to alternative interpretation. Rather than incorporating the new arguments and views discovered in deliberation into a renewed consideration of one's existing preferences in the light of one's basic values and long-term goals, individuals may, in a largely unconsidered way, simply learn and then adopt the preferences of others. Certainly, a good deal of the social psychological research mentioned earlier suggests that opinion shifts are more likely to be the result of obeying authority, seeking social approval, and thus more a matter of simple conformity than considered reflection. Indeed, several experimental studies of deliberation support this interpretation (for example, Price and Cappella, 2002; Barabas, 2004; Mendelberg and Karopowitz, 2007). This complements earlier work that indicates that group interaction tends to amplify shared bias (Kerr et al., 1996). This suggests that deliberation may not, as hoped, be fostering more adequate reasoning and rational consideration but, rather, functions as a herding operation which brings otherwise deviant individual ideas into line with dominant norms and values.

Though it examines dialogues rather than multiperson deliberations, the developmental psychological research is germane here. Much of that research involves in-depth interviewing that typically lasts no less than half an hour and often can take several hours over two or three sessions. During this time, the interviewee is not only asked to express their view of a topic but also to respond to numerous requests to clarify the meaning of their statements, to justify their preferences and to consider scenarios that challenge the views they express (for example, Kohlberg, 1984; Turiel, 1983; Kegan, 1994; Rosenberg, 2002). The focus of the interview is to assess the quality of their evaluative reasoning and the understandings it generates. The important point here is that, despite the extended and intensive engagement that occurs in the interview, and hence the opportunity and demand it places on the interviewee, the evidence suggests that the quality of their reasoning and judgement does not change over the course of the interview. This suggests that the more casual, less demanding and less supportive conditions of deliberation are unlikely to provide the cognitive quick fix that some advocates of deliberation suggest. This conclusion is supported by a recent study of nurses using the California Critical Thinking Skills Test which found that participation in a public deliberation had no effect on critical thinking (Goodin and Stein, 2009).

Apart from any impact on analytical and evaluative skills, deliberation is also hypothesised to have an effect on how people orient emotionally to the strangers in attendance. Supporting this claim in an aside in his oral presentation, Goodin (2005) reported that the final meeting of an Australian deliberation ended with participants hugging each other, exchanging e-mail addresses and promising to meet socially in the future. Observing several deliberations, I have also noted the formation of positive social bonds between former strangers. Complementing this anecdotal evidence is Hickerson and Gastil's (2008) survey of three thousand jurors which indicates that even individuals who are members of more marginalised groups view participation in a deliberation to be a satisfying, positive experience.

The presumption in the foregoing research is that the formation of positive bonds among participants is likely to render them more sympathetic to the views of others. In this vein, Muhlberger (2005) suggests that deliberation enhances citizen or community identification in a way that produces a small, but significant, increase in political perspective taking. In their study of deliberation about a more controversial topic, however, Mendelberg and Oleske (2000) observed that the discussions did not produce greater tolerance for opposing views or a mitigation of conflict. This result is supported by a recent study of deliberation that indicates that the quality of deliberation declines as the ideological division among participants increases (Esterling et al., 2010).

In sum, the empirical research on the effects of deliberation suggests that it can compensate for some of the inadequacies people exhibit in non-deliberative settings. It does lead people to develop positive social ties with one another, at least when topics are not too contentious. In addition, participants become more informed about the issue at hand and how opinions on the issue are socially configured. They also tend to change their opinions. This appears, however, to be more a matter of conforming to norms than guided by logical reflection or rational judgement. In this context, it is important to remember that there is little direct evidence on the effect of deliberation on the core components of deliberative capacity: logical reasoning, rational judgement and communicative competence. This should be a priority for future research.

The implications for citizen deliberation

Our review of relevant research on people's basic analytical skills suggests that people tend to think in simple terms. They prefer homogeneous categories and look for single concrete causes and effects. Moreover, people construct these categorical and causal linkages in a typically flawed way. They tend: (a) to focus on what is apparent, concrete or more cognitively available; (b) to process this information either by utilising cognitive short cuts or by uncritically applying prior personal experience or culturally available explanations; and (c) unconsciously to skew final judgements so as to maintain their self-esteem or prior evaluations of persons or groups. In sum, individuals' thinking appears to lack the objectivity, complication, integration and abstraction to enable them to appreciate the complexity of social problems and to imagine effective, novel ways of addressing them. Consequently, when deliberating, people are likely to generate analyses of problems that are simplistic, unimaginative and distorting in a way that reinforces their personal biases and their community's cultural definitions and social practices.

The research on evaluation suggests similarly negative conclusions. People are largely unselfconscious in the development or use of their preferences. There is little attempt to construct a subjective frame of reference for considering or creating preferences. Rarely do they draw upon higher-order, longer-term or abstract values or principles of relationship to organise their preferences. Lacking the broader framework in which to place initial preferences, possibly relevant evaluative concerns are typically not introduced. Lacking the consideration of abstract principles, there is little critical evaluation of specific preferences or their justifications. In sum, people's preferences tend not to be the product of personal reflection. Instead, they are evoked or simply cued by external circumstances that reflect learned social conventions. As a result, when deliberating, people are likely to generate evaluations of social conditions and possible future courses of actions that are narrow-minded, particularistic and uncritical in a way that reinforces their personal prejudices and the dominant cultural norms of their group.

There is not much research on citizen deliberation that examines communicative practices themselves. My own research focused on this and yielded results that are consistent with those of the empirical work on individual capacities. I observed and analysed the communicative exchanges in deliberations among several unusually well-educated and motivated groups of citizens discussing how to improve their children's schooling. The assumption was that, given their privileged backgrounds, these individuals would provide a best-case example of deliberative practices. Nonetheless, the manner in which they deliberated with one another was disappointing. They recognised disagreement over particular preferences or specific beliefs but did not seem to be aware of how others may have very different perspectives or ways of understanding the world. Consequently, speakers tended to offer simple, short, unelaborated statements of their views of an event. Similarly, listeners made little attempt to interrogate speakers' statements or to check the validity of their interpretation of them. Arguments were also simplistic and insufficiently sensitive to the listener's perspective. Claims were accompanied by reasons; these consisted, however, of little more than a link to what was assumed to be a shared preference or a commonly accepted cultural norm. These were not justified. When the difference of other people's values or norms was encountered, it was typically not addressed. Rather there was a tendency politely to avoid disagreement and, in a cognitive dissonance driven way, to judge those values and the people who advocated them in negative ways. Throughout, there was little collective reflection on the communicative interaction taking place. There was no discussion of the quality of what people were saying, the manner in which it was taken up by others or how influence or power was distributed among the participants (for example, Rosenberg, 2007).

Considered together, this research has important implications for expectations regarding deliberation. Consider first the case of deliberations involving people who have similar social backgrounds, and therefore share common perspectives, but have different preferences. Because individuals tend not to explore the meaning of the claims they are making, the deliberation is unlikely adequately to reveal the full extent and nature of their differences. Because they tend not to introduce more fundamental or generalisable concerns when considering their own and others' claims, they are unlikely to be able to bridge those differences that do emerge. As a result, discussion will not produce a common, integrative and possibly innovative understanding of problems and their solutions but, instead, will yield a patchwork of particular views, one or two of which will dominate the choice of action to be adopted. Any conflict of preferences will be either managed by politeness rules that dictate who must defer to whom under what circumstances, or adjudicated by a simple reference to shared values or cultural authorities. As a result, deliberations among citizens who share a common background or 'life horizon' will frequently produce agreements on policy. These choices will tend, however, to be superficial, uncreative and uncritical in a way that reflects dominant social norms and the existing distribution of social power. Thus, deliberation in such cases is likely to be more a mechanism of social control than the hoped-for critique and emancipation.

Deliberation will not fare any better when it includes people who have different backgrounds and who therefore draw upon different beliefs, values and moral authorities. Lacking the requisite self-reflection, perspective-taking or collaborative communicative engagement, the resulting discussion is unlikely to comprehend or bridge these differences. Thus, deliberation will fail to generate a shared understanding of problems or agreements on policy. To the contrary, and in a manner feared by some critics of deliberative democracy (for example, Sunstein, 2002), deliberation is more likely to accentuate incompatibilities and foster greater mutual alienation. Hearing beliefs and preferences that are different from one's own can alienate, especially when these views are justified by reference to moral values or assumptions regarding the dynamics of social life that one does not share or fully understand. The result can only emphasise the strangeness of the others and the basic incomprehensibility of their views in a way that further alienates from one another people of different backgrounds. When combined with people's tendency to draw simple, contrasting categorical distinctions and their cognitive-dissonance-driven tendency to denigrate others who advocate values that contradict one's own, this process is mutually alienating and likely to engender mutual suspicion and dislike. The result, as observed in some empirical research (for example, Mendelberg and Oleske, 2000), is likely not to mitigate conflict but to exacerbate it.

Can deliberation be fixed?

It is clear from the discussion thus far that there is a pressing need to rethink how to institutionalise democratic deliberation. The current practice of simply creating opportunities for citizens to discuss social problems with the aim of affecting public policy is not adequate. The likely deliberative result is a series of simplistic, prejudicial, uncritical and egocentric contributions leading either to conformity and superficial agreements on conventional courses of action or to insurmountable disagreement and mutual alienation. Like Sunstein and Thaler (2008), I suggest that we draw on psychological research to identify the mistakes citizen deliberators are likely to make and then craft institutional inducements or guides for 'nudging' citizens to deliberate in ways that better serves both their individual and collective interests. Like Warren (2007), however, I believe it is also important to do this in a way that is consistent with democratic norms and that recognises people's developmental potential. The short-term attempt to 'nudge' must be designed in a way that is consistent with longer-term efforts to develop people's capacities so that they can meet better the requirements of democratic citizenship.

Here I provide a few illustrative examples of how to organise deliberation in a way that is sensitive to the abilities and needs of those involved. A first step in organising a deliberation involves the solicitation of participants. Apart from the oft-stated democratic concern of inclusion, the pedagogical need to compensate for the tendency to think in narrow, unreflective ways may be addressed by including people of very different backgrounds. Such a mix ensures that participants are not offered the easy validation that the self-selected associations of everyday life typically afford (for example, Mutz, 2006). Confronted with their differences, participants in the deliberation are encouraged to reflect on their own and on others' views and, in so doing, to construct the deeper understandings needed to comprehend and bridge their differences.

A caveat must be introduced here. Just bringing together a disparate group of participants is not enough. As suggested earlier, the ensuing confrontation of difference may produce mutual suspicion and conflict rather than productive engagement. To address this possibility, deliberations should be designed to foster the formation of positive socio-emotional relationships among the participants. There is a number of ways this may be accomplished. Deliberative groups could be scheduled to meet a number of times. This encourages people to be more responsible to one another and provides the time for personal relationships to emerge. For similar reasons, deliberative groups should also be kept small. Larger deliberations should incorporate regular breakaway sessions in which the larger group divides into smaller ones. Participants should also be required to perform extradeliberative tasks together (for example, preparing meals or planning a site visit). To be most effective, these tasks should involve individuals working together as equals for a commonly valued goal that can be successfully achieved (Pettigrew, 1998).

Procedural rules can also be designed so as to foster a more desirable deliberative engagement. An example is the decision rule. Deliberations typically call for collective decision-making. Often this involves rule by majority. The concern here is that such a decision rule fosters a competitive atmosphere that encourages the building of alliances with like-minded others for the purpose of defeating the opposition. As a result, there is little incentive to take the perspective or to communicate clearly with those who are most different. In contrast, decision by consensus tends to restructure the demands governing the deliberation. If anything is to be accomplished, everyone must agree. This provides clear incentive for people to engage one another, even the most different among them, in a serious and accommodating way.

Again a caveat must be introduced. Whereas decision by consensus creates incentives for disparate members of a deliberative group to agree, this may be accomplished without a reflective working through of differences but rather by simple acquiescence and conformity. This suggests a general problem. Institutional arrangements typically provide very general incentives and offer little specific direction as how one should behave. Consequently, these arrangements may be variously understood and yield unanticipated results.

The insufficiency of general arrangements may be addressed by institutional fine tuning. This would involve scheduling specific, delimited tasks that target specific deliberative limitations and provide clearly defined incentives for alternative practices. For example, a task may be introduced to address the difficulty people have setting aside their own perspective to understand that of another, particularly one who takes an opposing position. Here, deliberation is interrupted and participants are asked to engage in a 'role-playing' task where they must adopt and then defend the position of their opponent. Another example is a task that addresses the tendency of people to ignore how they are communicating with one another. Here, participants are asked, at an early point in their deliberation, to create the rules to be used to govern their discussions. To deepen their considerations, they are asked to first consider what they think conversing with one another can ideally accomplish and then to design rules that will help them accomplish those goals.

Though helpful, the introduction of specifically targeted tasks cannot fully address the difficulty of anticipating people's reactions. There are no assurances that individuals will understand even these more specific tasks in the manner the organiser intends and thus respond appropriately. This suggests that the design of a deliberation should include the direct, personalised intervention that can be provided by a facilitator. In fact, facilitators are commonly used in citizen deliberations. Typically a citizen volunteer, the individual is asked to be a neutral referee who intervenes only to ensure that every participant has an opportunity to speak, that basic civility is maintained and that the group progresses towards a final decision. Concerned only with the distorting influence of status and power, this definition of the facilitator role reflects a democratic concern for the equality of the participants and the possibly disproportionate influence of the facilitator. Our concern, however, with the basic capacities of participants and the commonly substandard quality of deliberative exchanges demands a more expanded facilitator role. As well as being a referee who works to maintain the equality of participants, the facilitator must also be a teacher who helps the participants develop the analytical, evaluative and communicative capacities needed to yield creative, reflective bridge-building and potentially emancipatory deliberation. This will include regular, personally tailored interventions that ask individual participants to clarify their claims, explain their inferences, justify their evaluations and reflect critically on the adequacy of their assumptions about social life and the morality of their socially acceptable values. It will also involve interrupting exchanges to encourage interlocutors to explore their potential misunderstandings and to work collaboratively to build, rather than simply critique, each other's views.

Concluding remarks

I have attempted to offer a constructive critique of deliberative democracy. I began by clarifying the nature of the demands democratic deliberation places on individual citizen participants. Reviewing a broad range of psychological research, I concluded that people typically do not have the capacities to the meet those demands. Consequently, their deliberations are unlikely to be deliberative, democratic or productive in the way imagined by the theorists and practitioners of deliberative democracy. To address this problem, I offered suggestions as to how to design citizen deliberations with the aim of improving citizens' deliberative performance in the short run and encouraging the development of their basic capacities in the longer run. More generally, I suggest that citizen deliberation be viewed not only as a vehicle for collective decision-making but also, and perhaps more importantly, as an opportunity for democratic pedagogy.

CHAPTER 7

'Scaling up' deliberation

André Bächtiger and Alda Wegmann

Ten years ago, deliberation was seen as an exotic topic promoted by utopian philosophers and romantic democratic dreamers, and certainly not a topic of great relevance for mainstream political scientists. This view has dramatically changed in the past decade. As Pateman (2012) notes: 'we are surrounded by democracy-talk'. Not only has a veritable deliberative industry emerged, deliberation has also made significant inroads into standard political science (see Bächtiger et al., 2010). As such, deliberation is increasingly becoming a mainstream concept itself. But does that mean that deliberationists can take a back seat and enjoy the fruits of their years-long struggle for recognition in the discipline? In our view, the case for deliberation cannot be closed until one can convincingly demonstrate that deliberation is an important logic of action in contemporary politics and that it actually matters for policy outcomes. While many scholars now agree that deliberation is an important component of democratic quality, many disagree about its viability in real-world politics. We call this the 'scaling up' *problématique* of deliberation (see also Niemeyer, 2012). The 'scaling up' of deliberation has two dimensions: on the one hand, it depicts the viability of deliberation as a broad and sustained logic of political and social action. Thus, 'scaling up' is related to contextual incentives as well as to individual abilities for performing successfully in deliberation. On the other hand, 'scaling up' refers to deliberative action that has a discernible impact on policy outcomes. In particular, deliberationists need to demonstrate that deliberatively reached judgements in one forum (such as deliberative opinion polls, for instance) affect the policies in other arenas and are potentially turned into binding decisions for the whole polity. Of course, it would be foolish – as well as normatively undesirable – to argue for a perfectly deliberative political system where all deliberative inputs are 'heard' and where all decisions are made in a deliberative fashion. When investigating the 'scaling up' *problématique*, we are interested only in identifying 'examples of reasonably good practice' (Parkinson, 2012), that is, in finding political systems and policy cases where deliberative logics have informed the decision-making process and also had some discernible impact on policy outcomes.

By drawing from various findings of our own empirical research and research from others, this article tries to give an overview of the 'scaling up' of deliberation in the political and civic sphere, both at the national and the global levels. It tries to map under what *conditions* deliberation 'scales up' and when it does not. Our review shows that sustained elite deliberation is a rare event and that the impacts of citizen deliberation on policy-making have been relatively modest. At the end, our article discusses various solutions to deal with frequent lack of 'scaling up', namely a systemic approach to deliberation and new visions of democratic and representative politics.

Does deliberation 'scale up' in the nation state?

A first question concerns the 'scaling up' of deliberation in the nation state. Our contention is that deliberation is theoretically viable both in the political and the civic spheres but that countervailing forces are strong. In the political sphere, this mainly concerns an incentive problem; in the civic sphere this mainly concerns an ability and impact problem. In the following, we first concentrate on 'scaling up' deliberation in the political sphere and then turn to 'scaling up' deliberation in the civic sphere.

Elite deliberation
There is a long tradition in liberalism that is concerned with 'elite deliberation'. Elite deliberation is concerned with small, elite bodies that consider competing arguments on an issue at hand (see Fishkin, 2009). In his *Considerations on Representative Government*, John Stuart Mill developed a 'deliberative' view of politics. His 'Congress of Opinions' was supposed to embody a microcosm of the nation's views 'where those whose opinion is over-ruled feel satisfied that it is heard, and set aside not by a mere act of will, but for what are thought superior reasons' (Mill, 2010 [1859]: 156). Despite such claims, almost no political scientist would argue that deliberation has been (or, is) a dominant logic of action in modern elite politics. As Fishkin und Luskin (2005: 286) hold: 'much of the discussion among political elites is posturing or negotiation rather than deliberation ... Legislators are representatives, after all, and elected to support or oppose certain things.'

To understand why elite deliberation is so difficult to realise in modern democratic politics, we need to look back in history. In *Beyond Adversary Democracy* Mansbridge (1980) shows that an adversary and competitive ideal has dominated western democratic thinking since the seventeenth century and has developed alongside the conception of representative government. Adversary democracy implied a philosophy that human beings are driven by a desire for power and that 'political institutions must build on this conflict rather than resist it'. In adversary theory, interests are in constant conflict and there is no common good or public interest. Deliberation, too, is absent in this conception of politics. After World War II, the profession of political science began to describe the democratic process primarily in adversary terms. The adversary and competitive ideal is also prevalent in the self-description of politicians in liberal democracies. In this view, politics is generally about conflict and adversarial debating, rather than about co-operation with political opponents and deliberation toward common understanding and consensus.

Pincione and Teson (2006) radicalise this idea and speak of 'discourse failure' in politics. They argue that citizens face high costs to obtain reliable knowledge about political issues. This combines, say Pincione and Teson, with a tendency by politicians to take advantage of this 'rational ignorance' of the public. Thus, for political and personal gain, politicians will posture and use vivid arguments rather than engaging in rational discussion, because the former are more accessible to citizens and have a greater emotional appeal. Following Pincione and Teson, the absence of deliberation in the political sphere is not due to a lack of deliberative abilities on the part of politicians – in general, professional lawmakers might possess the ability to engage in rational discourse; rather it is due to a fundamental incentive problem.

This trend is reinforced by the trend towards the mediatisation of politics. Hjarvard (2008: 113) defines mediatisation as a process 'whereby society to an increasing degree is submitted to, or becomes dependent on, the media and their logic'. Commercial and competitive media have a need for compelling, attention-grabbing, and dramatic stories. Following the 'news value theory', this means simplification, polarisation, conflict orientation, negativism, and personalisation of politics. Mediatisation also affects the performance of contemporary politics. To grab media attention, politicians will increasingly follow the precepts of media logic and will use polarisation and simplification strategies as well. Rather than promoting reasoned and reflective discourse, the mediatisation of politics is strongly conducive to polarisation and simplification of political messages.

But this may be too narrow an account of the potential for elite deliberation in the political sphere. First, modern politics has some demand for deliberative action. To enhance the 'governability' of contemporary fragmented societies with increasing problem complexity, scholars have argued that deliberation is a tool that contributes to competent policy-making (see Papadopoulos, 2003). It can help actors to overcome uncertainty and bounded rationality, to expand their perspectives and learn about unforeseen consequences (Vanberg and Buchanan, 1989), and to generate new alternatives. Second, politics is not only about narrow self-interest and opportunistic behaviour in the form of re-election. Several students of legislative policy-making in the United States found that politicians are not only interested in re-election but also have policy interests (for example, Fenno, 1973). Third, and most importantly, we can also think of specific institutions that support deliberative action in politics (see Williams, 1998). Indeed, allegations of deliberation's impossibility – such as Pincione and Teson's 'discourse failure' – are generally based on the experience with current American politics. But this experience may not generalise to other political systems.

A good starting point to understanding under what conditions deliberation can become an extended logic of action in politics is the concept of *institutional order*. By institutional order, we understand an institutional arrangement that encompasses both formal and informal rules. In this view, institutions do not only affect the preference calculations of actors but may also alter their cognitive scripts. This is also emphasised by Rothstein (1998: 17) in his study of 'just institutions'. In Rothstein's conception, welfare-state programmes, for instance,

> are not merely rule-systems determining which strategies of action are rational, but are established normative arrangements as well. They also affect what values are established in a society, that is, what we regard as a common culture, collective identity, belonging, trust, and solidarity.

In other words, institutional orders can turn deliberation into a normatively acceptable, and even prescribed, logic of action to deal with political and social conflicts.

So, which institutional orders are conducive to sustained deliberative action and which are not? Drawing from our previous research (Steiner et al., 2004; Bächtiger et al., 2005), classic consociational democracy is an institutional order that entails deliberative ideals, while competitive and majoritarian democracy does not. Consociationalism comprises a set of institutional devices – in particular, grand coalition and mutual veto – as well as co-operative attitudes of political elites, leading them to transcend the borders of their own groups, to be receptive to the claims of others and to accommodate the divergent interests and claims (see Bächtiger et al., 2003). Indeed, classic deliberative ideals are embedded in the very structure of consociational democracies. As a former Swiss federal councillor, Samuel Schmid, aptly put it, Swiss consociationalism comprises 'moderation', 'respect', 'listening', 'constructive working-together', and 'accommodation'.[1] By contrast, competitive systems thrive on competition and conflict. When the political game is about winning or losing, political actors have barely incentive to enter into rational discourse with the political opponents.

Another institutional order which might be conducive to deliberative action is American presidentialism. As Sunstein (2007: 49) has noted,

> [t]he very structure of the U.S. government, with its bicameral legislature and its complex allocation of authority among the three branches, can be seen as an effort to ensure a high degree of deliberation with reference to relevant information, as well as a large measure of accountability.

Similarly, Warren and Pearse (2006: 2) argue: 'As an element of institutional design, the separation of powers is likely to increase democratic responsiveness and competence of government, all other things being equal.' The mechanism behind a separation-of-powers framework is mainly a formal one: to function effectively, complex institutions with multiple veto players have a quasi-functional need for communication and deliberation. Moreover, the lower degree of fraction discipline in presidential systems means that legislators have more leeway to transcend party boundaries and to be open to arguments of the 'other side'. Contrast this with parliamentary systems. Here, ministers and legislators of the same party are 'in the same boat' in a continuous election campaign against other parties (Saalfeld, 2000: 357). Thus, legislators are not only pressured to defend the proposals of their government, party competition also requires them steadily to attack the political opponent, even if legislators would privately value or even agree with the arguments of that opponent.

In the past decade, systematic empirical research has tried to shed light on these claims. Focusing on parliamentary debates in four countries, Switzerland, the United States, Germany, and the United Kingdom, the Swiss consociational democracy scores higher on several deliberative quality indicators (especially with regard to the respect dimension) compared to the other three countries where political competition is higher (at least at the level of parliaments). Bogas (2009) also finds clear differences in deliberative quality between the consensus-oriented legislature in the Netherlands and the competitive House of Commons in Britain: the former scores higher on several deliberative quality indicators (justification, rationality and respect) than the latter.

While empirics show that there is an association of consociationalism with deliberative politics, this is only partly true for American presidentialism. Our data show that deliberative quality in the US Congress is much lower compared with our best case, Switzerland (see Steiner et al., 2004). There are still clear hints, however, that American presidentialism has a higher deliberative quality than parliamentary systems, especially with regard to British Westminster democracy, but also with regard to the more consensual German parliamentary system. Though it is the world's most popular political project (Strom, 2000: 261), parliamentary democracy tends systematically to undermine deliberation.

Considering effect sizes, there is no sea change in deliberative quality between consociational and competitive institutional orders. For instance, on a nine-point respect scale, differences between the Swiss consociational democracy and more competitive systems are only about 0.3 and 0.5 points. This clearly underlines that, despite variety in institutional design, parliamentary discourse shares many similarities. By the same token, it also means that, even in consociational democracies, deliberation is far from being a dominant logic of action.

But how much are the differences between consociationalism and competitive institutional orders driven by the formal and informal part of institutional orders? This is a crucial question, relating to portability of deliberation-enhancing institutional designs. If deliberative quality is driven mainly by the informal – or, cultural – part of an institutional order, then deliberation is a deeply embedded, idiosyncratic logic of specific political systems which cannot easily travel to other contexts. We have run a batch of re-analyses of debates where institutional situations vary within a country or cultural context (Bächtiger and Hangartner, 2007). Our analyses show that formal institutions can have a profound effect on respect scores, regardless of the cultural or country context. The insertion of 'consociational elements' into competitive settings – in the form of 'consociational' (or bipartisan) arrangements or as explicit attempts at depoliticising issues – has positive and powerful effects on deliberative quality. Some analyses show, however, that the informal part of the institutional order may still matter. This is especially true for the American context where adversarialism and mediatisation pressures are particularly strong. First, compared with Swiss and German debates, American debates score significantly lower on justification rationality. Not only are there (self-imposed) time limits for plenary speeches in the US Congress, members of Congress also have a tendency to use 'catchy' sound bites to make their political messages appealing and accessible to 'rationally ignorant' citizens [exactly as Pincione and Teson (2006) have predicted in 'Discourse Failure']. Second, even under conditions of bipartisanism, American debates score lower on the respect dimension than comparable Swiss debates. This indicates that the competitive American political culture may, indeed, provide disincentives for deliberation.

But, despite the fact that formal institutions sometimes do have a profound effect on deliberative quality, the effects of formal institutions on deliberative quality are far less straightforward than one might surmise. This particularly concerns the internal working of coalitions, the hallmark institution of the consociational model. Rational-choice theorists have long argued that coalition settings entail mixed-motive games (for example, Martin and Vanberg, 2005: 94). On the one hand, they have reason to co-operate with their partners to pursue successful common policies. On the other hand, each party faces strong incentives to move policy in ways that appeal to party members and to the constituencies on which the party relies for support. This second motive creates an incentive to uphold a distinct partisan identity which sets an important constraint on coalition parties' deliberative capacities. This line of reasoning suggests that coalition arrangements do not automatically lead to the 'scaling up' of deliberation. Rather, the deliberative capacity of coalition arrangements will be strongly affected by appropriate partisan strategies and motivations. Indeed, in the Swiss consociational democracy, not all parties in the grand coalition adopt the same strategies (see Bächtiger and Hangartner, 2010). The deliberative work is done primarily by moderate and middle parties that are willing to take governmental responsibilities. Thus, while grand coalition settings provide some incentives for deliberative action, they primarily create a 'space of the possible' for deliberation which then must be filled with relevant partisan strategies and motivations.

In current times, elite deliberation seems to be on the wane, even in Swiss consociational democracy. Notice that the study of Steiner et al. (2004) was performed on decision cases in the 1990s and early 2000s. As Vatter (2008) has argued, the Swiss political system has increasingly moved to the competitive pole in the past decade. One reason for this shift is the rise of the populist Swiss People's Party, forcing moderate parties to give up their (partly) deliberative attitudes. Another reason is the increasing mediatisation of Swiss politics: even though the Swiss media system is still a far cry from the highly mediatised American system, there are discernible trends in the direction of a higher conflict-orientation, negativism, and the personalisation of politics. This creates incentives for politicians to posture and to use polarisation strategies. Indeed, glimpsing (in an unsystematic manner) at deliberative quality in the current Swiss parliament, a modicum of deliberation seems preserved only in non-public debates in the second chamber where party polarisation is lower. In the first chamber, by contrast, the logic of competitive debating has become the dominant mode of policy-making. The irony here is that the consensual and partly deliberative nature of consociationalism provides a favourable context for the mobilisation of populist parties (see Fröhlich-Steffen, 2006). In other words, the partly successful 'scaling up' of deliberation may have unintended, yet even perverse, effects.

The situation in the current United States Congress is even worse. There is increasing dependence on special rules that limit debate time for bills. Mann and Ornstein (2006: 170) have called this the vanishing of 'regular order', which comprises 'discussion, debate, negotiation, and compromise'. According to Mann and Ornstein (2006: 175), this trend started in the 1970s and has continued ever since, even when party control shifted in the US Congress. But, regular order is important 'because it is necessary for the full and fair deliberation of issues … ignoring regular order excludes many representatives from the legislative process, especially members of the minority party, and risks enacting substandard legislation'.

As mentioned before, modern political systems facing complex problems have an inbuilt need for deliberative action to enhance their 'governability'. If this cannot be achieved within representative institutions, then deliberative logics and problem-solving activities tend to retreat to so-called 'governance networks' and other non-public arenas which are (at least partly) shielded from mediatisation pressures and the public. Nonetheless, deliberative democrats (as well as their critics) may not speak of the 'scaling up' deliberation when the sustained deliberation is possible only in the back corridors of politics. Without a strong dose of publicly visible deliberation, it may be difficult to call a political system truly deliberative.

Let us finally address the second scaling up' question, namely whether elite deliberation also affects policy outcomes. There is, however, a dearth of studies addressing this topic in a systematic way. An exception is Spörndli's (2004) study of the German Conference Committee (Vermittlungsausschuss), a 'consensual' body that tries to reconcile conflicts between the Bundestag and the Bundesrat. With regard to formal outcomes, he found that in the Conference Committee unanimous or nearly unanimous decisions were typically associated with a high level of deliberative quality in the preceding debates. With regard to substantive outcomes, however, Spörndli found no association between high-quality deliberation and more egalitarian decisions (in the sense that the most disadvantaged in society are particularly helped).

In sum, the 'scaling up' of elite deliberation seems to be closely associated with a 'pre-modern' and 'gentlemen's club' model of politics rather than with modern mass democracies where disciplined parties compete for power (see Bächtiger et al., 2005). In addition, if sustained deliberation is possible primarily in the context of low issue polarisation, then the 'scaling up' of elite deliberation is a truly rare and highly contextualised event. In addition, mediatisation pressures and party polarisation have further diminished deliberation's role in representative politics, relegating it to the back benches and back corridors of politics. Even in Swiss consociational democracy, where deliberation occasionally 'scaled up' in the past, the drift towards adversary democracy is undeniable.

Citizen deliberation
If the political sphere is largely inimical to a fully fledged realisation of deliberative ideals, then we may want to turn to deliberative action among ordinary citizens. Citizens are not constrained by party politics, and thus can talk more freely and be open to the better argument. Another reason to turn to citizen deliberation has to do with a malaise in current representative politics. The most common way of participating, voting at elections, has fallen in most democracies since the 1970s. In addition, citizens have become more critical of political parties, politicians and parliaments. To counteract these tendencies, many political analysts are advocating more participatory forms of democracy where citizens are effectively included in political decision-making. In this regard, citizen deliberation might help to narrow the gap between politics and citizens. Citizens might become aware of the complexities of real-world politics and become more trusting of political decision-making processes and outcomes.

But there is also a number of challenges to citizen deliberation. There is an ongoing controversy whether ordinary citizens want to deliberate and whether they have the requisite abilities to engage in high-quality deliberation, that is, to advance complex arguments with a focus on the common good and to listen to other participants' arguments with respect. Regarding citizens' motivations to deliberate, Hibbing and Theiss-Morse (2002) claim that people do not want to deliberate. In their influential book, *Stealth Democracy*, they argue that citizens are perfectly happy to be passive bystanders of politics, as long as they trust the institutions that do the decision-making and can live with the outcomes. Only when the institutions start failing them, by making bad decisions or through dishonesty, will citizens become frustrated. With regard to the ability to engage in high-quality deliberation, psychologists and feminists have argued that citizen deliberation will be biased. From this vantage point, only higher education, higher class, well-developed cognitive capacities and appropriate motivations will create the necessary individual capacities to perform successfully in deliberative processes.

Let us address these two challenges. The manifold experiences with citizen deliberation have produced a wealth of data allowing us to check whether ordinary citizens want to deliberate and, if so, whether they are able to do so in a sophisticated way. With regard to the motivation to deliberate, it is certainly true that participation rates in citizen deliberative events are significantly lower than in normal elections. According to Hüller (2010: 94), 'even the representativeness with regard to social categories (education, income, etc.) would not make the assembly statistically representative, because highly attentive citizens appear at these events'. But it is equally true that deliberative events attract more diverse strata of participants than any legislative body in representative politics. Moreover, on the basis of an experiment and deliberative sessions of citizens with American Congressmen, Neblo et al. (2010: 582) show that Hibbing and Theiss-Morse are wrong and that there is a desire to deliberate among citizens: '[the] willingness to deliberate is much higher than indirect evidence from political behavior research might suggest, and that those most willing to deliberate are precisely those who are turned off by standard partisan and interest group politics'. Second, are ordinary citizens capable of deliberating? Most deliberationists argue that, with a little help, ordinary citizens can approach philosophical ideals of deliberation. Indeed, practitioners have developed a number of institutional devices to organise deliberative events effectively. In deliberative polls, the most prominent format of citizen deliberation, there are several institutional devices designed to support citizens' deliberative potential (see, for example, Fishkin, 2009: 160): participants receive balanced briefing material helping to narrow the gap in citizens' epistemological resources and capabilities; there are trained facilitators in the small discussion groups, bolstering substantive inclusion of all participants as well as stimulating a discussion atmosphere which is open and considerate (Smith, 2009: 197 ff.); finally, there are experts from different areas serving as additional information resources for citizens.

According to Dryzek (2010), many empirical studies contradict sceptics who highlight citizen incompetence. The most important finding is that there are large changes of opinion and voting intentions in the deliberative polls, and that these changes are also largely uninfluenced by sociodemographic factors (including education, economic status, or gender). Niemeyer (2011) also shows that citizen deliberation can overcome strategically crafted symbolic claims, leading to a greater level of 'integrative thinking' among citizens. Furthermore, citizen deliberation does not seem to be the preserve of highly educated and wealthy participants. To take just one example, in Andhra Pradesh in India a citizen jury was convened in 2001 to deliberate on the very complex issue of genetically modified organisms in agriculture, and to produce some policy recommendations (Pimbert and Wakeford, 2002). Fourteen of the nineteen participants were women, and most were poor farmers. They had few problems in grappling with the complexities of the issue. In a new study on the deliberative abilities of European citizens, Gerber et al. (2012) found that, in Europolis, a pan-European deliberative poll, a considerable number of citizens reached relatively demanding standards of deliberative quality (such as complex reasoning, common good orientation, and explicit respect toward other participants' arguments). Some important biases still pop up, however: in Europolis, working-class participants from eastern and southern Europe had a much lower deliberative quality than higher-class participants from western Europe.

The most serious obstacle in citizen deliberation, however, concerns the second 'scaling up' dimension. As Dryzek (2010: 170) notes: 'Direct influence on and in policy making is a hard test for mini-publics to pass. While examples exist of influence and impact, they are outnumbered by cases where a mini-public is established but turns out to have little or no effect on public decision-making.' Indeed, as Pateman (2012: 10) holds, mini-publics are 'not part of the regular political cycle in the life of a community'. According to Parkinson (2012: 156), the main problem for the frequent lack of policy impact is the interference of deliberative mini-publics with established venues of policy-making:

> The decisions and deliberations of real mini-publics impact on established interests and preconceptions, sometimes significantly. When confronted by deliberated agreements that contradict their positions, organized interests react in three ways: by putting forward opposing perspectives; by calling into question the motivation and competence of the mini-public …; and by applying other kinds of political pressure via routes to which they have privileged access.

In addition, serious legitimacy issues also arise when recommendations from mini-publics confront the rest of the community who have not deliberated: 'the casually-observing public – the great majority – frequently dismiss counter-intuitive results of deliberation as the ravings of madmen' (Parkinson, 2012: 156). Even worse, the 'great majority' does generally not even know that a deliberative citizen event has happened. (For further consideration of the role of mini-publics in deliberative democracy, see Chapter 10, 'Mini-publics: issues and cases', by Stephen Elstub).

A prominent example for such dynamics is the famous British Columbia

Citizens' Assembly on Electoral Reform (Warren and Pearse, 2008; Fournier et al., 2009). In 1996, the Liberal Party promised to create a citizens' assembly on electoral reform if the party came to power, which they did in the next election in 2000. The citizens' assembly was intended to address the conflict of interest that elected politicians have if they design their own electoral system (Snider, 2009). After eleven months of discussion, the citizens' assembly recommended that the first-past-the-post electoral system be replaced by a single-transferable-vote system. The citizens' assembly proposal was then submitted to a popular referendum. In the first referendum, it received 57.1 per cent of the vote but needed 60 per cent to pass. The government then put the citizens' assembly's recommendation to a ballot again in 2009 when it received only 39 per cent of the vote. There were several reasons for this failure: on the one hand, after being in office, the Liberal Party's enthusiasm for citizens' assemblies quickly withered away, especially when the recommendations did not fit the political agenda any more. Hence, the Liberal Party did not endorse the citizens' assembly's proposal in the referendum campaign even though it had initiated the reform. As Snider (2009: 14) writes, data from British Columbia also indicate that if voters in the majority party believe the reforms will hurt their party, they will oppose these reforms in a referendum. By contrast, 'such reasoning did not appear to characterize the deliberations of the citizen assembly juries, where members of all the major parties voted overwhelmingly in favor of reform'.

With regard to the second 'scaling up' dimension, there is, however, variation in institutional orders whether and how much citizen deliberation affects policy designs in the political sphere. Dryzek (2010) lists a number of examples where mini-public recommendations were taken up in the policy process. In Denmark, for instance, there are clear cases of consensus conference recommendations finding their way into legislation. By contrast, in France, mini-public recommendations have not been taken up by the political elite. According to Dryzek, this striking variation can be attributed to the different institutional orders. Dryzek classifies states as inclusive and exclusive to social interests; they can also be either active or passive regarding social interests. The best scenarios for 'scaling up' citizen deliberation are actively inclusive states, such as Denmark, whereas passively exclusive states, such as France, undermine attempts to use citizen deliberation productively. Dryzek (2010: 174) ends on a fairly pessimistic note: 'There is no realistic hope of rendering most other liberal democratic states into the actively inclusive Nordic form that makes the full integrative use of the consensus conference possible in Denmark.'

A striking example of the 'scaling up' of deliberative mini-publics is China. Here, recommendations made by deliberative mini-publics were taken up and implemented by the Chinese Communist Party. But why would elites in an authoritarian regime ever be receptive to the outcomes of citizen deliberation? He and Warren (2011) argue that development-oriented elites, such as China's

Communist Party, don't just need compliance but the 'willing compliance of multiple actors'. Thus, if deliberation generates legitimacy, then elites will have incentives to employ deliberative schemes to expand the governance capacities of the state (He and Warren, 2011: 280). By the same token, deliberative schemes may yield additional benefits to elites in authoritarian regimes: they co-opt dissent and maintain social order, generate information about society and policy, and they enable leaders to deflect responsibility on to processes and thus avoid blame (He and Warren, 2011).

Finally, participation in deliberative events may have other, more indirect 'scaling up' effects. In their book, *Talking Together*, Jacobs et al. (2010) argue that 'small-scale deliberation' can have large-scale impacts by creating 'the very kinds of empowered citizens that make discursive democracy at the large scale work'. Focusing on the United States, Jacobs et al. (2010: 117) find empirical evidence in this direction:

> The engagement of large numbers of Americans in talking about, discussing, and debating public issues is prompting them to do more to make contacts with elites (from boycotting to calling a public official or the media), to participate in civic activities (from volunteering to working with others to solve a community problem), and to engage in electoral politics (voting and working on a campaign).

Furthermore, public talking 'increases citizens' store of political capital, which in turn further increases their resources and motivation to act in the political and civic world' (Jacobs et al., 2010: 117). So, even if many deliberative events do not produce results in the second scaling dimension, they may nonetheless help to improve the overall democratic quality of our polities.

'Scaling up' deliberation beyond the nation state?

In the literature, there are two major arguments questioning whether deliberation can work and 'scale up' in the realm of international politics: (1) relationships of power are particularly prevalent in the international sphere; (2) there is no common lifeworld where actors share a common language, history, or culture. Some deliberative democrats, including Jürgen Habermas (2006), have remained sceptical about how well international and transnational deliberation can work. The argument is that the common cultural and historical background as well as the dense solidarity networks that facilitate national democracy may be difficult to transpose to the international and transnational level.

In a highly influential article, Risse (2000) has claimed that deliberation might play a role in international politics despite the aforementioned objections. Ulbert and Risse (2005) demonstrate empirically that processes of persuasion changing actors' perceptions of the situation and definitions of interests have discernible consequences in multilateral negotiations, leading to unexpected outcomes. Critical for successful persuasion is the 'credibility' of speakers and their ability to put forward arguments that resonate with existing norms and general standards of appropriateness. Again, institutional context plays an important role in international negotiations too: a 'dense framework of previously agreed-upon principles, norms and rules' (Ulbert and Risse, 2005: 363) creates points of reference for arguing which then strongly affect negotiation outcomes.

In a groundbreaking study, Naurin (2010) demonstrates that deliberation is not a marginal phenomenon in the Council of the European Union. Focusing on working groups in the council, in about half the cases where member-state representatives intervened at a working group meeting, they acted in a deliberative way, that is, they gave reasons for their positions with the intention of changing the minds of other actors. There is also substantial variation in this general picture, however, both between institutional settings and different types of actors. Naurin found the highest amount of deliberative action when political pressure was low. Moreover, in stark contrast to the hopes of normative theorists, the highest quality of deliberation was found among the most powerful and best-connected actors.

Moreover, in a detailed reconstruction, Deitelhoff (2010) shows that the creation of the International Criminal Court (ICC) is an exemplar of a deliberatively driven legalisation process. According to Deitelhoff, the creation of law cannot be reduced to a functional, cost–benefit equation. Equally important is the 'inherent normativity of law, based on norms of due process, shared legal principles and broader normative understandings' (Deitelhoff, 2010: 43). Deitelhoff (2010: 60) could identify traces of successful rational discourse and persuasion during the negotiation process of the ICC. To be sure, the negotiation outcome was not a rational consensus where actors agreed with the underlying reasons of other positions and viewpoints but it was a 'carefully designed compromise that was affected by rational argument'.

In past years, scholars of international governance have increasingly turned to deliberative theories to address the 'democratic deficit' of the international level. The hope is that deliberative processes enhance the legitimacy and rationality of international decision-making processes. There are essentially two pathways to achieve this goal. On the one hand, there is a 'liberal' pathway seeking to realise deliberative ideals within international and global institutions (Cohen and Sabel, 2005). A prominent idea in this regard is the 'popularly elected global assembly' in Richard Falk and Andrew Strauss (2001). On the other hand, there is a 'critical' pathway focusing on deliberation in transnational civil democracy without recourse to formal institutions in the global sphere (Dryzek 2006). In this regard, Dryzek et al. (2011) propose the establishment of a 'Deliberative Global Citizens' Assembly' (DGCA) composed of ordinary citizens randomly drawn from all the countries of the world (for a similar proposal, see also Goodin and Ratner, 2011). Dryzek et al. (2011) list a number of distinctive advantages of a DGCA. The key advantage is the installation of a truly deliberative setting and the enrichment of global politics with the authentic voices of ordinary citizens. By contrast, a 'popularly elected global assembly' will hardly be a deliberative forum. According to Dryzek et al. (2011), this would require an institutional design 'which deviates from standard institutional settings (and prescriptions) in the political and international sphere, requiring consensual, non-partisan settings with highly independent representatives'. As detailed before, this has already proved very difficult to realise and sustain in the context of the nation state. Another hope is that a DGCA would contribute to ameliorate the United States and China problem in world politics. Historically, the United States has been unwilling to cede formal authority to international bodies. China would also be a sticking point for any elected global assembly. It is hardly imaginable that the Chinese Communist Party would agree to organise China-wide competitive elections to a global body. By contrast, a deliberative global citizens' assembly would ameliorate the United States problem because an assembly based on random selection from the citizenry does not look like a direct challenger to the US Congress. The China problem would be ameliorated by the fact that no elections would need to be organised in China (see Dryzek et al., 2011). As detailed before, the Chinese government has been willing to experiment with a variety of deliberative forms of consultation at the local level.

These advantages notwithstanding, citizen participation in international politics may suffer from similar 'scaling up' problems as citizen participation at the national and local levels. An instructive example in this regard is the European Union. In the previous decade, the European Commission has promoted direct citizen involvement in European Union affairs via institutions such as deliberative polls, citizen conferences, online consultations or citizens' initiatives. Hüller (2010: 100) evaluated two participatory instruments, European Citizens' Consultations and the Commission's online consultations. In his account, '[t]he main problem of the demotic ECC is that the entire process has remained almost completely unrecognised by both politics and the public sphere'.

Solutions

Taking stock of the various experiences with deliberation in the political and civic spheres, we have seen that 'scaling up deliberation' is a difficult venture. While politicians and citizens do possess a potential for deliberative action, there are many hindrances for deliberation to 'scale up' even if institutions create a 'space of the possible' for deliberation. In politics, this primarily concerns the first 'scaling up' dimension, namely the willingness of politicians to engage in sustained deliberative action. In the civic sphere, this mainly concerns the second 'scaling up' dimension, namely the frequent lack of policy impact of deliberative citizen events. In the following, we sketch two escape routes from these deadlocks.

Systemic approach

The systemic approach somewhat circumvents the 'scaling up' problem in an elegant way. The systemic approach asks empirical and normative questions about the relationship between the various sites of deliberation and about the functioning of the system as a whole rather than focusing on isolated and discrete instances of deliberation such as synchronic, face-to-face interactions. Conceived this way, according to Neblo (2005: 180), 'the hopes for the quality and breadth of deliberative participation may not seem so perversely utopian'. The basic thrust of the systemic approach is that different parts of the system may have different deliberative strengths and weaknesses, and that even parts which perform poorly in terms of deliberative quality at first glance may nevertheless make an important contribution to the overall deliberative system (Mansbridge et al., 2012). For example, highly partisan rhetoric, 'even while violating some deliberative ideals such as mutual respect and accommodation, may nonetheless help to fulfill other deliberative ideals such as inclusion' (Mansbridge et al., 2012: 3). Or, 'certain disruptive and only weakly civil … protests enhance the deliberative system if they can be reasonably understood as giving voice to a minority opinion long ignored in the public sphere, or as bringing more and better important information into the public arena' (Mansbridge et al., 2012: 19). Conversely, parts of the system which perform well on deliberative quality at first glance may not always perform a deliberative function in the whole system. For instance, 'an institution that looks deliberatively exemplary on its own, such as a well-designed minipublic, can look less favourable in a systemic perspective when it displaces other useful deliberative institutions, such as partisan or social movement bodies' (Mansbridge et al., 2012: 3). In other words, the systemic approach forces us to rethink the 'scaling up' *problématique* in novel ways. For instance, it can help us to grapple normatively with the empirical finding that the 'scaling up' of deliberative mini-publics is strongly aligned with partisan support. While many practitioners of citizen deliberation are wary of aligning a deliberative event with a specific political party (because this would impair its impartiality) a systemic approach will see such political alliances in a much more positive light.

Nonetheless, the systemic approach builds on one potentially questionable assumption. It presupposes political systems that are minimally capable of fulfilling deliberative functions. In this regard, Mansbridge et al. (2012) refer to five potential pitfalls of a deliberative system: (1) a part of a deliberative system is too tightly coupled, that is, the self-corrective quality is lost; (2) parts of the system are decoupled from one another, that is, that good reasons arising from one part fail to penetrate the others; (3) there is institutional domination where a state, party or leader controls not only government but also the media and even civil-society organizations; (4) there is social domination, that is, a particular social interest or social class controls or exerts undue influence over many parts of the deliberative systems; (5) there is a division of citizens, legislators, and administrators (by ideology, ethnicity, religion, or any other cleavage), that is, that they will not listen to positions other than those coming from their side.

But what if these defects are widespread in our contemporary political systems? This is exactly what Pincione and Teson (2006) claim in their attack on the viability of deliberation. Clearly, empirical findings tend to contradict Pincione and Teson's claims but they nonetheless suggest that the realisation of deliberative politics is highly context dependent and sensitive to additional conditions, especially the absence of partisan polarisation. Moreover, as argued before, recent trends in contemporary political systems point to further hollowing of the three institutional preconditions. Mediatisation, for instance, systematically undermines the deliberative capacities of political elites, forcing them to follow media logics and engage in posturing and conflict. Or, as we have shown above, parliamentary democracy entails institutional domination of the government, thus undermining the deliberative potential of parliaments. In other words, the system may not easily produce deliberatively desired effects. This still calls for thinking of transforming existing institutional settings to make them more deliberative. In the following, we sketch some new visions for the deliberative renewal of democratic politics, with a specific eye on representative politics where success in the first 'scaling up' dimension – the sustainability of deliberation as broad action logic – increases the chance that direct and immediate effects translate into the second 'scaling up' dimension – deliberation's impact on policy outcomes.

New visions of democratic and representative politics

There is general agreement in the literature that large-scale institutional reform is utopian. For instance, it may be true that in a properly functioning consociational democracy, elite deliberation occasionally 'scales up' but it is hard to imagine that consociational practices will find easy acceptance in other institutional orders. Therefore, any attempt for 'scaling up' deliberation in modern polities will require a differentiated and moderate reform approach. In the context of American politics, several scholars have advanced such a moderate reform approach, dubbed 'regular order' (for example, Eilperin, 2006). 'Regular order' is not so much about institutional reforms but advocates a return of American politics to reduced partisan polarisation and a shift of individual conduct and expectations of party behaviour. First, 'moderate minded legislators may be less wedded to partisan victory and more open to input from the opposite party' (Eilperin, 2006: 223). Second, legislators should also return to independent judgement and less party loyalty. As Eilperin writes, '[i]n today's

House, the most widespread individual norms appear to be based on party loyalty and success. Voting against the party on important votes, for example, can be met with severe scorn from fellow party members as well as party leaders' (Eilperin, 2006: 223). But the House did not always operate in this way. Writing in the 1960s, Fenno observed that the House followed several informal rules, including 'no man is required to show complete party loyalty' and one should 'disagree without being disagreeable' (Fenno, 1965: 73–5).

In the political sphere, one can think of a strengthening of second chambers which can inject a modicum of deliberation and reflection into the political process. As Parkinson (2006a: 6) holds: 'Parliament does require, and would greatly benefit from, a second chamber better able to perform the roles of scrutiny and deliberation, holding the Government to account and probing its legislation and policies.' Elected second chambers also have the advantage that they are fully accountable to their constituents whereas governance networks lack this essential base for legitimate decision-making.

Of course, in times of polarisation and mediatisation, calling for less partisan polarisation as well as a shift of individual conduct may sound as utopian as calling for large-scale institutional reform. But we should not forget that substantial parts of the electorate are increasingly turned off by partisan polarisation, mediatisation and the resulting deadlocks in politics. Thus, there may be an electorally based opening for a more deliberative orientation of future democratic politics. One way to achieve this goal may be a clever division of labour between different political venues – partisan and reflective ones. While partisan arenas serve the goal of defending constituency and partisan interests, reflective forums serve the goal of enlarging perspectives and identifying common interests and values. If the two venues are nested, that is, one arena is constrained by the decisions of the other (as we frequently find in the context of bicameralism), this may lead to the partial realisation of deliberative virtues while simultaneously tying deliberatively reached decisions to constituency and partisan interests.

But we may also start thinking in different directions, expanding the boundaries of classic deliberation. Though it is beyond the scope of this chapter to develop in full, let us give a brief sketch of a new vision for democratic politics, dubbed 'noble politics'. Contrary to classic definitions of deliberation, our ideal of 'noble politics' is not about a small and socially homogeneous 'gentlemen's club' with 'calm consideration' of the issues at hand and a strong gear towards consensus; rather, it puts a strong prime on passionate contestation and confrontation in a highly diverse setting. It shifts deliberation's frequent focus on a collaborative and 'play-well with others' approach (see Mucciaroni and Quirk, 2010) to a conception of deliberation which fully revalues adversarial and confrontational practices and turns deliberation into a critical and rigid inquiry, similar to cross-examination in court (Bächtiger 2011). As psychological scholarship has demonstrated, contestatory forms of engagement may produce epistemically superior outcomes compared to those from consensual dialogue (see, for example, Schweiger et al., 1986).

This new version of 'noble politics' has three distinct advantages. First, as elaborated before, trying to infuse politics with consensual deliberation is problematic, and the respective dependency on specific institutional orders may be (too) strong. Second, this version of 'noble politics' is less anti-partisan than classic visions of deliberation and thus more compatible with current liberal politics. Indeed, contestatory forms of deliberation require partisanship and even polarisation strategies to present positions and arguments in their strongest form. Third, our version of 'noble politics' may also better satisfy the logics of the media system than consensual deliberation. Contestatory forms of deliberation, if properly deployed, are a 'first-class theatre' where conflicting arguments clash and where disputants use rhetorics and emotional speech to engage hearers by that speech (see Bächtiger, 2011). This fully corresponds to the needs of the current media system, priming conflict and controversy over moderation and co-operation. The key difference to standard adversarial debating, however, is that contestation in noble politics retains the quest for truth, learning and self-transformation. The goal is 'productive controversy', not sterile confrontation as in classic adversarial debating (Bächtiger, 2011). As such, our version of 'noble politics' may still be dependent on a 'play of politics' which upholds some classic deliberative virtues, especially a modicum of open-mindedness and a minimal willingness to be swayed by the 'better argument'.

In conclusion, our inquiry shows that the 'scaling up' of deliberation in the real-world politics is burdened with many obstacles. Nonetheless, a systemic perspective, in combination with a novel and expanded understanding of deliberation as well as partial transformations of institutional settings (including shifts in politicians' conduct), might give a more nuanced and rosy picture of deliberation's 'scaling up' potential in the real world. At any rate, 'scaling up' deliberation will remain a top priority on all future agendas of deliberative democracy (see also Niemeyer, 2012).

Note

1. See *Neue Zürcher Zeitung*, 26 March 2011.

CHAPTER 8

Sequencing deliberative democracy to promote public openness

Jürg Steiner

Research on the deliberative model of democracy now enters a third phase. Initially, the discussion focused on the normative-philosophical aspect of deliberation. Then attempts were made to get an empirical handle at the phenomenon of deliberation with the emphasis at the micro-level of specific speech acts. In a third phase that is barely beginning the attention turns to the macro-level with the concept of deliberative system. The question is what do we mean if we characterise a country as having a deliberative system? The question can also be asked at other systemic levels, such as the level of academic departments. When we move in our academic careers from department to department, we may intuitively be struck that some departments have more of a deliberative character than others. If we approach the question from the empirical side, how do we know whether an academic department has a deliberative system? At departmental meetings there will always be some decisions made by majority vote. Some bargaining may go on. Students may organise a protest about a particular faculty appointment. Do such occurrences disqualify an academic department from having a deliberative system? The argument of this paper is that pure deliberation at the systemic level is not possible and not even desirable. Any social system also has other elements besides deliberation, and this is good. How strong has deliberation to be that we can speak of a deliberative system? The discussion on this issue has only just begun. I consider it as a fascinating development that we begin to think about the concept of deliberative system.

At the Workshop on Frontiers of Deliberation at the European Consortium for Political Research (ECPR) Joint Sessions in St Gallen, Switzerland in April 2011, Jane Mansbridge et al. forcefully made the argument that we should turn our attention to the concept of deliberative system. They emphasise that, in a deliberative system, not all elements need to have a deliberative nature: 'for example, highly partisan rhetoric, even while violating some deliberative ideals such as mutual respect and accommodation, may nonetheless help to fulfill other deliberative ideals such as inclusion'. To illustrate their approach, Mansbridge et al. (2011: 25) stated:

> take a closer look at protest. Protest often appears to violate several standards of deliberation. First, the slogans protestors use to excite enthusiasm and convey a dramatic message often undermine epistemic subtlety. Second, when protest explicitly or implicitly threatens sanctions or imposes costs, it acts as a form of

coercion. Third, protest sometimes involves levels of disruption and contestation that fail to meet deliberative standards of civility and civic respect, [but] protest can begin to correct inequalities in access to influence by bringing more voices and interests into the decision making process.

Thinking of deliberation in systemic terms is a useful exercise but it makes it difficult to identify what is deliberative and what is not. To take the illustration of Mansbridge et al., a protest action may appear as non-deliberative at the micro-level but as contributing to deliberation at the systemic level. Furthermore, it is not easy to determine whether a particular protest action contributes to deliberation at the systemic level.

This third phase of deliberative research should lead to the determination of the appropriate level of a political system. This level may very well depend on the specifics of a political system. To use the example of protests, alluded to by Mansbridge et. al., some countries may be so stuck in their daily routines that mass street protests may be a refreshing event stimulating spirited public discussions. Western European countries in the 1950s were in this situation in the sense that the mass protests of the 1960s were positive from a deliberative perspective (Crepaz and Steiner, 2012). By contrast, with its programme of reintegration of ex-combatants of leftist guerrillas and the rightist paramilitary, Colombia is currently in such a delicate political situation that mass protest could easily disrupt the slow process of democratic development (Steiner, 2012).

In this chapter, I use as an illustration the deliberative element of *public openness* to discuss the concept of deliberative system. I shall argue that it is not necessary for a deliberative system that all actions take place in full public openness. For some parts of a political decision process it may be appropriate that they take place behind closed doors because this may help other deliberative elements. The important point is that, overall, there is enough public openness so that ordinary citizens see at critical junctures what is going on and have the opportunity to intervene. Though I make some general statements, I am aware that the desirability of public openness depends on the characteristics of the political system, in particular its media system. If the media strongly personalise and sensationalise what is going on in politics, restrictions on public openness are more appropriate than if the media are focused on the substance of the issues under discussion. Restrictions on public openness can also be tolerated more if a country is at war or if its financial system is in great turmoil.

What has the philosophical literature to say about the function of public openness in the deliberative model of democracy? Jürgen Habermas insisted throughout his career that good deliberation should be public and transparent. He continues to emphasise this point strongly in a recent publication where he demands 'publicity and transparency for the deliberative process' (Habermas, 2006: 413). He justifies the logic of publicity in claiming that this is a necessary condition to 'generate legitimacy' (Habermas, 2006b: 413). This Habermasian view was for a long time shared by virtually all deliberative theorists, and many of them still stress the importance of publicity and transparency as a key element of the deliberative model. Claudia Landwehr (2010: 105–6), for example, argues:

> The strongest incentive for actors to name generalizable reasons and engage in argumentation of them exists where interaction is public … publicity forces actors to give the best possible justification for their premises and decisions … is not an option to renounce publicity as a defining element of discursive interaction and as a requirement for political decision making … Accessibility could be guaranteed if doors remain ajar, for example, if a committee meeting that is not organized for a large audience is nonetheless open to interested members of the public, journalists or researchers.

Though Landwehr adheres to the logic of publicity, she acknowledges that, in practice, publicity may be relative. Her point is that, even if doors are not fully open but only ajar, the logic of publicity should still apply in the sense that reasons should be 'generalizable and transferable' (personal communication, 10 March 2010).

There are now, however, a few theorists who acknowledge that, sometimes, deliberation is facilitated when it does not take place in the public eye. Simone Chambers (2005: 255) was one of the first to raise this issue in asking: 'Is it better for public deliberation to go behind closed doors and to insulate deliberators from the harmful effects of the glare of publicity? Or should deliberation be in open forums to insure maximum transparency and citizen scrutiny?' Chambers (2005: 256) acknowledges that 'all normative theories of deliberative democracy contain something that could be called a publicity principle. The principle has many forms but almost always involves a claim about the salutary effects of going public with the reasons and arguments backing up a policy, proposal or claim.' Chambers (2005: 256) sees 'general agreement among most deliberative theorists about what is salutary about [publicity]: having to defend one's policy preferences in public, leans one towards using public reason … that this public at large can accept.' Though Chambers agrees with the prevailing view among deliberative theorists that publicity has many beneficial effects, she is also concerned that the glare of publicity may lead to what she calls a plebiscitory debate. By this she means 'demagoguery, misinformation, inflammatory rhetoric, and flattery put in the service of a predetermined agenda', or also that 'the speaker says what the audience wants to hear' (Chambers, 2005: 262). The question then is, under what conditions publicity has good or bad effects? Chambers (2005: 255) hopes 'that normative theory can learn something from empirical research'. Normative theory needs a more nuanced idea of publicity and its effects on speakers. Empirical research can help build a new typology of publicity that in turn helps us understand the conditions under which openness enhances deliberation and the conditions under which it might harm the quality of debate.

Robert Goodin (2005: 193) is another theorist who sees limits to the publicity principle. To be sure, he concedes 'that the "ideal speech situation" would be best. The very best deliberation, let us suppose, would indeed be a cooperative game among all players in which all the deliberative virtues would be simultaneously and continuously on display.' Goodin's

> point is simply that politics is not like that, at least not in the sorts of representative democracies that now predominate. But while we cannot seriously expect all the deliberative virtues to be constantly on display at every step of the decision process in a representative democracy, we can realistically expect that different deliberative virtues might be on display at different steps of the process. (Goodin, 2005: 193)

According to Goodin, this would hold for the virtue of publicity. For good deliberation, it would not be necessary that all phases of a decision process would be completely open to the public. Political parties could

> work out their positions behind closed doors. [Their] arguments are then put to the maximally expansive deliberative body, the public at large, at an election … Once voters have electorally determined the distribution of power in parliament, party leaders convene a probably only semi-public session to cut deals. (Goodin, 2005: 193)

Goodin's 'larger point is simply that a staged deliberative process, with different deliberative virtues on display at different stages, might add up to a good enough deliberation' (Goodin, 2005: 193–4). With respect to the publicity principle, this means that it can be tolerated from a deliberative perspective that some parts of a decision process take place behind closed doors as long as other parts are truly open to the public eye. John Dryzek (2009: 1385) also takes such a sequential view of the publicity principle when he writes of 'the paradox that effective deliberation sometimes benefits from moments of secrecy (as long as) publicity can enter later or elsewhere in the deliberative system'.

What is empirical research telling us about the relationship between public openness and other deliberative elements? In our research group, we analysed the level of deliberation of parliamentary debates in Germany, Switzerland, Britain and the United States (Steiner et al., 2005). Thereby, we developed a Discourse Quality Index (DQI). We have seen that there is trade-off among three deliberative virtues, namely logical justifications of arguments, references to the common good, and respect for the arguments of others. Plenary sessions were characterised by high levels of logical justification and frequent references to the common good but little respect for the arguments of others, while committee meetings had exactly the opposite characteristics, high levels of respect but low levels of logical justification and infrequent references to the common good. These findings fit the argument of Robert Goodin that, realistically, we can not expect to have all deliberative virtues all the time. A weakness of the above findings is that committee meetings and plenary sessions do not only vary in the level of publicity but also in other important aspects. Most obviously, committee meetings are much smaller in size than plenary sessions. Committee meetings also have quite different functions in the parliamentary decision process than plenary sessions; most notably, committees do not make any final decisions on bills while plenary sessions do. Therefore, we cannot exclude that at least part of the variation in deliberative virtues is not due to the difference in publicity between committee meetings and plenary sessions but to some other differences between the two types of parliamentary institutions.

Ellen Meade and David Stasavage were able to remedy this weakness in profiting from a quasi-experimental situation in real-life politics. In 1993, the United States Congress decided that the verbatim minutes of the US Federal Reserve's Open Market Committee (FOMC) must be published, though only after five years in order not to create financial market volatility. As was subsequently revealed, all pre-1993 meetings had been taped and, contrary to the expectations of participants, these earlier records had been preserved and had to be published as well. Meade and Stasavage (2006: 123) describe this quasi-experimental situation as follows:

> As a result, the FOMC transcripts provide a rare opportunity to compare decision-making in two environments: after 1993, when officials knew that their statements would eventually become public, and before 1993, when officials believed (erroneously as it turned out) that their statements would remain private.

The FOMC is the committee of the Federal Reserve that has the responsibility for setting short-term interest-rate policy. It has eight regularly scheduled meetings each year and has twelve voting members: the seven members of the Board of Governors of the Federal Reserve and five of the twelve presidents of the regional reserve banks. During the period studied by Meade and Stasavage (1989–97), the meetings were always chaired by Alan Greenspan, Chairman of the Federal Reserve, who, at the beginning of a meeting, made an interest-rate policy recommendation. The other committee members then had the opportunity to express dissent. Meade and Stasavage make the reasonable assumption that the higher the number of such dissents, the higher the level of deliberation because a wider range of views is expressed. Controlling for factors like inflation and productivity during the period under study, Meade and Stasavage (2006: 130) found that publicity had, indeed, a strong effect. They

> estimate that a Fed Governor would have had a 10% likelihood of verbally dissenting before the 1993 change and only a 3% likelihood of verbally dissenting after transcript publication began. This is a very significant drop. When

we conduct a similar exercise for voting Bank presidents, we observe that they would have a 17% likelihood of dissenting before 1993 and a 13% likelihood of dissenting after transcript publication began. This is a smaller but still significant reduction in the probability of dissent.

Meade and Stasavage (2006: 131) conclude from their investigation 'that while there may be clear benefits to establishing greater transparency in government, advocates and institutional designers should also take into account the possibility that openness can entail important costs'. This conclusion fits the concern of Simone Chambers that not all publicity has beneficial effects.

Robert J. MacCoun (2006: 112) gives an informative overview of the psychological literature on the effects of publicity. He begins his essay in the following way: 'In a democratic society, the desirability of openness and transparency in government decision making would seem nearly self-evident.' He then shows that 'some attempts to achieve transparency may have unintended and undesirable consequences' (MacCoun, 2006: 113). MacCoun (2006: 113) relies heavily on experimentation with college students, and he is very much aware of the limits of such experiments for real life in politics:

> These studies provide strong causal inferences about cognitive mechanisms, but weak external validity. Importantly, these experiments inevitably exclude organizational structure, historical context, and most of the tactical and dramatic elements that characterize the 'rough and tumble' of real-world politics. Thus, the ideas presented here should be considered hypotheses for further consideration rather than firm conclusions about political systems.

Being aware of the limited validity of experiments with students for political decision-making, MacCoun (2006: 116) still claims that 'a basic finding in social psychology is that public commitment to a position makes people more resistant to moderating their views in light of subsequent argument'. Should this finding indeed apply to politics, we would have to conclude that a key deliberative element is damaged by publicity because actors would be less willing to change their positions based on the force of the better argument. The summary conclusion of MacCoun (2006: 121) with regard to the effects of publicity is mixed: 'Efforts to increase transparency can and probably do eliminate many decisions from the worst end of the continuum, but it is conceivable that they do so at the expense of impairing high quality decisions at the other extreme.' Here again, empirical data show that it is problematic to consider publicity as an unquestionable virtue in the deliberative model.

Though not much empirical research is available on the effect of public openness on deliberation, the available research still allows for having some doubts on whether public openness is always good for deliberation, as claimed by many theorists, or whether there are situations where deliberation profits from a certain confidentiality. The question then is when, in the interest of good deliberation, it is advisable to keep a discussion out of the public eye. We need to think here in terms of different phases of a political decision process, as Robert Goodin has suggested. We have seen that he has interesting ideas about phases in which deliberation is particularly important and phases where it has less importance. I now attempt to elaborate on Goodin's ideas with regard to the specific aspect of public openness and to determine under what conditions we can speak for this aspect of a deliberative system. I ask when public openness is important, less important or not desirable.

I find it important that the early phase of a decision process takes place outside the public eye. This is the phase where new creative ideas should be discussed. As the psychological research of MacCoun has shown, a non-public environment makes it more likely that actors do not stick to their original positions but are willing to consider new ideas. Politicians are always in danger of being considered unprincipled and wishy-washy if they change their positions so that, in public, they have the tendency to stick to their stances. Behind closed doors, however, they have more of the luxury to speculate about new ideas. Therefore, I agree with Goodin that it may be better if political parties work out new positions behind closed doors. In this way, they can play with new ideas without immediately being criticised by other parties. Informal 'brain-storming' groups may be helpful in this respect.

In an earlier research project, I could study such a 'brain-storming' group by participant observation in the Free Democratic Party of the Bern canton in Switzerland (Steiner and Dorff, 1980). For two years, I could attend all 111 party meetings. Among these meetings was a regular working luncheon of the party president, the party secretary, and the two Free Democratic cabinet members of the cantonal executive. At the beginning of these working luncheons, my silent-observer status was somewhat awkward but, after a while, the four top party leaders became accustomed to my presence so that their discussion could take its normal course. I assured them that no details of these luncheon meetings would ever be revealed and that I was interested only in establishing causal relations among various characteristics of the observed meetings. Comparing these luncheon meetings with more formal party meetings, I was struck by the highly deliberative nature of the luncheon meetings. There was no fixed agenda. The conversation usually began with non-political issues like sport events and, in these initial conversations, I also took part which made my role as observer less awkward. Slowly, the discussion then turned to political issues. No formal decisions were ever made because these informal luncheon meetings had no authority to do so. The purpose was to hear new ideas about future policy positions of the party. When stating new ideas, the four leaders often emphasised that these ideas were not yet carefully thought out and possibly would lead nowhere. In a quick, interactive give and take, the discussion was usually spirited, with the leaders listening carefully to each other. In sum, the level of deliberation tended to be high. It was clear that the confidential nature of these working luncheons helped with their deliberative quality.

In recent public debate, not only in Switzerland but in many other countries as well, such informal party discussions are criticised as back-room politics. In my view, however, political parties are well served if they prepare their long-term positions in such informal, non-public, 'brainstorming' meetings. Such meetings, of course, should not only involve top party leaders but also lower-level party leaders, and most importantly, ordinary party members and supporters as well. Here the idea of mini-publics can be implemented. (For a consideration of the role of mini-publics see Chapter 10, 'Mini-publics', by Stephen Elstub.) Randomly selected groups of party members and supporters would be given the task of coming up with new ideas for the party programme.

When political parties have established their policy positions in a broadly based internal process, at election time, as Goodin puts it (2005: 193–4), they can submit those positions 'to the maximally expansive deliberative body, the public at large'. Here, then, there is a high degree of public openness. In other respects, however, the level of deliberation is low in election campaigns. This is particularly true of the willingness to yield to the force of the better argument. When party leaders debate their respective election platforms on television, one should not expect that they be convinced by the arguments of the other side. And it is right that this is the case. If election campaigns thus became more fluid it would be hard for voters to make up their minds because they would be unsure where the individual parties really stand. One has also to expect that, in the heat of the election campaign, some of the rhetoric may be low in mutual respect. There seems to be a trade-off between public openness and other deliberative elements. If public visibility is low, other deliberative elements flourish, and when public visibility is high, other deliberative elements suffer.

When the election is over, a cabinet must be formed. In parliamentary systems, this often means bringing together a coalition of two or more parties. If a single party is strong enough to form the cabinet alone, intraparty negotiations are still necessary. Negotiations to put a cabinet together are also necessary in presidential systems. According to Goodin (2005: 193), in all these cases 'party leaders convene a probably only semi-public session to cut deals'. Empirically, this is probably true, and some of these negotiations may even take place behind closed doors. Normatively, however, I think that negotiations to put together a cabinet should be in full public view. Voters, after all, should be allowed to see how the policy positions of the various actors are put together into a cabinet programme. Voters should be suspicious of deals where, for example, support for the cabinet is bought out with appointments of unqualified people to governmental positions or with wasteful governmental subsidies. Therefore, party leaders should make it clear to the public what criteria are used to put together the cabinet programme, and they have to explain why some electoral policy programmes are included and others dropped. Cabinet formation should be more than deal-making where each group attempts to maximise its own utilities. In my view, in cabinet formation, the level of deliberation should be at a high level. Negotiations should be in full public view, arguments be justified in an elaborate way and, in terms of the common good, the policy positions of all negotiating partners be considered with respect, and negotiators be willing to yield to the force of the better argument. Under these conditions, there is hope for a coherent cabinet programme.

When a cabinet and its policy programme have been established, the next phase is the preparation of enabling legislation. For this phase, public openness should be at a minimum. To prepare good legislation, much creative detailed work is necessary. The government bureaucracy, often helped by outside advisory committees, should be able to focus in a concentrated way on this work without constantly being questioned by journalists and lobbied by interest groups. The responsible cabinet members and the cabinet at large have great responsibilities in preparing draft legislation. For this task, they should also be shielded from constant public scrutiny. In my view, cabinet meetings should be kept confidential. Leaks to the media hurt the free and creative exchange of ideas among cabinet members. With the same argument, minutes of cabinet meetings should not be verbatim but should record only cabinet decisions. Later in the decision process, cabinet members will be highly exposed to public view. But, when they prepare draft legislation for parliament, they should be able to do this among themselves in a confidential way, which should help with the coherence of what they decide upon.

Draft legislation then passes on to parliamentary committees. Sometimes, parliamentary committees take it on themselves to draft legislation. Whatever course is chosen, it is a matter of debate whether or not parliamentary committees should be open to the public. In most countries, parliamentary committees meet behind closed doors. Claudia Landwehr (2010: 105–6), however, advocates that doors to parliamentary committees should stay 'ajar', allowing access to researchers and journalists. From a deliberative perspective, trade-offs are involved. As we have seen earlier in the paper, meetings behind closed doors help parliamentary committees to reach a high level of reciprocity compared with public plenary sessions. Opening the doors on parliamentary committees may very well take away this advantage which would be detrimental to interactive give and take when discussing draft legislation. A possible solution may be to give access only to a single so-called 'pool' journalist. This method is sometimes chosen in delicate situations where giving access to all journalists would be disruptive. A trusted member of the journalistic corps is then chosen to report for all. For parliamentary committees, limits could be set for such a 'pool' journalist in the sense that he or she could report only on the arguments discussed but not on who advances those arguments. In this way, the public could begin to make up its mind on the merits of the various arguments. At the same time, committee members could still feel free to have a spirited exchange of views without immediately being exposed to public criticism.

When draft legislation reaches plenary sessions of parliament, there is agreement among theorists that the debates must be in the full public light. This is, indeed, the time when the public learns in a final way what the arguments are and who supports what. From a deliberative perspective, there is a different trade-off from that in the committees; as we have seen earlier in the chapter, the full glare of publicity encourages parliamentarians to justify their arguments in an elaborate way and to refer often to the public good as substantive justification; at the same time, however, there is less mutual respect during plenary sessions.

Having described the entire decision process with regard to public openness, the question now is where exactly do ordinary citizens fit in? In which decision phases do they have the best opportunities to take an active part in the decision process? As I wrote above, when political parties develop their policy positions behind closed doors, ordinary party members and supporters should also be involved in the form of randomly chosen mini-publics. The discussions could take place face to face or, often more conveniently, online. When political parties present their policy positions in election campaigns, this is the time for all citizens to become thoroughly involved. Citizens should deliberate with one another about the policy positions of the various parties. In this context, Bruce Ackerman and James Fishkin (2004) have presented the idea of a Deliberative Day as a national holiday in the United States. They present their idea not only to an academic audience but also in a spirit of practical politics to popular outlets, such as in *The American Prospect*, where they argue for their idea as follows:

> Deliberation Day [would be] held two weeks before presidential elections, it would replace President's Day on our national calendar. Americans would now honor Washington and Lincoln by gathering at neighborhood meeting places to discuss the central issues raised by the leading candidates for the White House. Deliberation Day would begin with a nationally televised debate between the presidential candidates, conducted in the traditional way. But then citizens would deliberate in small groups of 15, and later in larger plenary assemblies. The small groups would begin where the televised debate left off. Each group would spend an hour defining questions that the candidates had left unanswered. Everybody would then proceed to a 500-citizen assembly to hear their questions answered by local party representatives. After lunch, participants would repeat the morning procedure. By the end of the day, citizens would have moved far beyond the top-down debate of the morning. Through a deliberative process of question and answer, they would have achieved a bottom-up understanding of the choices confronting the nation. (Ackerman and Fishkin 2004: 1)

I support this idea of a Deliberative Day though, in practice, it may be organised only by some local communities and not nationally. The crucial point in the present context is that citizens do not merely listen to the election campaign in a passive way but get actively involved in discussing with other citizens the policy positions of the various parties.

When it comes to the preparation of draft legislation to implement the government programme, ordinary citizens can again be involved though I argue above that this phase should be shielded from continuous public scrutiny. Involvement of ordinary citizens can be done here, too, with randomly drawn mini-publics. This involvement can be carried out in a formal way. Just as experts are consulted when preparing legislation, randomly chosen mini-publics of ordinary citizens could also be consulted. I agree with the following state-ment of Maija Setälä (2010: 15) who also wishes to make mini-publics part of the formal decision process: 'The impact of mini-publics could be strengthened by the institutionalization of their use and by developing ways in which their recommendations are dealt with in representative institutions.'

When parliamentary debates begin, usually in committees first and then in plenary sessions, ordinary citizens tend to come into play only through survey data. It is a key message of this chapter that opinions of ordinary citizens should not simply be taken spontaneously in raw form. Citizens should first discuss their opinions with others so that those opinions are more considered. Here, randomly chosen mini-publics can again be of crucial importance. During par-liamentary debates, mini-publics should be organised throughout the country and, in this phase of the decision process, their discussions should be widely publicised with the help of newspapers, radio and television. It is also important that moderators of mini-publics steer the discussions in such a way that they arrive at clear positions with regard to the issues debated in parliament. If mini-publics represent a random sample of the entire citizenry, their policy positions will have a significant influence on the outcome of parliamentary debates.

Ordinary citizens have an even greater say if parliamentary decisions are submitted to a referendum, as is regularly the case in Switzerland (Crepaz and Steiner, 2012). Other countries increasingly use the referendum. Even Britain, the classic example of a pure parliamentary system, submitted to a national referendum in May 2011 the reform of its electoral system. From the perspec-tive of deliberative democracy, I support an increased usage of the referendum because referendum campaigns give citizens good opportunities to deliberate on policy issues. For Swiss referendums, Hanspeter Kriesi (2005: 299) found 'evidence that Swiss voters are less minimalist than generally expected', and that 'argument-based voting' is quite frequent. Of great importance is his finding 'that the quality of the deliberation of individual voters crucially depends on the quality of the arguments exchanged among members of the political elites in the course of the debate preceding the vote'. This finding suggests the possibility of a positive feedback loop between political leaders and voters. If the leaders discuss at a high deliberative level, this stimulates good deliberation at the citizen level, which may send a signal to the leaders to improve even further the quality of their discourse because they become aware how reflective citizens have become. In such positive feedback processes, randomly chosen mini-publics should play an important role. I agree with Yves Sintomer (2010: 484) that a combination of referendums and mini-publics offers an 'interesting path' for democratic renewal. This path was chosen in British Colombia where, for the discussion of a new electoral system, a citizens' assembly, chosen by lot, was coupled with a referendum of the population as a whole (Warren and Pearse, 2008). All in all, I am optimistic about the potential of referendums, combined with mini-publics, to increase the level of deliberation in a country. The caveat is, however, that the referendum needs a long practice to be a useful vehicle to increase the quality of deliberation. One-shot referendums, as in the Netherlands on the Constitution of the European Union, may even be detrimental to good deliberation (Crepaz and Steiner 2012: 303).

This chapter should have shown that public openness is certainly an important deliberative element but cannot have the same importance in all phases of a political decision process. From a systemic level, the crucial point is that overall public openness is good enough if ordinary citizens have sufficient access points to see what is going on at critical junctures and how they can make their influence felt. For a deliberative system, it is not necessary, nor even desirable, that all phases of a political decision process are open to the public. A certain confidentiality in some phases is quite compatible with the requirements of a deliberative system.

What I postulate here for the aspect of public openness, also applies for other deliberative elements (Steiner 2012). The expression of anger, for example, may be a useful part of a deliberative system though, at first sight, to be angry does not seem to be compatible with the respect towards others. But, as Mansbridge (2010) argues, anger may prepare the terrain for later deliberation, and 'angry moments' may help to include 'perspectives that can be accessed only through anger … Anger distorts cognition but, like many other emotions, also motivates thought.'

My overall conclusion is that this third phase of deliberative research is extremely challenging and that we are only at the start of thinking systematically about how we should proceed in this endeavour. One thing is already clear, however, namely that it is not desirable that a deliberative system is constantly deliberative in all aspects. We also need competitive elections, strategic bargaining, aggregative voting, and street protests. The big question then is what is the best mixture of all these elements? In my view, no general answer can be given. The desirable mixture rather depends on the specifics of a particular political system. Switzerland needs a different mixture from the European Union, the

United States a different one from Mexico. The challenge of further research is to investigate the details of individual political systems.

Such a research agenda brings back into focus classical case studies which have been somewhat neglected in recent years. To be sure, we should attempt to generalise as much as possible but we should also be aware that each political system is unique. If we want to be relevant for political practice, we need also to study the specifics of political systems. If we are asked, for example, how deliberation can be improved in the European Union and how the various deliberative elements should be combined with other democratic elements, we need to do an in-depths study of the European Union. (See also Chapter 7, '"Scaling up" deliberation', by André Bächtiger and Alda Wegmann.) Conclusions derived from a general theory of deliberative systems will not be enough. Such conclusions will have to be filled in with the specifics of the European Union. A general theory of deliberative systems may serve as a checklist of where to look in specific cases.

CHAPTER 9

The public sphere as a site of deliberation: an analysis of problems of inclusion

Maija Setälä

Introduction

Deliberation can be understood broadly as 'communication that induces reflection on preferences, values and interests in a non-coercive fashion' (Mansbridge et al., 2010: 55). The concept of deliberative democracy, in turn, involves the idea that deliberation eventually leads to binding collective decisions. Furthermore, deliberative democracy requires the *inclusion* of all different values and interests relevant to a collective decision. Arguments put forward in democratic deliberation should be considered equally on their merits; in other words, by the consistency and the epistemic qualities of arguments and the reasonableness of the claims put forward. Democratic deliberation can thus be distinguished from strategic communication which is not based on the merits of arguments but rather on power resources, such as economic and physical power, which can be mobilised in support of claims.

In other words, in deliberative democracy, collective decisions are based on a process of reciprocal reason-giving among equal and autonomous citizens or their representatives. Democratic deliberation can be expected to enhance fairness and rationality of public decisions. Ideally, democratic deliberation can be expected to help to achieve public decisions which can be reasonably accepted (or at least cannot be reasonably rejected) by all bound or affected by a decision. Though democratic deliberation can be expected to increase consensus among deliberators, most deliberative democrats admit the necessity of voting in democratic decision-making (see Habermas, 1996: 306). As a positive 'side effect', democratic deliberation can be expected to increase individual deliberators' understanding of different viewpoints as well as their knowledge about the facts and causalities relevant to the issue (Andersen and Hansen, 2007).

The public sphere is a central concept in theories of deliberative democracy, and it originates from Habermas's book *The Structural Transformation of the Public Sphere (Strukturwandel der Öffentlichkeit)* which was published in German in 1962. In this book, Habermas analysed the bourgeois public sphere in early representative systems and its decay in modern democracies where mass communication dominates. In general, the term 'public sphere' refers to the political communication in civil society, outside formal political institutions. The public sphere can be understood to involve public discussion within media as well as political and civil society organisations. The public sphere, however, also encompasses other forums and situations where people engage in political discussions, including everyday political talk. Recently, the Internet has become a forum where people increasingly engage in informal discussions on politics.

This chapter addresses two broad questions. The first, normative question pertains to why deliberation in the public sphere *should* be inclusive. The first part of this chapter addresses this normative question; it explains why inclusiveness is such an important condition and why it has become a central issue in democratic theory. Furthermore, the first part discusses the role of the public sphere in the system of deliberative democracy, and describes processes of public deliberation which follow from the normative ideal of inclusiveness. There are some important differences among deliberative theorists in this respect: there are theorists who emphasize deliberation within the inclusive public sphere whereas other theorists stress the importance of non-inclusive forms of communication. The second main question addressed in this chapter is more empirical and it pertains to whether and how inclusiveness *can* be achieved. The second part of the chapter analyses the challenges of inclusive deliberation in current political decision-making. Most notably, the problems following from so-called enclave deliberation are discussed as well as the 'new' challenges of inclusion following from the increasing interdependency of nation states.

Ideas of inclusion, representation and the public sphere

Notions of inclusion and exclusion

As a contrast to the 'classical' or Athenian democracy, where a large share of the adult population was excluded from the democratic process, the idea of inclusiveness is a central normative principle in the modern conception of democracy. For example, according to Dahl (1989: 119–31), inclusiveness means that all those who are bound by a collective decision should have equal rights to influence processes of public decision-making. In practice, this means that all adult members of a political unit where a binding decision is made (for example, a nation state) should have a say in the democratic process. Many democratic theorists have argued, however, that the democratic process should also include people affected by decisions, not only the ones bound by them.

In her book *Inclusion and Democracy* (2000), Iris Marion Young distinguishes different ways in which people can be excluded from the democratic process. Young makes a distinction between *external* and *internal* exclusion. External exclusion means that certain relevant perspectives are not allowed to be put forward in the public deliberation or decision-making. The grounds for external exclusion have been widely discussed by democratic theorists (for example, Dahl, 1989), and the idea of inclusion of all bound by a collective decision has been used to justify the equal political rights of all adult citizens within a certain political unit. Young (2000: 54–5) mentions the disenfranchisement of certain groups of people, and the de facto exclusion of citizens (or their elected representatives) from actual decision-making processes as examples of external exclusion. New kinds of issues of external exclusion have arisen because the problem of the definition of the demos (boundaries of political units) has become increasingly pressing (see below).

The concept of internal exclusion is tightly related to the theory of deliberative democracy. According to the theory of deliberative democracy, arguments put forward by all bound (or affected) by a decision should be considered equally on their merits. To put it simply, internal exclusion means that this is not the case because certain viewpoints and interests are favoured in a deliberative process while others are dismissed or ignored. Young (2000: 55–6) argues further that certain normative ideals of the 'standard' version of deliberative democracy may lead to patterns of internal exclusion. For example, the emphasis on rational argumentation in the Habermasian account of deliberative democracy may give an advantage to the arguments of well-educated people with a good access to the relevant sources of information, and lead to the dismissal of perspectives by those with less education or without access to information. For this reason, Young (2000: 61) suggests that the forms of communication which indicate recognition, such as greetings, as well as emotional and figurative forms of communication, such as rhetoric and narratives, are essential elements in inclusive deliberation.

One of the major issues in contemporary democratic theory concerns the definition of the demos. There seems to be an increasing consensus that the inclusion of all bound by a decision is not sufficient in the contemporary world which can be characterised by increasing economic and environmental interdependency of nation states. As a consequence, democratic theorists have called for influence by, not only all those who are bound but also those who are affected by, a collective decision. For example, Young (2000: 5–6) argues as follows: 'The normative legitimacy of a democratic decision depends on the degree to which those affected by it have been included in the decision-making processes and have had the opportunity to influence the outcomes.'

The principle of the inclusion of all affected is obviously quite vague, and at least it seems to be necessary to qualify the ways in which people should be affected in order to be morally entitled to influence a collective decision-making process. For example, what kinds of interests and values must be at stake in order to allow people outside the demos, predefined by the boundaries of a nation state, to influence policy-making? Without going deeper into the philosophical debate among those defending nation states and those supporting more cosmopolitan viewpoints (see, for example, Young, 2000: 236–75), it seems obvious that at least some political decisions, concerning, for example, environmental or economic standards, have potentially such effects on people living in other countries that they should have a say in decision-making. Moreover, certain collective decisions have a potentially drastic impact on people belonging to future generations (Gutmann and Thompson, 1996: 144–51).

The idea of inclusion of all affected suggests that there are serious problems of external exclusion in the current systems of representative democracy which are based on nation states. It has also some radical implications concerning the political boundaries, as well as the possible systems of representation of the viewpoints, of people who live in other countries or belong to future generations. It seems to be an open question how the inclusion of the viewpoints of all affected could be organised. Most importantly, current forms of supranational governance seem to fall short of the procedural standards of representative democracy exercised at the level of nation states (Dahl, 1999). At the same time, the representation of the viewpoints of those outside the demos has not been properly institutionalised in the systems of representative democracy at the national level (Ekeli, 2005). Indeed, the practical or procedural aspects of inclusion seem to be at least equally as important as the more abstract debate on the principles that guide the definition of the demos. The issues related to boundaries are discussed again in the second part of the chapter. (The issues around the 'scaling up' of deliberative democracy are considered in the chapter by Bächtiger and Wegmann.)

Deliberative accountability

The idea of the authorisation of representatives to make decisions on citizens' behalf is central in contemporary theories of democracy, including theories of deliberative democracy. Political units are too large and political problems too complex to allow all citizens directly to participate in most decisions affecting their lives. Some deliberative democrats have pointed out that, because deliberative processes require time and attention, representative democracy should be understood as a system based on the idea of 'the division of deliberative labour' (see, for example, Warren, 1996; Richardson, 2002).

In a well-functioning system of deliberative democracy, the institutions of representative democracy are the most central arena where the deliberative process of weighing and judging of arguments takes place. The normative goals of deliberative democracy are reflected in the design of representative institutions, most notably parliaments. Especially committee work is expected to foster deliberation among members of parliament representing different viewpoints, and parliamentary plenary sessions provide a forum that enhances accountability, that is, the justification of policy choices for the general public (Elster, 1998).

According to this idealised view of parliamentary decision-making, parliamentary procedures, as such, can be expected to enhance reciprocal exchange of arguments between parliamentarians and the public at large. When looking at the reality of parliamentary procedures in representative democracies, however, factors such as government–opposition division and party discipline shape par-liamentary discussions. There is also some empirical evidence suggesting that processes of policy-making in parliaments are based on a mix of deliberation and various forms of strategic communication, such as bargaining (for empirical evidence, see Holzinger, 2004. See also Chapter 8 by Jürg Steiner.)

The system of representative democracy is based on the principle of public accountability which allows citizens to question and to challenge the decisions made by representatives. In deliberative democracy, accountability is under-stood in terms of reason-giving. Gutmann and Thompson (1996: 128) define the idea of accountability in deliberative democracy in the following terms: 'Citizens and officials try to justify their decisions to all those who are bound by them and some of those who are affected by them.' According to the theory of deliberative democracy, accountability means that political decisions should be acceptable (or at least not unacceptable) in terms that are reasonable from the perspective of all bound (or affected) by decisions.

In deliberative democracy, people should expect their representatives to be able to justify political decisions publicly in terms that are acceptable to all. At the same time, citizens should be engaged in public deliberation where the justifications given by representatives are critically reviewed and discussed (Young, 2000: 131). In the process of public deliberation, citizens should become reflective concerning their own political viewpoints, and should weigh those in relation to other, different viewpoints raised in public deliberation as well as justifications given by the representatives. Deliberative accountability therefore requires that citizens should be able to use 'public reason' (Rawls, 1993: 217–19) which means that citizens are ready to be reflective of their own interests and values and are capable of making reasonable judgements. Citizens should be able to accept that, sometimes, their own values and interests may not be the ones that have the most weight in the deliberations preceding collective decision-making policies which can be justified in terms of values and interests other than their own. (For a discussion of psychological studies relating to these issues see Chapter 6, 'Citizen competence and the psychology of deliberation', by Shawn Rosenberg).

In a representative system based on the division of deliberative labour, however, it is impossible that citizens would go through the same deliberative process of weighing and judging of arguments as their representatives, or even to follow or to mimic these processes. In reality, the acceptance of political decisions in democratic systems is not necessarily based on the use of the public reason, emphasised by theorists of deliberative democracy, but political trust also plays a crucial role (Warren 1996). Furthermore, the prospect of 'throwing the rascals out' in subsequent elections seems to be an important legitimising factor in representative democracies (Grönlund and Setälä, 2007). Deliberative democrats emphasise, however, that deliberative processes and public reason should play a central role in issues concerning people's rights and constitutional issues (for example, Rawls, 1993) and in contested issues where people's vital interests are at stake (Warren, 1996).

Consequently, citizens' inability to accept reasonable justifications seems to be a potential problem for a deliberative democracy. It may be argued that current systems of representative democracy are not, in fact, particularly well designed, considering the idea of accountability of representatives to all who are bound (or affected) by a decision. In most representative democracies, representatives are electorally accountable to their constituents who consist of people living in a particular electoral district. Furthermore, representatives normally try to appeal to certain types of people, that is, people with particular interests or values. This may lead to dilemmas if constituents' interests and values are very different from what is reasonable from the point of view of some people who are bound (or affected) by the decision.

In such situations, constituents may set too stringent constraints on their representatives and leave too little scope for compromise at the arena of representative institutions. These kinds of problems are aggravated if different groups of constituents are polarised (see below). Sometimes the insulation of decision-making from public accountability has been suggested as a cure for these kinds of problems (Stasavage, 2007). This kind of a solution is, of course, fundamentally undemocratic. For example, Gutmann and Thompson (1996: 137–44) argue that 're-iterated' public deliberation, where representatives justify their choices to voters, is a solution to the problems of accountability and, in the long term, the insulation of policy-making from public accountability would create problems of its own.

All in all, in a well-functioning system of deliberative democracy, citizens should be relatively reflective of their interests and values and ready to judge them in relation to the interests and values of all others bound (or affected) by decisions. The question then follows: how do citizens learn to exercise public reason? Many deliberative democrats would argue that this requires actual participation in processes of inclusive public deliberation where different viewpoints based on different values and interests are heard. This viewpoint has also gained empirical support as there is evidence from deliberative mini-publics that deliberation enhances participants' capacity of understanding other viewpoints (for example, Andersen and Hansen, 2007).

Inclusion in the public sphere

Habermas (1996: 359) used the term 'public sphere' to describe the structures of political communication in networks and associations of civil society. According to Habermas, the role of the public sphere is to 'feed in' and to monitor the representative institutions. Habermas (1996: 359) describes the function of the public sphere in the following terms:

I have described the political public sphere as a sounding board for problems that must be processed by the political system because they cannot be solved elsewhere. To this extent, the public sphere is a warning system with sensors that, though unspecified, are sensitive throughout the society. From the perspective of democratic theory, the public sphere must, in addition, amplify the pressure of problems, that is, not only thematize them, furnish them with possible solutions, and dramatize then in such a way that are taken up and dealt with by parliamentary complexes.

In other words, the Habermasian public sphere is a site where citizens' concerns and perspectives are articulated and transmitted to the forums of political decision-making. Considering the problem of inclusiveness, it seems to be relevant to ask whether we should understand the public sphere in singular or in plural. Habermas seems to understand the public sphere as one, unitary entity. Nancy Fraser (1992) emphasises the plurality of public spheres in her famous essay 'Rethinking the Public Sphere'. In this essay, Fraser also introduces the important distinction between strong and weak publics. Weak publics are exclusively involved in opinion-formation and not in decision-making whereas strong publics are involved both in opinion-formation and in decision-making. In particular, parliaments are strong publics because their deliberations culminate in legally binding decisions (Fraser, 1992: 134–5). Fraser raises a number of issues on the relationship between various kinds of publics and the institutional arrangements that support accountability of democratic decision-making bodies (strong publics).

The idea of multiplicity of publics and their relationship has recently been elaborated by Jane Mansbridge and others (2011) who discuss the notion of a 'deliberative system'. A deliberative system consists of distinguishable and differentiated forums and moments of deliberation which, however, are interdependent. In a well-functioning deliberative system, '[...] persuasion that raises relevant considerations should displace suppression, oppression and thoughtless neglect' (Mansbridge et al., 2011: 6). Mansbridge et al. suggest that deliberative systems include arenas which are directly involved in making binding decisions as well as arenas of formal or informal talk related to issues of common concern. In Fraser's terms, the deliberative system entails both the weak and the strong publics.

Mansbridge et al. claim, however, that a deliberative system is not necessarily related to binding decisions made by nation states but it can go beyond the boundaries of the state and include social institutions other than states, such as corporations. Mansbridge et al. (2011: 17) admit that the notion of a deliberative system complicates the question of the normative standards by which the quality of deliberation can be measured. They claim that low-quality and non-inclusive forms of deliberation may sometimes contribute to healthy deliberation from a systemic perspective. Furthermore, they argue that the defects of one part of the deliberative system can be compensated for by other parts. For example, the role of expert deliberation is important in a deliberative system, especially when it comes to the epistemic standards of deliberation. The requirement of expertise creates a potential problem, however, if it leads to disrespect for 'ordinary' citizens' perspectives (Mansbridge et. al., 2011: 18–24. For further consideration of the role of experts in deliberative democracy see Chapter 3, 'Expertise and deliberative democracy', by Mark Brown.)

Several deliberative democrats, including Mansbridge and her colleagues, have also emphasised the role of so-called enclave deliberation in deliberative systems. The term enclave deliberation, first introduced by Sunstein (2002), is increasingly used by deliberative democrats to refer to deliberation among the like-minded. Like-mindedness may be based on shared opinions on political issues or by shared identities which, in turn, may be based on language, nationality, class, gender and so on. Among theorists of deliberative democracy, there are rather different views on the role of enclave deliberation in democratic systems. Some theorists stress the virtues of enclave deliberation whereas others perceive it as a potential source of problems.

For example, Young (2000) argues that deliberative theorists should support the coexistence of inclusive deliberative forums and non-inclusive 'counter-publics'. Young argues that, from the perspective of inclusion, it is important that those who belong to marginalised or oppressed groups form counter-publics that challenge prevailing political discourses. There is also recent empirical evidence that seems to support the view that the presence of like-minded people helps politically marginalised and oppressed groups (for example, ethnic minorities and women) to articulate and express their concerns (Mendelberg and Karpowitz, 2007; Karpowitz et al., 2009). Enclave deliberation seems, therefore, to be needed for the articulation of new and alternative viewpoints which challenge dominating perspectives and ideologies.[1]

The idea of counter-publics had already been put forward in Fraser's criticism of the Habermasian idealisation of the bourgeois public sphere. Fraser (1992, 118: 120–2) criticises the Habermasian account of the public sphere for ignoring the fact that inequalities prevailing in society are more likely to be amplified than to be mitigated in the public sphere. Fraser argues that there are many subtle forms of political control that may prevail in formally inclusive arenas. In cases of social inequalities, it is not possible to reach fairness in participation in the public sphere and, in such societies contestation among competing publics may be a better way to promote participatory parity. (See Chapter 2, 'Inequality and deliberative democracy', by Peter McLaverty for further consideration of equality and deliberative democracy). Fraser (1992: 123) refers to historical examples where subordinated groups have constituted alternative publics where they '[...] invent and circulate counterdiscourses to formulate oppositional interpretations of their identities, interests and needs'.

She calls these kinds of publics 'subaltern counter-publics'. As examples of such counter-publics, Fraser mentions groups demanding rights for women workers as well as ethnic and sexual minorities.

Mansbridge et al. (2011: 31–4) also analyse problems of institutional and social domination in deliberative systems. Institutional domination is apparently a problem in authoritarian states where the state institutions exert control over the media and civil society. The position of the government dominates public discourse and decision-making, and precludes alternative viewpoints. In Young's terms, institutional domination can be understood as a problem of external exclusion. Social domination means that values and interests of particular social groups play a disproportionate role in various parts of the deliberative system. Public spheres are dominated by a particular perspective or ideology, and alternative perspectives are not taken seriously in public deliberation. In Young's terms, social domination seems primarily to be a problem of internal exclusion.

There are historical examples of situations where ideas and viewpoints incubated in enclaves of marginalised people have first challenged dominant discourses but then have gradually been accepted and become a part of the 'mainstream' discourse in the public sphere. This has been the case, for example, for movements campaigning for civil rights of various oppressed groups in western democracies. Often, this process has involved forms of communication which fall beyond the scope of the Habermasian notion of rational discourse, such as rhetoric and storytelling. Many deliberative democrats are ready to welcome these forms of communication in the repertoire of deliberative democracy as they may help other people to situate themselves in the position of subordinated groups. Furthermore, even arguments referring purely to self-interest seem to be acceptable when they inform about the position of disadvantaged people (Mansbridge et al., 2010; see also Fraser, 1992: 129–31).[2]

The potential benefits of enclave deliberation may not be limited to marginalised groups but, in fact, enclave deliberation seems to be a central element of the system of representative democracy. In the context of representative democracies, Habermas (1996: 171) discusses the importance of deliberation among the like-minded within political parties. Habermas argues that party competition encourages parties to articulate social problems and to find solutions to them. In a well-functioning democracy, the claims and demands articulated in enclaves of political parties should be reconciled in the context of more inclusive public spheres and in representative institutions that facilitate inclusive forms of deliberation and decision-making. Heather Gerken (2005: 1101) has used the term 'second-order diversity' to describe the situation where diversity of opinions is achieved at the level of the democratic system rather than in each individual political group.

Despite her emphasis on the contestation between publics, Fraser (1992:

126–7) does not deny the possibility of additional, more comprehensive arenas where members of different publics communicate across the lines of diversity. Fraser argues further that it is an empirical, rather than a conceptual, question under which circumstances such communication is possible. At the same time, she considers social equality as a precondition to the democratic accommodation of cultural diversity. Fraser may be right about the importance of social equality for deliberative democracy; there is also some empirical evidence about the fact that social inequalities affect deliberation even when special efforts have been made to neutralise them (Setälä et al., 2010).

From the perspective of deliberative theory, however, and especially bearing in mind the idea of a deliberative system, it seems to be important to be able to sketch normatively desirable patterns of communication between different groups. Young (2000: 109–10) seems to hold the view that groups of like-minded people should be able to articulate their interests and to situate themselves in the inclusive public sphere. Young argues that the concept of publicity, as such, entails the idea that the public at large is at least implicitly involved in communication. Young argues as follows (2000: 179): 'For their expressions to satisfy the publicity condition, however, they cannot assume the history, language, and shared perspective of a particular interest group but instead must recast the particularity of their concerns in generally accessible images, concepts and issues.' In other words, the publicity condition entails the requirement that communication is not directed to a particular audience of like-minded people only but, at least hypothetically, to a wider public consisting of people with different interests and values. (See Chapter 8, 'Sequencing deliberative democracy to public openness', by Jürg Steiner for further consideration of publicity within deliberative democracy.)

From the perspective of the theory of deliberative democracy, enclaves should thus be connected to more inclusive forums of public deliberation, where other enclaves are present, and to forums of public decision-making. Those who deliberate in enclaves should anticipate and prepare themselves for the situation where they have to justify their position at inclusive forums of deliberation and decision-making, involving people representing different viewpoints. As Young (2000: 113) argues: 'If participants are to make objective judgements appropriate to their context, they must express their own particularity to others and learn of the particularity of those differently situated in the social world where they dwell together.'

Problems of enclave deliberation

Though non-inclusive forms of deliberation seem to have an important role in the system of deliberative democracy, it seems also necessary to discuss the possibility that these forms of communication can sometimes become dysfunctional or pathological. Enclave deliberation seems to be problematic from the point of view of those theorists of deliberative democracy who emphasise reasonableness (for example, Rawls, 1993; Gutmann and Thompson, 1996) and from the perspective of 'republican' versions of deliberative democracy which emphasise the common good. For example, Cass Sunstein (2007) argues that deliberation among like-minded people potentially erodes the capacity of citizens to deal with conflicting viewpoints and, consequently, the basis of democratic citizenship.

The tendency towards enclave deliberation has gained support from recent research in political psychology which suggests that it is rather unusual for people with different political viewpoints to discuss political issues together. Based on the analysis of survey data and experimental studies, Diana C. Mutz (2006) claims that people find it uncomfortable to face political disagreements when they discuss politics with their colleagues, friends, neighbours and so on. Indeed, people are likely to try to avoid situations where political disagreements come up. These kinds of findings of political psychology suggest that people are not likely to 'hear the other side' when they communicate on politics spontaneously in everyday situations. Mutz (2006: 109–18) makes another important observation, namely, that those who repeatedly encounter political disagreements (cross-cutting exposure) are less likely to participate in politics. Facing disagreement decreases proneness to political action especially among individuals who want to avoid social conflicts. Mutz's findings have been confirmed by other studies (for example, Morrell, 2005) which show that participation in deliberative forums may actually decrease people's sense of political efficacy.

On these grounds, Mutz (2006: 135–9) argues that there is an underlying tension between the normative goals of participatory and deliberative democracy. To put it simply, those who are prone to 'hear the other side' may not be particularly active in politics, and the other way around. In a way, Mutz's findings only confirm the insights by Fraser, Young and others who emphasise the importance of enclave deliberation for political articulation and mobilisation. These findings, however, also raise questions on whether and how enclave deliberation can be reconciled with reflection and reasonableness which are also expected by citizens in deliberative systems.

Sunstein (2002, 2007) has analysed the consequences of 'group thinking' which are involved in deliberation in groups of like-minded people. Sunstein has pointed out two possible negative outcomes following from discussions among the like-minded: namely, group polarisation and the amplification of cognitive errors. Group polarisation refers to the social psychological mechanism in which deliberation in a group of like-minded people reinforces those attitudes and opinions that prevail in the group at the outset. There are different reasons for group polarisation. One reason is that, in a like-minded group, discussion is based on a limited and biased pool of arguments which does not necessarily encourage deliberation and reflection (see, for example, Mercier and Landemore, 2012). People's desire to strengthen their in-group identity by conforming to the opinions of the majority may further contribute to group polarisation. The so-called 'spiral of silence' means that, in fear of social isolation, people who think that their political views are unpopular remain silent (Noelle-Neumann, 1984).

The amplification of cognitive errors refers, in turn, to the corroboration of biased or erroneous epistemic beliefs. This may follow from the fact that alternative viewpoints and counterarguments do not come up in the discussions among the like-minded. This is because the pool of arguments present in the discussion is limited, and the 'spiral of silence' may further reinforce this effect. Sunstein (2007: 84–5) also points out the problem of large-scale misconceptions, or 'informational cascades', that come up when people just follow the cues provided by others in the absence of contrary evidence.

These negative consequences of enclave deliberation have gained support in social psychological experiments on political talk which Sunstein himself (2007: 60–2; 2009: 161–8) refers to. In the context of experiments involving deliberative mini-publics, however, participants' cognitive errors have usually been corrected rather than amplified, and groups have depolarised rather than polarised (for example, Luskin et al., 2002). Apparently, this may have been because the inclusion of different viewpoints is ensured in deliberative mini-publics. Also, other procedural features of deliberative mini-publics seem to encourage reflection and deliberation. In particular, some information on the issue is provided to deliberators which widens the pool of arguments put forward in discussions, and the use of moderators in small-group discussions encourages the exchange of arguments and their judgement on merit. (For further discussion of mini-publics see Chapter 10, 'Mini-publics: issues and cases', by Stephen Elstub).

Based on the systemic approach to deliberative democracy, defective forms of enclave deliberation can be identified by the fact that communication is targeted only to those who already belong to a particular group, and it is not even expected to convince those with different identities or interests. Following Young's idea of publicity, enclave deliberation may become 'non-public' in the sense that people deliberating with the like-minded actually assume that, to understand their point, the audience needs to share their history, language or perspective.

Sunstein (2007) uses the term 'balkanisation' which entails not only that enclaves become more extreme in their opinions but also that they lose the capacity and willingness to justify their opinions to other publics and, ultimately, insulate themselves from more inclusive public spheres.[3] This is likely to cause problems of accountability as balkanised groups are not necessarily ready to accept reasonable justifications given for political decisions. In the worst-case scenario, the whole system of deliberative democracy may break down as weighing arguments based on merit ceases to be a method of arbitration between conflicting values and interests. Ruptures in the system of deliberative democracy are likely to increase non-deliberative, strategic forms of political communication based on promises and threats.

Considering the risks related to polarisation and balkanisation, it seems to be necessary to understand the reasons behind defective forms of enclave deliberation. Why does civil society sometimes become 'bad' (cf. Dryzek, 2005)? Young (2000: 236–55), for example, argues that non-inclusive deliberation can be problematic if it is based on exclusionary identities that are explicitly based on strict dichotomies between 'us' and 'them'. Exclusionary identities are likely to lead to enclave deliberation which further reinforces prevailing opinions and attitudes. According to Young, nationalism is often based on a strict distinction between 'us' and 'them' and nationality is, therefore, a typical example of an exclusionary identity. Nationalism seems to create a serious obstacle for inclusive deliberation within some multi-ethnic states and in supranational units of governance, such as the European Union. In general, exclusionary elements of national identities can be regarded as obstacles for the democratisation of the supranational governance.

Of course, there are also other exclusionary identities, such as the ones based on class, ethnicity and religion, which may hinder interaction with other groups and the emergence of inclusive public spheres. As deliberation requires a common language, obstacles for inclusive deliberation are obvious in multilingual political units, both in multilingual nation states, such as Belgium, and in supranational political entities, such as the European Union. The problems of the emergence of a Europe-wide civil society and public sphere have been analysed by many political theorists (for example, Habermas, 2004). The difficulties related to the lack of a common language and the absence of forums for public deliberation, such as Europe-wide political media or truly European electoral campaigns, are widely recognised.

Sunstein (2007) points out that the argument concerning people's proneness to avoid conflicting opinions also applies in mediated modes of political communication. After all, face-to-face political communication analysed by Mutz is not the primary mode of political deliberation in the current civil society but political deliberation in large-scale societies is usually mediated (Young, 2000: 167–8). People hear different political viewpoints from their representatives and political activists and, typically, this communication takes place in the mass media or, increasingly, on the Internet.

Sunstein argues that new communication markets may actually amplify the risks related to enclave deliberation. Unlike many other democratic theorists, Sunstein is quite critical about the patterns of political communication on the Internet. Democratic theorists have often expressed a lot of optimism concerning the new communication technologies because they may be used to enhance transparency of public decision-making and to facilitate new forms of citizen

engagement (see, for example, Barber, 1984). From the point of view of deliberative democracy, it has been argued that, compared with mass media, communication technologies allow more horizontal forms of communication.

Reflecting on the developments in the United States, Sunstein (2007: 51–4)
points out how people with different ideological orientations (Democrats and
Republicans) are affected by the news network labels (CNN and Fox, most
notably) as they are drawn to those labels that they consider ideologically
close to themselves and avoid those that they find distant. Sunstein (2007:
63–4) argues further that the Internet further enhances the tendency to communicate with the like-minded, which potentially leads to group polarisation.
The Internet makes it easier for people to find like-minded people and helps to
insulate them from competing opinions. Many political discussion sites on the
Internet are expected to attract like-minded people only. According to Sunstein,
similar logic applies to blogs as people are likely to follow those blogs that they
are likely to agree with.

These kinds of websites are likely to become 'echo chambers' where people
primarily seek reassurance for their own opinions and attitudes. The most
extreme examples of the risks related to enclave deliberation on the Internet are
various hate groups that are based on strictly exclusionary identities (Sunstein,
2007: 73–6). There are some reasons why the risks of group polarisation and
balkanisation seem to be much more pressing in the case of enclave deliberation
on the Internet compared to enclave deliberation in political parties, for
example. First, many online discussions are often anonymous which may undermine social norms of mutual respect, tolerance and so on. Second, online discussions focus typically on one particular issue whereas political parties need to
address a wide range of issues which, in turn, increases the likelihood of eventual
disagreement among participants. Third, unlike most online discussions, parties
in representative democracies are usually connected to the forums of inclusive
deliberation, most notably to institutions of representative democracy.[4]

The reasons for polarisation and balkanisation may sometimes be found in
how those who deliberate in enclaves perceive their position in the deliberative system. Most notably, defective forms of enclave deliberation can also be
a manifestation of the view that other publics, most importantly strong publics
with decision-making power, are not receptive or responsive to the viewpoints
of certain subordinated or marginalised groups. People in these enclaves do
not have much faith in being heard in public deliberation influencing collective
decision-making.

This kind of a perception of exclusion can simply be based on a lack of
understanding of, or alienation from, the processes of democratic deliberation
and decision-making. Such a perception, however, may result from actual
patterns of external or internal exclusion. As pointed out above, deliberative
democrats are open to the possibility that enclave deliberation may help sub-

ordinated groups to articulate their interests, and they are even ready to accept non-argumentative modes of communication to make marginalised viewpoints heard. Subordinated groups, however, may be tempted to reject any notion of non-coercive persuasion in case they suspect that these forms of influence will not be helpful.

The risks related to enclave deliberation are likely to be aggravated, too, if public spheres are simply not influential with respect to public policy-making. When democratic institutions are weak, policy-making processes tend to be unresponsive to the viewpoints raised in the public spheres of the civil society. Mansbridge et al. (2011) regard this kind of a dysfunction as a kind of 'de-coupling' of the parts of the deliberative system. In Young's terms, this can be regarded as a form of external exclusion as it means that citizens are de facto excluded from decision-making forums. In these situations, people deliberating in enclaves cannot anticipate a situation where their arguments are heard in inclusive forums of deliberation and decision-making.

For example, policy-making in institutions of supranational governance, such as the European Union, seems to be quite detached from the public spheres. This seems to be due partly to the weakness of the institutions of representative democracy at the EU level, despite the fact that the European Parliament is arguably the most advanced institution of supranational representative democracy. Though the European Parliament is inclusive, in the sense that it allows articulation and discussion on political viewpoints from the whole union, it has restricted powers in European Union policy-making and, therefore, it is a 'strong public' in only a limited sense.

In addition, some of the European Union institutions, especially the Commission which is the primary agenda setter in the EU policy-making process, are designed not to be accountable to the public. For this reason, it does not seem to be meaningful for civil society associations to try to influence the 'European' public opinion. Rather, these organisations seem to try to influence European Union institutions directly, through lobbying, for example. At the same time, public deliberation on European Union policy-making takes place primarily within enclaves based on national boundaries, and there are only a few, and typically quite elitist, forums for public discussion at the European level. In the context of national public spheres, European Union issues are primarily discussed from a national perspective which also seems to dominate European Union policies of the member state governments.[5]

At least in theory, the organisation of high-profile deliberative mini-publics could be one way of starting up processes of reciprocal justification between groups deliberating in enclaves. This was one of the motivations for organising two EU-wide deliberative polls, Tomorrow's Europe (2008) and Europolis (2009). These deliberative polls were sponsored by the European Union Commission in the aftermath of the No votes in the referendums on the

European Constitutional Treaty in France and the Netherlands in 2005. Both these two deliberative polls dealt with a variety of policy issues. Participants came from twenty-seven European Union member states and they used more than twenty languages (Fishkin, 2009, 175–89). It seems that EU-wide deliberative polls had very little influence on public discourse which can be explained partly by the weakness of the European public sphere. Deliberative polls and other mini-publics, however, have had a relatively modest impact on public discourses also in the context of representative democracies, apart from some cases where mini-publics have been used in conjunction with inclusive forms of citizen participation, such as referendums (see, for example, Fishkin, 2009: 133–9; Warren and Pearse, 2008).

Concluding remarks

A deliberative process requires exchange and reflection of arguments. According to the systemic approach to deliberative democracy, the processes of inclusive deliberation do not need to happen at one particular forum or at one particular point in time. Rather, the emphasis is on the sequencing of deliberative moments and the interaction between different kinds of publics. In this chapter, it has been pointed out that deliberative democrats have provided two kinds of accounts on deliberation among the like-minded: one emphasising its importance for the articulation and mobilisation of political viewpoints and interests; and the other emphasising the risks involved in enclave deliberation.

Even those deliberative democrats, however, who highlight the positive aspects of enclave deliberation stress that deliberative forums and moments should be communicatively connected to each other. Inclusiveness of at least some of the public spheres, especially strong publics with actual decision-making power, seems, therefore, to be a central element in deliberative democracy. In a well-functioning deliberative democracy, those deliberating in enclaves should anticipate that, eventually, their arguments need to be put forward at more inclusive forums. This requires sufficient confidence that other political groups, representing different interests and values as well as decision-making institutions, are responsive and ready to communicate in fair terms.

Mutz shows that people have an inclination to avoid conflicting viewpoints and, in this respect, certain tendencies towards enclave deliberation seem to be 'built in' in human psychology. Sunstein seems to argue that these tendencies play a key role in shaping new information markets and warns about the risks of group polarisation and balkanisation involved in these forms of enclave deliberation. These are likely to occur when enclave deliberation becomes a pervasive pattern of political communication or when enclaves are detached from more inclusive forums of deliberation and decision-making. Defective forms of enclave deliberation can also be a reaction to the perception that a particular viewpoint is excluded from public deliberation and decision-making. Arguably, this kind of a perception may be based on a misconception of how democratic deliberation works. It may also follow, however, from actual exclusion of certain viewpoints from collective decision-making (external exclusion) or their unfair treatment in public deliberation (internal exclusion).

Group polarisation and balkanisation create problems of deliberative accountability and potentially decrease the capacity of the representative system to resolve political problems. Sometimes, the insulation of public decision-making from public accountability (or in Mansbridge's terms, 'de-coupling') is regarded as a cure in such situations. This may only further aggravate the balkanisation of the public sphere, however. Gutmann and Thompson argue that, in such situations, representatives should be particularly careful in justifying their policy choices. Moreover, inclusive and 'reiterated' public deliberation at different forums should be encouraged in all possible ways.

In the contemporary world, the increasing need for supranational policy-making creates more challenges for inclusiveness. The scope of many collective problems is much larger than the boundaries of nation states. Democratic processes in nation states seem to enjoy a high level of legitimacy, partly because many democratic nation states seem to host relatively well-functioning systems of deliberative democracy. The impacts, however, of public policies which reach beyond people currently living within the boundaries of a certain nation state may create a moral obligation to include the perspectives of people in other countries or of future generations. These impacts seem to have created more or less permanent problems of external exclusion both at the level of decision-making in nation states and at the level of supranational governance.

Notes

1. Enclave deliberation could be seen as a possible cure for ideological domination (Przeworski, 1998) which essentially means that people are 'duped' into holding certain beliefs that may sometimes be against their real interests.
2. Dryzek (2000) argues, however, that, from the perspective of the theory of deliberative (or discursive) democracy, even these forms of communication should be non-coercive and capable of connecting the particular to the general.
3. Mansbridge et al. (2011: 33–4) call zealous polarisation 'entrenched partisanship'.
4. Indeed, as these kinds of online discussions do not necessarily induce reflection (cf. Mansbridge's definition), it may be asked whether they can be regarded as examples of enclave *deliberation*.
5. Mansbridge et al. (2011) name this kind of a defect in a deliberative system as 'tight-coupling' which means that a particular perspective dominates the entire deliberative system and, consequently, the policy-making process.

CHAPTER 10

Mini-publics: issues and cases

Stephen Elstub

In its third generation, deliberative democracy has an increasing institutional orientation (Elstub, 2010a). Mini-publics comprise the institutional device that has received the most attention from deliberative democrats in terms of being the most advocated method to institutionalise deliberative democracy but also as the subject of the most empirical studies. Much of the empirical turn in deliberative democracy hailed by Dryzek (2010) can therefore be attributed to the study of mini-publics. Indeed, this is not surprising given that mini-publics are an institutional type that very much reflects the third-generation interpretation of deliberative democracy (Elstub, 2010a). For example, the initial ideal of deliberative democracy developed by Habermas is that public reasoning could resolve the differences, disputes and conflicts between stakeholders, leading to consensus, with the unforced force of the best argument winning out. As described in the introductory chapter here by Elstub and McLaverty, however, the second generation of deliberative democrats revised this theory to be more in line with reality. Faith in public reasoning to promote the common good between partisans has been lost. The dominant view in the third generation of deliberative democracy is that partisan deliberators are unlikely to amend their preferences in the light of reasoning. Mini-publics fit well here because they attempt to achieve impartiality, preference change and public reasoning by bringing together a random selection of non-partisan citizens to discuss key issues. As this book is on issues and cases of deliberative democracy, and mini-publics represent most of the cases studied, and because the dominance they have gained in discussion of institutionalising deliberative democracy, the fact that there is a chapter dedicated to them here is clearly justified. They are not in themselves an 'issue', however, not in the sense of the other issues covered in this book. Mini-publics are a device that may or may not help deliberative democracy overcome or resolve the other issues covered here. The focus of this chapter, then, is to review the relationship mini-publics have with the nine other key issues of deliberative democracy, addressed in the other chapters of the book, by drawing on evidence from a range of cases. I conclude that mini-publics comprise an indispensable institution for deliberative democracy but that they need to be combined with other institutions and that more comparative research on the different types of mini-public is required to locate them most effectively in the policy process. The chapter starts, though, by defining mini-publics, outlining the different types, and offering a typology.

Typology of mini-publics

The relatively recent rise of mini-publics is based on the resurrection of the Athenian method of representation by lot. In theory, this rise was instigated by Dahl (1989) and his idea of a 'minipopulus'. For Goodin (2008: 11) mini-publics are democratic innovations that are made up of ordinary, non-partisan, lay citizens and are 'designed to be groups small enough to be genuinely deliberative and representative enough to be genuinely democratic'.[1] Therefore, their goal is to strike a balance between the competing choice of rule by deliberative elites or by non-deliberative masses. Either a random or a stratified sample of the population is selected to achieve a 'deliberative microcosm' of the population, with each citizen having an equal chance of being selected. Smaller mini-publics are not intended to be statistically representative of the population but are still 'demographically diverse' (Hendriks, 2005: 96). Participants are remunerated, the discussions are facilitated, and experts provide evidence and advocacy of relevant information and positions and are then cross-examined by the lay citizens (Fishkin and Luskin, 2000; Elstub, 2006). They are usually issue specific, and are dissolved as soon as the issue has been deliberated (Dryzek, 2010: 59). Despite these common features, there is a variety of types of mini-public including citizens' juries, planning cells, consensus conferences, deliberative polls and citizen assemblies. Each is covered briefly in turn below.

Citizens' juries

Citizens' juries (CJs) were first established in 1971 in the United States by Ned Crosby of the Jefferson Center before the deliberative turn started but have been employed in many other countries since then including the United Kingdom, Netherlands, Ireland, France and Australia (Crosby and Nethercut, 2005). They cost approximately £16,000 to £30,000 (Davidson and Elstub, 2013). Approximately twelve to twenty-five randomly stratified selected participants are assembled for four to five days to discuss an issue and produce a collective recommendation. According to its originators, CJs are designed to provide jurors with some control over the process, including facilitation, choice of witnesses, and the nature of interaction with the witnesses (Crosby and Nethercut, 2005: 114).

Consensus conferences

The Danish Board of Technology devised consensus conferences (CCs) in the late 1980s just as the deliberative turn started. Though they were originated in Denmark, and the vast majority of CCs have been held there, they have been employed in a number of countries including Australia, Argentina, New Zealand, Korea, Israel, Japan, Canada, the United Kingdom and the United States. They cost between US $70,000 and $200,000. Danish consensus conferences, are divided into two stages. Ten to twenty-five citizens are selected by stratified random sampling. Firstly, the citizens 'meet for two preparatory weekends to learn about the topic, the process, and the group', which involves selecting the experts and interest groups from a list to advise and present to the citizens in the second stage of the conference (Hendriks, 2005: 83). The second stage of the conference lasts four days and the citizens hear the presentations from their selected advocates and experts before questioning them and then compiling a collective report which outlines their collective decision. Both consensus conferences and CJs (at least in the United States) use an external advisory committee that selects the citizens, compiles the list of experts from which the citizens choose, develops information packs and selects facilitators. This committee tends to be made up of academics, practitioners, issue experts, and even interest-group representatives (Hendriks 2005).

Planning cells

Planning cells (PCs) originated in Germany and were created by Peter Dienel of the Research Institute for Citizens' Participation at the University of Wuppertal in Germany in the 1970s before the deliberative turn began. PCs have been held predominantly in Germany but also in Austria, Switzerland, Spain and the United States. They cost between US $180,000 and $240,000. A series of planning cells, usually six to ten, with about twenty-five citizens participating in each, runs concurrently on the same issue for about four days, usually resulting in the participation of one hundred to five hundred citizens in total. This is not exclusive to PCs as CJs have also been run concurrently on the same issues (Crosby and Nethercut, 2005: 113) but, where it is the norm with PCs, it is an exception for CJs. They are also facilitated differently from CJs and CCs, with the facilitators more likely to be issue- than process-specialists. The planning-cell convenors aggregate all the preferences across all the cells into a report which is then approved by a selection of the citizens from the various cells before being published and distributed to relevant decision-makers and stakeholders (Hendriks, 2005: 84–6).

Deliberative polls

The deliberative poll was first set up by James Fishkin and the Center for Deliberative Polling in 1988 in response to the deliberative turn. A deliberative poll (DP), with its more representative 130 to 500 sample, 'is designed to show what the public *would* think about the issues, if it thought more earnestly and had more information about them' (Luskin et al., 2002: 258). The first ever DP in the world was held in Britain in 1994; since then they have been run in many countries, including Canada, the United States, Denmark, Hungary, Bulgaria, Greece, Brazil, Australia and China. They cost approximately £200,000 (Smith, 2009: 105).The process involves taking a probability sample of voters, surveying their opinions on an issue, sending them balanced information about the topic in question, gathering them together in small groups to discuss the issues with each other and with a balanced range of experts in plenary sessions, and then surveying their opinions again. Ideally they are televised, or at least receive broad media coverage to contribute to informing the broader public (Luskin et al., 2002: 258–9). The participants' preferences are aggregated, as they are not required to come to a collective decision themselves, through deliberation, as in CJs and CCs.

Citizens' assemblies

Citizen' assemblies (CAs) are the newest (since 2004) and potentially the most radical and democratically robust of all the mini-public types developed to date They are difficult to assess as there have been only three instances in British Columbia, Ontario (both in Canada) and the Bungerforum in the Netherlands, and all three have addressed the issue of electoral reform. The two Canadian cases preceded a referendum on electoral reform, for which the assembly determined the options on the referendum, as well as making recommendations for the referendum outcome. In the Dutch case the citizens' recommendation was passed to the government for consideration. An assembly will last for months or even a year. The three cases so far have assembled 100 to 160 participants. In all the assemblies, the citizens were selected randomly from the electoral register; a further random selection is then made from those who express an interest in participating, meaning they are not strictly a random sample. Nevertheless, it is still considered that all three assemblies were representative of the broader population in terms of age, gender and geographical location. The process progresses in three phases: the learning phase which takes six weekends and enables the participants to get to grips with the complexities of the different electoral options; the consultation phases where the randomly chosen citizens run public hearings in their local constituencies to gather information and opinions from other members of the public; and the deliberative phase when the citizens discuss the issue and agree their final proposal. Following the deliberation, a vote among the participants was conducted to decide a final outcome of the assemblies (Fournier et al., 2011).

Now that each type has been broadly outlined, each mini-public can be compared across salient features. Citizens' juries, consensus conferences and planning cells are closely related types of mini-public but there are still important distinctions (Hendriks, 2005; Smith, 2009) and the differences with DPs and CAs are even greater. The similarities and differences among all types of mini-public are highlighted in Figure 10.1 below.

	Citizen juries	Planning cells	Consensus conferences	Deliberative polls	Citizen assemblies
Developed by (first instance)	Crosby (the United States, 1971)	Dienel (Ger., 1970s)	Danish Board of Technology (1987)	James Fishkin (the United States 1994)	Gordon Gibson (Canada, 2002)
No. of citizens	12–26	100–500	10–18	100–500	103–160
No. of meetings	4–5 days	4–5 days	7–8 days	2–3 days	20–30 days
Selection method	Random selection	Random selection	Random + self-selection	Random selection	Random + self-selection
Activities	Information + deliberation	Information + deliberation	Information + deliberation	Information + deliberation	Information +consultation +deliberation
Result	Collective position report	Survey opinions + Collective position report	Collective position report	Survey opinions	Detailed policy recommendation
Destination of proposal	Sponsor and mass media	Sponsor and mass media	Parliament and mass media	Sponsor and mass media	Government and public referendum

Figure 10.1 Key features of mini-publics

(Based on Fournier, 2011: 11).

	High number of participants (>100 participants)		
Common statement	*Citizens' assembly*	*Deliberative Polling* *Planning Cells*	*Individual Voting*
	Consensus Conference Citizens' Jury		
	Low number of participants (<30 participants)		

Figure 10.2 Mini-publics sortal typology

(Based on Lindell, 2011)

Figure 10.1 compares the main features of each mini-public, together with the different forms of citizen involvement. This figure includes just the raw facts; we need to explore the significance of these similarities and differences.

Figure 10.2 provides a sortal categorisation of the mini-publics with respect to the number of participants in each mini-public with the decision-making method. We can see here that CJs and CCs suffer comparatively with respect to representativeness because they assemble a smaller number of citizens:

> These methods often suffer from the same problem ... they begin with self-selection and then employ such small numbers that any claims to representativeness cannot be credibly established. Another problem is that these research designs do not permit evaluation of how those agreeing to participate compare to those who do not. (Fishkin, 2006: 43)

The way in which decisions and collective judgements are reached in a mini-public also influences the quality of the deliberation. As discussed above, the CJ, CC and CA participants reach a collective recommendation. For Smith (2009: 100) this means that they can be more creative and develop novel ideas and solutions. Moreover, the final recommendations are supported by reasons. In DPs and PCs, preferences are just surveyed using set questions so these dimensions do not occur: 'The preset nature of the survey instrument raises questions about the extent to which it fully captures considered judgement' (Smith, 2009: 100). For example, it is unlikely that those setting the survey can predict the changes in preferences that might occur during deliberation, meaning that a strength of mini-publics is that they are not a useful tool for co-option (Goodin, 2008: 35). Figure 10.2, however, fails to provide sufficient information because, in reality, the differences between the mini-publics are scalar with respect to representativeness of the population at large, level of control, and policy impact of the mini-public. A scalar analysis is therefore provided in Figure 10.3.

From the comparison on these aspects, it seems apparent that the CJ initiators are correct to argue that CAs are 'breaking new ground in empowering citizens who meet in a deliberative format' (Crosby and Nethercut, 2005: 117). Figure

Mini-public	Representativeness	Citizen control over process	Decision-making impact
CJ	Low/ Mod	Mod	Low
CC	Low/ Mod	High	Mod
PC	Mod/High	Mod	Mod
DP	High	Low	Low
CA	Mod/High	Mod	High

Figure 10.3 Mini-publics scalar typology

10.3 indicates that, taking all these criteria into account, CAs are, on aggregate, the democratically superior mini-public: 'It is the only method of citizen policy-making that combines all the following characteristics: a relatively large group of ordinary people, lengthy periods of learning and deliberation, and a collective decision with important political consequences for an entire political system' (Fournier et al., 2011: 10). CAs might be less representative in comparison to DPs but that is the only criterion they can be beaten on, and that is because pure random sampling was considered impractical because of the huge time commitment required from assembly participants (Fournier et al., 2011). But DPs are not perfect with respect to sampling either. DPs usually sample from the entire population but this is not always the case, sometimes for principled reasons, such as when the DP in Northern Ireland on Education Reform simply sampled parents of school-aged children, and sometimes because of pragmatic reasons, such as cost, as the Power 2010 DP sample in Britain was selected from an online polling company's virtual panel (O'Flynn and Sood, 2012).

Nevertheless, it is mini-publics in general that we are interested in here. The remainder of this chapter, therefore, considers the key issues from the other chapters in this book in terms of what we have learnt from mini-publics in practice and with respect to how mini-publics can help address these issue more generally.

Mini-publics and conflict

Though there are clear advantages to the neutral nature of randomly selected participants in mini-publics, such as the reduction of corruption of officials and domination of special interests (Fishkin et al., 2006; Delannoi et al., 2012), the danger is that partisanship is eliminated and, therefore, mini-publics fail to deal with conflict. As Georgina Blakeley alludes to, in Chapter 1 of this book, non-partisan processes, such as mini-publics, might fail to deal with conflict as they do not bring together the stakeholders who are in conflict so that they may dispute together to resolve their disagreement and agree on a way forward. This is a criticism levelled at deliberative democracy more generally (Mouffe,

1999) which might be harsh, as Blakeley herself concludes, because, as Dryzek suggests, 'theoretical presentations of deliberative democracy normally assume that deliberators are partisans' (Dryzek, 2007: 246). It could, however, be an apt criticism of deliberative democrats' most favoured institution, the mini-public. Deliberative democrats who feel that mini-publics are the only method available to institutionalise deliberative democracy seem to lack faith in the power of public reason, instead thinking it seemingly necessary to ensure a focus on the common good and a willingness to change preferences by ensuring that those deliberating do not have an interest in, or opinion on, the decision itself (Elstub, 2010b). Though having non-partisan participants does, indeed, facilitate this, partisanship cannot be removed from the political process; we must, and should, have faith in the deliberative process itself to encourage preference transformation and recognition of the common good. Elstub's (2010b: 321) comparison of partisan citizen forums with mini-publics indicates that, in general, partisan forums are able to deal with agenda-setting, decision-making, implementation and review more successfully than mini-publics. In contrast, mini-publics are more inclusive and deliberative.

Neither can mini-publics avoid conflict just by having randomly selected participants. Mini-publics engage a range of interest groups and experts to advise and give testimony in the process, and these actors might act strategically. Such strategic motivations of interest groups include improving their public image, distributing information, improving their understanding of public opinion, stimulating policy reform and avoiding non-participation costs (Hendriks, 2006: 580–4). Partisanship in politics is therefore inevitable, we cannot dismiss and eliminate these natural human motives, and neither is partisanship necessarily bad (Elstub, 2008: 221). Partisanship can also aid deliberation, motivating people to participate in the first instance and being a key reason why people would stick to deliberative obligations, such as offering reasons to persuade others and reciprocating to listen to theirs (Festenstein, 2002). It seems that mini-publics can contribute to dealing with conflict if they are facilitated appropriately but, owing to the non-partisan citizens that they engage, other institutions and policy processes, which include partisan stakeholders involved in conflicts, will always be required.

Mini-publics, pluralism and inequality

Pluralism and inequality are distinct values which is why they are treated separately in this book. They are closely related, however, especially with respect to their relevance to mini-publics, that is: are there equal opportunities for participation; are mini-publics sufficiently diverse; and, once assembled, is the process equal and compatible with diverse groups? Thus, they are dealt with together here.

Mini-publics use random or stratified sampling to assemble their participants, meaning that everyone has an equal opportunity to participate. Random
selection is very good at ensuring 'descriptive representation' (Stone, 2010).
In this sense, then, mini-publics can be very inclusive, achieving the 'politics
of presence' that Phillips (1995) has thought essential to democracy. With the
smaller numbers participating in CJs and CCs, it seems essential to employ
stratified sampling to ensure all the relevant social groups are included but
even some social characteristics might be missed which means that 'certain
perspectives are not articulated' (Smith, 2009: 81). It is then vital to ensure that
stratified sampling selects people on all the salient criteria otherwise important
views and groups will be excluded and, consequently, compromise the deliberative process (Parkinson, 2006b: 76). With the larger sample in DPs, this is less
of a problem but including a proportional representation of people from some
social groups is perhaps not sufficient to ensure a genuine politics of presence
for these groups (Phillips, 1999), with quotas or thresholds possibly required to
make mini-publics more inclusive (James, 2008: 120–3). This is vital if deliberative democracy is to be approximated to ensure the reasons of the minorities are
genuinely articulated: 'one voice can be isolated in a larger assembly' and, as
larger mini-publics break into smaller groups to deliberate, 'quotas will help to
ensure a range of relevant reasons are heard by all participants' (Smith, 2009:
84). There is a danger here of false essentialism but, again, this is exactly why,
from a deliberative perspective, a threshold of certain social groups is required
to ensure inclusive deliberation because people from the same social group will,
indeed, have different perspectives (James, 2008: 120–3). Selection of participants in mini-publics is consequently an exclusive system because not all those
who want to participate can but, at the same time, selection meets inclusive
criteria by ensuring that no social group is 'systematically' excluded (Smith,
2009: 80).

There is also an inevitable problem of self-selection because even those who
are randomly selected must agree to participate. Though not ideal, this does
not ultimately affect the inclusiveness of the mini-public with respect to social
groups because those who decline the invitation to participate will be replaced
by someone with similar, social characteristics. Most people invited to participate, however, accept the invitation (Davies et al., 2006: 80–1), particularly in
mini-publics (Smith 2009: 82), because being invited is one of the main factors
that makes people participate (Lowndes et al., 2006). Nevertheless, self-selection
does raise the likelihood of having participants who are politically interested and
active, who also tend to be the more educated (Fishkin and Farrar, 2005: 74;
Smith, 2009: 80–1).

Random sampling in mini-publics does then contribute to distributive justice
because, whether participating in them is a privilege or burden, all have an
equal chance to participate (Delannoi et al., 2012: 6). Sortition promotes justice

in the Kantian sense of being an impartial selection process, and is compatible with the Rawlsian theory of justice, as sortition is compatible with the difference principle, because it seems that those in society who are worst off are more likely to be able to participate through random selection than through any other process. Perhaps, here, we see that the greatest strength of random selection and mini-publics is that they overcome the socio-economic barriers that prevent so many citizens from participating. They perhaps then are the most promising method for overcoming Macpherson's vicious circle of inequality that McLaverty discusses in Chapter 2. Though there is a danger that such a focus on identity leads to false essentialism, the politics of presence and descriptive representation can also aid the politics of ideas and reasons, namely deliberative democracy. It is thought that ensuring that all types of people are included in a mini-public will, in turn, ensure that a full range of reasons on a topic will be included, too.

Dryzek, however, strongly disputes the argument that descriptive representation will ensure that a full range of reasons are included in a mini-public: 'There is no guarantee or even strong likelihood that people with different social characteristics will in fact represent different discourses, or that a reasonably full range of social characteristics will guarantee a reasonably full range of discourses is present in the forum' (Dryzek, 2010: 52). Certainly marginal discourse could be missed through descriptive representation which is problematic for equality as 'representation of marginal discourses is especially important from the point of view of democratic equality to the degree dominant discourses embody privilege and power' (Dryzek, 2010: 58). Similarly, in Chapter 2 McLaverty notes that descriptive representation does not ensure that all opinions are included or considered equally: 'If none of the jurors initially supported an opinion that opinion might not get much of a hearing in their subsequent deliberations, even if the facilitator tried to ensure that this happened' (McLaverty). Consequently, Dryzek suggests a reform of mini-publics that, rather than randomly sampling citizens to ensure descriptive representation, would include participants that would represent relevant discourses to the issue in a 'Chamber of Discourses' (Dryzek, 2010: 52). Dryzek acknowledges that the inclusion of all relevant discourses can be secured through random sampling but large numbers, like those present in DPs and CAs, are required. To ensure good deliberation, however, these large groups are split into small groups and then it becomes hard to ensure that all discourses are included into each small group. Therefore, Dryzek's vision for a Chamber of Discourses is for it to be the size of a citizen jury (fifteen to twenty) with one participant related to a particular discourse on that issue.

Q methodology is advocated as the tool to identify the range of discourses and to select those who will represent them most effectively. Because 'discursive psychology suggests that the typical individual actually has access to more than one discourse' (Dryzek, 2010: 57), only selecting those with strong identification to a discourse will mean that we include only extremists unwilling to reflect on their preferences. To combat this, Dryzek suggests having two chambers of discourse on an issue. The first chamber would be made up of those who identify strongly with one discourse; this 'chamber of extremism' would be good at opening up the relevant range of issues. The second chamber would be the 'chamber of moderation', consisting of those who identify with more than one discourse, which would be best placed to reach reflective judgement. Alternatively, the extremists could act as advocates for different positions, with the chamber of moderation making judgement on these discourses, more in line with how mini-publics currently operate (Dryzek, 2010: 57). As with descriptive representation brought about by random sampling, discursive representation has no principle agent bonds but, according to Dryzek, accountability can be achieved through the authenticity of the articulation of the discourse (Dryzek, 2010: 57). This is something that is extremely difficult to measure, however, especially in a deliberative setting when the aim is that discourses will be transformed in response to other discourses and their associated reasons.

Once the participants for a mini-public have been selected, the issue of facilitation of mini-publics is crucial if they are to be equal and plural processes. As already highlighted, all mini-publics make use of facilitators or moderators to help ensure that the proceedings reflect deliberative norms and practices and that the process is fairly equal and compatible with pluralism. Facilitators have the role of ensuring that participant discussion is not dominated by a few members of the group, that each person is able to have a fair say, and that participants do not engage in abusive, dismissive or domineering activity. This has led some critics to argue that these types of 'deliberative' mechanisms are open to manipulation and are unlikely to reflect the freely arrived-at views of the participants (Furedi, 2005: 118–19). In particular, the facilitator can be seen as potentially having the power to control the process and to guide the deliberation in a specific direction. Evidence does not suggest that facilitators engage in widespread manipulation but, for some, the question of potential manipulation remains in need of satisfactory answers. As McLaverty argues in Chapter 2, however, mini-publics use facilitators to try to equalise deliberation. Manipulation of participatory processes, such as mini-publics, seems inevitable; it is the nature of that manipulation that is crucial.[2] The aim to 'manipulate' them along deliberative lines then seems positive. Though there is evidence to indicate that mini-publics do not always meet these standards of facilitation (Huitema et al., 2007: 305), this remains the goal, and rightly so. In general, a great strength of mini-publics is their ability to adapt to pluralism and promote an equal deliberative process but there are still key intensions and issues to be resolved here.

Mini-publics, expertise and interests

All mini-publics engage experts and interest groups as witnesses and informers in the process, and they provide the relevant information on which the citizens will deliberate, so it is not just the selection of the lay citizens that can influence the inclusivity of the process. From a deliberative perspective, it is vital to ensure all relevant views and salient information are given to the citizens.

It seems clear that the experts' presentations are indispensable to the process of mini-publics, with research from the CAs, in particular, indicating that these presentations were the most useful in the whole process in terms of informing the participants (the deliberative phase being the next most useful) (Fournier et al., 2011). According to Mark Brown, in Chapter 3, experts act as arbiters in mini-publics, dealing mainly with technical questions, which can facilitate lay deliberation, except when 'the issue involves extensive political controversy and scientific uncertainty' as experts lose neutrality in these situations. In such circumstances it becomes imperative that mini-publics have experts with competing political views (Fishkin, 2009: 120).

Mini-publics have been criticised for excluding partisan citizens with vested interests and technical expertise: 'There is a danger that even before citizens are directly involved, issues, information and witnesses might be mobilised out of the process' (Smith and Wales, 2000: 58; see also Price, 2000; Mansbridge, 2010b). This bias can be reduced by having an advisory group made up of a diverse range of interests and opinions relevant to the issue to reduce the influence, control and bias of the commissioning authority, such as in Danish CCs and American CJs. In Danish CCs the lay citizens also get to choose the final selection of experts and advocates. It is not always the case, however, that key interest groups are intentionally excluded from the process – they often exclude themselves (Hendriks, 2002, 2006; Elstub, 2010b): 'Serious substantive problems in the deliberative process arise from the blunt refusal of stakeholders to engage with the jury event. The fact that a jury can be strongly driven by speaker effects, despite great efforts to achieve balance, is itself a substantive problem' (French and Laver, 2009: 442).

Consequently, Brown argues that mini-publics could be set up as 'hybrid deliberative bodies that include both experts and laypeople' (Brown, 2009: 231–7; Turner, 2003: 67–9; Callon et al., 2009). This is similar to how experts are engaged in public hearings (Lightbody, 2012). Brown is fully aware of the danger that experts will dominate the deliberation but suggests that this can be overcome through good facilitation. Research indicates that interest groups and experts might be more inclined to participate in mini-publics in this type of reciprocal, equal, discursive format. For Hendriks the impact and influence of mini-publics on decision-making are often restricted precisely because it changes the role of interest groups and experts from their usual role in the policy process, as they are reduced to presenting to citizens: 'a number of policy actors resist taking up this new role because it constrains their control of and influence on the policy debate and their ability to participate freely in policy discussions' (Hendriks, 2005: 96). In general, mini-publics make good use of expertise but there are still concerns here and interests groups will try to circumvent mini-publics to influence policy as long they are included only in an advisory role.

Preference change and citizens' psychological attributes in mini-publics

Random selection contributes to the production of psychological benefits that facilitate deliberation by delivering non-partisan participants. Non-partisan participants are perhaps more likely to be reasonable in the reasons they offer, to respect reciprocity and to reflect critically on their preferences, which may make them more likely to revise them (Pelletier et al., 1999; Smith, 2000; Hendriks, 2002: 70; Hendriks, 2005: 82; Hendriks, 2006: 497; Hendriks et al., 2007; Dryzek, 2007). Nevertheless, we know from rational choice theory that citizens do not have the motivation to become informed over an issue because their influence on this issue via voting will be very limited (Pincione and Tesón, 2006). Once a citizen has been selected and agreed to participate in a mini-public, however, he or she can influence the outcome, and the process therefore gives them both the opportunity and the incentive to become informed (Fishkin, 2006: 45).

Preference change following deliberation certainly seems commonplace in mini-publics. In CJs in Britain participants nearly all change their preferences (Coote and Lenaghan, 1997; McIver, 1997; Stewart et al., 1994; Parkinson, 2006b: 98; Smith, 2009: 95; French and Laver, 2009) and preference change seems to occur in CCs and PCs (Hendriks, 2005: 90) and in mini-publics, in general (Barabas, 2004; Fishkin and Luskin, 2004; Muhlberger, 2005; Niemeyer and Dryzek, 2007; Price and Cappella, 2002; Fournier et al., 2011; Farrell et al., 2012). Most of the evidence on preference change comes from DPs and, on average across all DPs, about two-thirds of participants' preferences change after engaging in deliberation (Fishkin and Farrar, 2005). Not only do individual preferences change through the deliberative process but aggregative preferences do, too, to an extent greater than by chance, across all social groups. Moreover, the preferences become more informed and considered through the deliberative process, cognitive errors have usually been corrected and groups have depolarised, across all social groups (Luskin et al., 2002). Preferences also become more 'public' in orientation after deliberation because they do not represent social groups or interests. For example, in the Texas polls post-deliberation, a majority of citizens were willing to pay more for renewable energy, invest in conservation programmes and subsidise lower-income energy users (Ackerman and

Fishkin, 2004a: 55). The preferences also become more logically connected with respect to values, causal connections and policy preferences, leading Fishkin to conclude that 'the changes are far from arbitrary. They are the product of considered judgments' (Fishkin, 2006: 50). In addition, as Mansbridge (2010b: 56) explains, 'the opinions that do not change are also more valuable as democratic input, because the participants have had to confront alternative arguments'. For Richardson (2010: 182), the fact that mini-publics rarely make consequential decisions means that the recommendations they make will be undisciplined and effectively be mere wishes as 'being subject to the discipline of truth depends on having power'.

The evidence from DPs has also been criticised because it is hard to prove that preference change has been the result of deliberation and not just the distributed information packs, the media coverage, or other political or psychological factors (Shapiro, 2003; Jordan, 2007; Sanders, 2010). Research on an Australian citizens' jury, where participants were surveyed before, after, but also during the process, suggests that, again, significant preference change is likely to occur to those who participate in a mini-public but that the key factor for preference change was information gains from the information the jurors are provided with, and not deliberation itself, though the latter still did have some effect on preferences (Goodin, 2008: 46–51). This is just one case study, however, and similar methods need to be applied to many more cases. The result is supported by evidence from a DP in Britain, though, where again information, rather than discussion, had the greatest influence on preferences (Luskin, et al., 2002: 474–8) and the CAs (Fournier et al., 2011). More recently, research from another DP in Ireland in 2011 indicated that a control group provided with the same information packs as the DP participants did not undergo as much preference change, indicating that deliberation might still be crucial (Farrell et al., 2012).

In Chapter 6, Shawn Rosenberg criticises the results on preference change from mini-publics and the survey methodology employed because they fail to 'examine the cognitive process underlying the observed changes' which means for Rosenberg that there is an alternative and more valid interpretation of the evidence from mini-publics. O'Flynn and Sood (2012) also have concerns about the use of closed-end scales in the surveys DP participants complete, and advocate the 'greater use of open-ended, open format measures, soliciting people's opinions about the issues under discussion in more general terms'. Rosenberg argues that, rather than adapting preferences in the light of reasons, preference change could be about conformity whereby people may just 'adopt the preferences of others' (Rosenberg; see also Kerr et al., 1996; Price and Cappella, 2002; Barabas, 2004; Mendelberg and Karopowitz, 2007). This conclusion does not necessarily reflect evidence from DPs, though, where half of the preferences move towards the mean but half move away from the mean, indicating no overall pattern (Luskin et al., 2002; Fishkin, 2006: 50). If Rosenberg is right, however, it does not mean that mini-publics become useless or redundant because, out of all institutional devices, they perhaps fit best with his suggestions of 'how to organise deliberation in a way that is sensitive to the abilities and needs of those involved'. His remedies include having a diverse set of citizens to encourage them to reflect on their own views and those of others, establishing 'positive socio-emotional relationships among the participants' by meeting several times, the number of citizens should not be too large, small-group discussions should be used, and the assembled citizens should be given other tasks to organise collectively other than discussing the issue. These are all processes that are commonplace in mini-publics. Finally, the role of the facilitator is absolutely key to ensure equal inclusive debate but also to assist in developing analytical, evaluative and communicative skills.

As mini-publics rely on a sample of citizens, the question arises as to whether a different sample of citizens, with different experts and different briefing materials, would have different preferences post-deliberation (Sturgis et al., 2005: 33). The results from a series of DPs held in Texas on energy policy indicate, however, that similar preference changes might occur with different citizens as each group polled ended up with preference shifts from pre- to post-deliberation in the same direction (Fishkin, 2006). CJs, CCs and CAs are in a way more affected by the problem than DPs and PCs, because they do not use a scientific sample, but also less affected, because they result in collective judgements supported by reasons, and the reasons are then crucial in others being able to judge whether an appropriate judgement has been made. In DPs, because preferences are aggregated, we miss out on the key reasons to support the post-deliberative preferences. Because a different sample might end up with alternative post-deliberative preferences, the absence of these reasons makes DPs susceptible to this problem. Ultimately, Smith argues that we are expecting too much from mini-publics if we take this criticism too seriously: 'all we can really hope is that they come to considered judgments that reflect the demands of their particular context' (Smith, 2009: 101) because elected legislative assemblies would also reach differing judgements depending on the make-up of the assembly. This is undeniably true but legislative assemblies are elected, and the make-up of them has then been chosen and determined, to an extent, by the citizenry themselves. Moreover, part of the reason why those politicians have been chosen is precisely because of the sorts of considered judgements that they make. Evidence from mini-publics does suggest that citizens participating will change preferences but more evidence is still needed on exactly why these preferences change.

Mini-publics in the policy process

Can the micro-deliberation in mini-publics have macro consequences? To what extent can the results, decisions and recommendations from mini-publics be incorporated into the policy process? Can mini-publics be scaled up? Can they feed into debates in the public sphere? Can mini-publics be sequenced appropriately with other institutions to influence policy? Given that mini-public are institutional devices that attempt to achieve deliberative democracy in practice, these questions are extremely pertinent and will be considered in turn.

Scaling up mini-publics

Though different types of mini-publics have different relationships to decision-making, 'rarely does the mini-public itself share sovereignty over the decision at hand' (Goodin, 2008: 12; see also Ryfe, 2005: 61; Dryzek and Goodin, 2006: 7; Smith, 2009: 89; Dryzek, 2010: 170). The founders of CJs reluctantly admit that, in the United States, there has been very little impact on public policy, and they attribute this as the cause of the closure of the Jefferson Center (Crosby and Nethercut, 2005). Some deliberative opinion polls have had a direct influence on policy-making. For example, the Texas series of DPs, held on electricity provision, influenced the decisions of the electricity companies to pursue more renewable energy sources and state legislature promotion of renewable energy sources (Goodin, 2008: 22). In the Chinese DP in Zuego, the local government that ran the poll had committed themselves to implement the resulting majority preferences on budgeting (Fishkin et al., 2006; Goodin, 2008: 29). Both the Canadian CAs also determined the options of the referendums on electoral reform (Fournier et al., 2011). These represent the exceptions for mini-publics, however.

Lessons can be learnt from planning cells, though, which evidence suggests have greater, but still limited, influence on decision-making. This is facilitated by contracts between the authority that commissioned the planning cell and the organisers and participants of the cell who require the authority to explain and account for its response to the cell's recommendations. Ultimately, though, the authority can still reject the recommendations, so the link to decision-making is only slightly strengthened (Smith, 2009: 93). In Denmark, because they are organised by the Board of Technology, CC reports are regularly consulted by parliamentarians and parliamentary committees, and it does mean that they have influenced legislation. Outside Denmark, without this 'institutional anchor', CCs have had little or no influence on legislation (Hendriks, 2005: 91–2). Moreover, commenting on the citizens' reports produced by CCs and PCs Hendriks (2005: 91) comments that they are conceived as advisory, and their 'recommendations invariably compete with other forms of advice from political parties, expert committees, and interest groups...when some of these other sources of policy advice happen to recommend the same policies and celebrate the same values articulated in the citizens' reports, it can be difficult to determine which recommendation held more sway.' The commissioning authority of a mini-public therefore usually picks and chooses which recommendations from the mini-public to accept (McLaverty, 2009; Smith, 2009) which, for some critics, means they are too easily manipulated (Price, 2000; Furedi, 2005: 118–19) and co-opted by government, as if their 'recommendations are not already supported by the government, they are likely to be ignored' (McLaverty, 2009; see also Smith, 2009: 93). Therefore, we must agree with Goodin that

> mini-publics lack formal power or authority in the macro-political system. They might sometimes have been established by some public authority. They might report to it. But when they do, their reports are purely advisory and lack even any presumptive law-making power of their own. The problem of how the macro-political 'takes-up' their micro-deliberative input thus arises in acute form. (Goodin, 2008: 15–16)

Not only do mini-publics not make decisions but they have little influence over what they make decisions about because citizens usually have little control over the agendas for mini-publics but follow agendas set by the sponsoring body (Price, 2000; Smith and Wales, 2000; Bau, 2012). For Richardson (2010: 184), this means that mini-publics 'will tell us little of value about the popular will'. The setting of the agenda is crucial for the quality of deliberation and, time and time again, evidence from citizens' juries demonstrates that, where there is not a clearly defined, narrow and focused agenda, there will be poor-quality deliberation (Davies et al., 2006: 112; Parkinson, 2006b: 132–3; Smith, 2009: 89, 97). Mini-publics 'require that well-defined boundaries can be drawn around issues' (Dryzek, 2010: 28). On a practical level, if the citizens participating in the mini-public were able to change the focus of the agenda that they had been charged with deliberating on, then the funding authority might decide to withdraw funding (Smith, 2009: 89). Moreover, the citizens assembled in mini-publics are non-partisan, and not informed about the issues overall, making it very difficult for them to be in a position to set the agenda for debate (Smith, 2009: 89). The process of citizens setting the agenda for deliberation in citizens' juries has been experimented with in the United States and ultimately failed for this reason (Crosby and Nethercut, 2005). In Britain this problem has been alleviated, but not resolved, through the use of pre-jury focus groups to contribute the jury organisation (Stewart et al., 1994; Smith and Wales, 2000: 58). This problem is likely to escalate as we move up the levels of governance and, at the transnational and global levels, citizens will be so distant from the issues that they will have a real lack of relevant information to determine the agenda in the early stages of the mini-public's discussion.

In Chapter 7, André Bächtiger and Alda Wegmann highlight that a key reason that mini-publics fail to have policy impact is that they are 'interfered' with by 'established venues of policy-making'. In particular, organised interests challenge the outcomes of mini-publics, questioning their competence and legitimacy, and using other avenues of the policy process, such as lobbying, to secure and advance their interests. Dryzek summarises this problem effectively: 'In a larger environment of partisan conflict, those not satisfied with the recommendation that a forum reaches can try to undermine its legitimacy' (Dryzek, 2010: 27).

Bächtiger and Wegmann further reflect on the disconnection between the sample included in a mini-public, which has deliberated on the issue, and the general public, who have not, with most people not being aware of the mini-public's existence. Similarly, Shapiro (1999: 33) is concerned about the legitimacy of a process that involves so few of those who are actually affected. As Dryzek puts it, mini-publics 'do not solve the scale problem because decisions still have to be justified to those who did not participate' (Dryzek 2010: 27). For these reasons, it is unlikely that mini-publics would be seen as legitimate if they did result in binding decisions because they go against traditional notions of democratic accountability. Ultimately, if a random selection of citizens were to make decisions, there is no mechanism to hold them accountable for the decision (Baber and Bartlett, 2005; Parkinson, 2006b; Goodin, 2008; Smith, 2009: 169, 176, 187, 191). Mansbridge (2010: 60) understands that mini-publics will gain formal institutional roles in policy-making only if and when randomly selected citizens are seen as 'legitimate representatives of the public. Such an evolution is still far away.'

The extent to which mini-publics can be scaled up and influence policy is determined by the nature of the political system. Dryzek categorises political systems into three broad types, based upon two types of dimensions: whether states are inclusive or exclusive in terms of integrating social interests into the policy process; and whether inclusivity and exclusivity are active or passive. Inclusive states accept a myriad of social interests in the policy process, while exclusive states limit the interests that are seen as legitimate participants in the policy process. States that are actively inclusive, such as Denmark, 'intervene in civil society to manage the pattern of interest organization, and also construct formal channels of participation that organize these interests into the state' (Dryzek, 2010: 171). If states are passively inclusive, for example the United States, channels exist for civil society to be involved in the policy process – such as by lobbying, legal action, consultation, political party activism – but their inclusion is not actively sought. States that are passively exclusive, such as France, enable only a few select groups to participate in the policy process. Actively exclusive states 'intervene in civil society to try to undermine the basis for the organisation of social interests' (Dryzek, 2010: 171). These inclusivity/exclusivity dimensions of a political system then significantly affect the transferability of mini-publics in enacting deliberative democracy (Dryzek, 2010).

There are then good reasons why mini-publics do not have macro-level effects and determine policy but there is still plenty of scope for them to have more influence than they currently do: 'The impact of mini-publics could be strengthened by the institutionalization of their use and by developing ways in which their recommendations are dealt with in representative institutions' (Setälä, 2010: 15). Their expanded employment was even advocated in the 2007 Green Paper, *The Governance of Britain*, the former prime minister, Gordon Brown (2007), calling for an increase in the use of citizens' juries in local government (Cabinet Office, 2001; Davidson and Elstub, 2013), and Segaline Royale advocated their increased use in France in her 2007 election manifesto (Dellanoi et al., 2012) but wide-scale use of mini-publics in any political system remains to be seen. Inevitably, and perhaps rightly, 'mini-publics of the sort here generally can have real political impact only by working on, and through, the broader public sphere, ordinary institutions of representative democracy, and administrative policy-making' (Goodin, 2008: 12). We have considered their impact on representative institutions and administrative policy-making, and we turn now to consider the influence mini-publics have on the public sphere.

The public sphere
For Niemeyer (2012) mini-publics can help to scale up deliberation by influencing the public sphere via supply and demand. With respect to supply, mini-publics filter out and launder many preferences and discourse from the debate, influencing the agenda of the public sphere. On the demand side, citizens have the opportunity to trust mini-publics' discussion and conclusions and use them as an heuristic or 'anticipatory public' (MacKenzie and Warren, 2012). Before 'trust' can be established, 'nonparticipants would need to understand the logic of random selection' (Dryzek, 2010: 27). MacKenzie and Warren's (2012) evidence from the British Columbia CA suggests that mini-publics could be 'trusted information proxies' for the public precisely because they are made up of 'people like them' which might be a reason to favour traditional, randomly selected mini-publics over Dryzek's discourse chamber model.

It is certainly the intention of DPs to have recommendatory force to the broader public and to decision-makers themselves because the poll indicates what people would think as a whole following deliberation (Fishkin, 1997: 162). Here, then, DPs can influence the rest of the public, who were not participants in the process, as well as government bodies, and evidence suggests that this has occurred to a degree in polls in the United States, China, Greece and Brazil (Fishkin and Farrar, 2005: 44–5). For example, following the series of DPs in Texas on energy policy, legislation was introduced, in line with the majority of deliberative opinions from the polls, to promote natural gas and renewable energy use on a significant scale (Ackerman and Fishkin, 2004a: 46), though it has been questioned whether this can be attributed to the deliberative poll (Dryzek and Goodin, 2006: 9; Smith, 2009: 93). By contrast, in the Australian deliberative poll on monarchy versus republic, the majority of voters in the referendum voted for the opposite of what the deliberative poll participants had preferred post-deliberation (Dryzek, 2010: 27). In general, the influence of mini-publics on public opinion and discourses does seem limited (Chambers, 1996, 2003), apart from some cases where they have been used in conjunction with inclusive forms of citizen participation, such as referendums (Fishkin, 2009: 133–9; Warren and Pearse, 2008).

The contribution mini-publics can make on the public sphere is very much dependent on the media: 'By giving substantial coverage to [mini-publics], the media could stimulate a broader debate about what information and knowledge people need to make informed pronouncements about … policy' (Fishkin et al., 2003: 19, cited in Goodin, 2008: 23). Media coverage of mini-publics varies extensively, however, and depends on the relevance of the issue to the media (Parkinson, 2006a). Mini-publics produce reports which are available to the public but these get little media attention, resulting in a lack of citizen engagement and awareness of mini-publics outside the citizens and interest groups that are involved in the process (Smith, 2009: 102). Websites are also used to aid the transparency of the processes but in CJs the deliberation between the participants themselves and the information from the recruited experts tend to happen in private, and this clearly undermines the transparency of the process (Chambers, 2005; Smith, 2009: 103). Plenary sessions and small-group debates, which occur in DPs, are more accessible and have even been broadcast on television and the Internet. Not only do the media hold the power of whether to cover mini-publics but, when they do, the media coverage is designed to meet the broadcasters' needs rather than to facilitate the democratic process, as research from Australian and British DPs indicates (Gibson and Miskin, 2002: 169; Parkinson, 2006a: 181–3). Indeed, Parkinson concludes that the democratic credentials of the media coverage of such events will always be compromised by the need to gain and keep viewers: 'if one relies purely on the media as the means of building bridges between deliberators and audiences, then one privileges those points of view which can easily be dramatized and narrated and excludes those which cannot' (Parkinson, 2006a: 183). CCs seem to get fairly extensive and positive media coverage in Denmark, leading to good levels of public awareness of them (Hendriks, 2005), but this does not mean that their interaction with the broader publics sphere is always positive because CCs 'might not relate or contribute to wider public debate, and it might be perceived by the public as just another remote administrative institution' (Joss, 1998, cited in Hendriks, 2005: 95). Perhaps then the greatest potential for mini-publics to have influence is via the public sphere but this potential has not been fulfilled on a widespread basis as yet.

Sequencing mini-publics

As mini-publics have been the most commonly and widespread means employed to implement deliberative democracy, it seems apparent that they do have a significant role to play within a deliberatively democratic polity, but, given the issues discussed above, further thinking is required to determine exactly what role they can and should fulfil. Mini-publics are unlikely to provide everything we need for a deliberative system, so the key is to understand how mini-publics can be sequenced with other institutions so that all the norms of deliberative democracy are enacted in a policy process (Goodin, 2005). Many suggestions are emerging.

In Chapter 8 of this book, Jürg Steiner suggests that mini-publics could be used by political parties to help form party manifestos, to contribute to the preparation of draft legislation and to supplement parliamentary debates, with the hope that the mini-publics will have 'a significant influence on the outcome of parliamentary debates' (Steiner). As with the recent use of CAs on electoral reform in Canada, Steiner argues that mini-publics should also be sequenced with referendums. Mansbridge (2010b) would like to see DPs used in advance of referendums, primaries, and administrative policy-making. The founders of CJs suggest that these could be used to assess state ballot and referendum initiatives in the United States (Crosby and Nethercut, 2005: 117). Leib (2004) envisions mini-publics functioning as the fourth branch of government in the United States where it would generate legislative proposals but also scrutinise the executive, legislative and judicial branches of government. Demos (Dryzek, 2012: 59) and Delannoi et al. (2012) see mini-publics as replacing the House of Lords in the United Kingdom, which is also similar to McLaverty and MacLeod's (2012) vision for mini-publics to review and revise government legislation, a role that Dryzek would like to see for his Chamber of Discourses (Dryzek, 2010: 59). In all these visions for mini-publics, they would primarily give accent to government legislation, reject it, or recommend that it was revised.

These are all interesting suggestions for sequencing mini-publics and would give them more power and influence than they have traditionally had. Nevertheless, before we can start with these suggestions, we still need to know much more about what each mini-public can deliver in a deliberative system. As Smith argues, 'there are then some potentially significant differences in the design of mini-publics' (Smith, 2009: 79) as highlighted by the typology set out earlier in this chapter. Moreover, from the discussion here, we can see that the different types of mini-public vary in their relationships with conflict, equality, pluralism, expertise, interests, and citizens' psychological attributes. Therefore, they need to be sequenced differently in the policy process. Lindlell (2011) notes that there is insufficient comparative analysis about the contextual factors in relation to all the empirical evidence that is emerging on mini-publics. She has

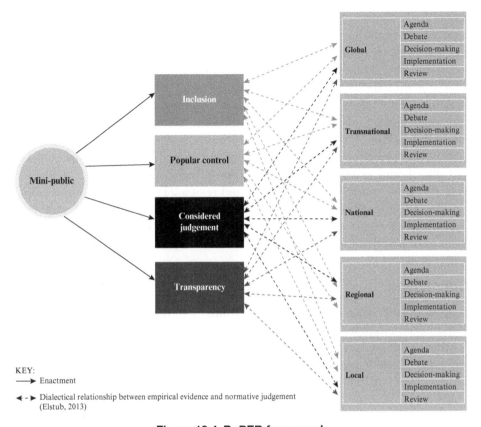

KEY:
——▶ Enactment

◀ - ▶ Dialectical relationship between empirical evidence and normative judgement
(Elstub, 2013)

Figure 10.4 DePER framework

started to plug this gap by employing qualitative comparative analysis, but more comparative understanding is still required.

Neither can we just rely on mini-publics to institutionalise deliberative democracy because other institutions are required (Chambers, 2009; Dryzek, 2010: 6; Elstub, 2010b; Mansbridge, 2010b). As Hendriks argues, the key now is to find their 'optimal location within a larger democratic system' (Hendriks, 2005: 98; see also Smith and Wales, 2000: 62) or even deliberative system (Mansbridge et al., 2011). We need a comprehensive and systematic comparison of what each mechanism could realistically achieve in the policy process and information about how these various mechanisms relate to each other. To facilitate the comparison of mini-publics and other institutional devices, Elstub (2013) has developed the 'Deliberative Pragmatic Equilibrium Review' (DePER) comparative framework. The process is demonstrated in Figure 10.4.

The figure employs Fung's (2007) 'pragmatic equilibrium' and 'practical reasoning' to review critically through a normative lens the empirical evidence already available on mini-publics, creating a dialectical relationship between theory and practice of deliberative democracy, and revising both accordingly until equilibrium is reached. Deliberative democracy will be in pragmatic equilibrium with mini-publics when the values prescribed by it are produced by mini-publics (Fung, 2007: 445). In the DePER framework this is achieved by reviewing the various mini-publics' abilities to enact deliberative interpretations of Smith's (2009) democratic principles (inclusiveness, popular control, considered judgement, and transparency), despite the contrasting features of complexity (pluralism, scale, inequality, need for expertise, globalisation) that are present at varying levels of governance (local, regional, national, transnational, and global) and at different decision-making stages (agenda-setting, deliberation, decision-making, implementation and review). From this it is hoped that a deeper understanding of the role mini-publics could play, in institutionalising deliberative democracy, will be achieved, and we can learn how to sequence them most effectively.

Conclusion

Understandably, mini-publics have been subject to the most focus on debates about institutionalising deliberative democracy. They do have important roles to play in dealing with conflict and pluralism, in enhancing equality, utilising expertise, in engaging interests groups, and enhancing citizens' relevant psychological attributes. All types of mini-public cannot play the same role, however. Neither are they the only institution required to approximate deliberative democracy and deal with these and other key issues. They must be sequenced with other institutions, old and new. Consequently, if we are to scale up mini-publics, connect them effectively with the public sphere, and sequence them more appropriately in the policy process, more comparative institutional analysis is required.

Notes

1. It is important to note that the definition of mini-publics used here includes only democratic innovations that are based on lot, not forums that are purely based on self-selection. In this manner, the definition of mini-publics here differs from Fung's (2003).
2. I'm grateful to Graham Smith for this point.

Conclusion: the future of deliberative democracy

Stephen Elstub and Peter McLaverty

Given that, in its third generation, the empirical turn in deliberative democracy has been occurring, we thought it time that the theory of deliberative democracy was reconsidered in the light of this empirical evidence, around ten key issues that have been affecting its progress and development. The chapters in this book reflect different approaches towards deliberative democracy. While each chapter has dealt with a distinct issue related to the theory and practice of deliberative democracy, authors approach the issues with different emphases and perspectives towards deliberative democracy. Within the overarching issues discussed in each chapter, there is a number of themes that come out of the chapter discussions which we would like to highlight here by way of conclusion. Those themes are important for future theoretical and practical work on the development of deliberative democracy. We start by looking at the idea of the 'deliberative system' which might represent the start of the fourth generation of deliberative democracy. We draw attention to some of the difficulties authors have raised about the achievement of a deliberative system. We also assert that the systemic analysis of deliberative democracy creates distinct interpretations of our ten issues. We next look at psychological factors that are seen as making the achievement of deliberation difficult. The negative and positive issues which authors have raised in respect of various divisions in societies, both national and international, are then considered. Finally, we consider what the authors had to say about the way forward for deliberative democracy. As Hegel famously noted 'the owl of Minerva spreads its wings only with the coming of the dusk', thereby suggesting that, at best, we understand a historical condition just as it passes. There is then the consideration that, rather than reflecting on the future of deliberative democracy, we are simply recording and understanding its recent past.

The deliberative system

Within recent academic work on deliberative democracy, a number of writers have turned their attention to the idea of the deliberative system (Chambers, 2003; Dryzek, 2010; Parkinson and Mansbridge, 2012; Steiner, 2012). In its widest form, the basic approach associated with work in this area is that deliberation, or deliberative democracy, should be placed within democracy or society considered as a system. Rather than simply focusing on the extent to which particular types of institutions do or do not meet standards of deliberative democracy, the focus is now on how to combine these institutions with other processes to ensure that the norms of deliberative democracy are prevalent across the deliberative system as a whole: 'A *system* here means a set of distinguishable, differentiated, but to some degree interdependent parts, often with distributed functions and a division of labor, connected in such a way as to form a complex whole.' While 'a *deliberative* system is one that encompasses the talk-based approaches to political conflict and problem solving' (Mansbridge et al., 2011: 4–5). In general, there are four parts to a deliberative system: the making of binding decisions; preparing to make binding decisions; informal talk related to binding decisions; and informal talk not related to making binding decisions (Mansbridge et al., 2011: 12). It is then the interconnected nature, interdependence, and division of labour between these parts that become key to systemic analysis, and this means our ten issues should be approached differently in a systemic analysis. Each part of a deliberative democracy system does not have to be deliberative, but some parts do, and the impact of the deliberative parts has to be strong enough for the whole democratic system to be defined as deliberative. Authors differ about what this might, or should, mean in practice. Similarly, if the deliberative system idea is used in the context of society, the starting point is conceiving of society as a system. For a society to be seen as deliberative, not all aspects of society have to be organised along deliberative lines. What matters is that parts of the society are deliberative, and the deliberative aspects are so influential that the society as a whole can be called deliberative. It is quite difficult to think of a deliberative society in these terms but easier to conceive of a deliberative democracy where not every aspect, process and institution conform to these strict norms.

The chapters by some of the authors in this book contribute to a discussion of the deliberative system. André Bächtiger and Alda Wegmann consider the role that deliberation might play, not just within nation states and national territorial levels of government, but also within the expanding institutions of global, or international, governance. They consider how elite and citizen deliberation can be combined, and argue for the importance of contestatory discourse, and they thereby echo Georgina Blakeley's argument made in Chapter 1. In Chapter 9, in her consideration of deliberative democracy and inclusion, Maija Setälä considers the opportunities and problems that 'enclave deliberation' can represent. She argues that different public spheres need to be able to influence public policy. She gives reasons for why this may not always be easy but her work suggests that a deliberative democratic system is unlikely to be sustainable or legitimate if it does not allow 'enclave public spheres', especially of the politically and socially marginalised and oppressed to be influential, and seen to be influential, in public policy terms.

In her consideration of the 15-M Movement in Spain, Blakeley's argument suggests that the achievement of a deliberative system is very unlikely, given the conflicts that are endemic within capitalism. As long as democracy is dominated by 'liberal democracy', other forms of politics will override deliberative politics. Deliberation has a role to play in politics but this role is always likely to be limited. Blakeley argues that this is not only more or less inevitable but strongly questions whether it is right to expect any more of deliberative politics in the world today. Similarly, in Chapter 2, Peter McLaverty questions how far 'deliberative democracy' can travel in societies where there is large-scale inequality. In such societies, he argues, the rich and powerful are likely to exercise disproportionate political influence and may well see their privileges threatened by a more deliberative form of democracy. He argues that, unless large-scale inequalities are significantly reduced, 'deliberative democracy', including the idea of the deliberative system, is likely to face major obstacles.

Systemic analysis is also relevant to how Mark Brown, in Chapter 3, considers how expertise is distributed throughout a system, and the need for non-deliberative modes of political activity. In Chapter 8, Jürg Steiner considers questions surrounding 'public openness'. He argues that, even in a deliberative system, not all deliberation has to be, or should be, out in the open and accessible to the public. In a deliberative system, he argues that different levels of public openness will apply at different points in the system. He also argues, however, that there should be a number of important points where the public can gain a view or understanding of what is happening in the public policy process; the system should also be open in the sense that citizens feel they can influence decisions that are made at different points in the system. In Chapter 10, Stephen Elstub concludes that, although a great deal of empirical evidence on mini-publics is now available, more comparative analysis is required to deepen our understanding of what each type of mini-public can contribute to a deliberative system. He outlines a comparative framework to facilitate this, which could also be applied to other types of institution. Considerations of deliberative democracy from a systemic angle certainly seem to be a principal part of the future of deliberative democracy, and this could even take it into a fourth generation of comparative, integrated and macro analysis that builds on the empirical evidence and specific institutional focus.

Psychological and intellectual obstacles to deliberation

One of the main criticisms made against deliberative democracy is that it is impractical and unworkable. Some argue that deliberative democracy demands a level of equality that can never be achieved. Such arguments are considered by Peter McLaverty in his chapter. Another criticism is that deliberative democracy is impossible because, psychologically, it is either impossible or very difficult for individuals to engage in deliberation or individuals lack the necessary intellectual capacity. Shawn Rosenberg, in Chapter 6, considers the relevant psychological literature and empirical studies, and concludes that deliberation between people is very unlikely to occur, even among those who have reached very advanced levels of education. His conclusion is that deliberation will not occur unless there are mechanisms in place to help overcome the psychological obstacles. He argues that deliberation needs to be created and that there is a crucial role for facilitators of deliberation. Rosenberg suggests that, if the developmental approach to individual psychological capacities is correct, it may be possible for individuals to learn and develop the skills associated with 'higher level' deliberation. Otherwise, unless facilitation can produce the necessary psychological states, deliberation is unlikely to happen. Several other authors argue that deliberation can produce 'other regarding' approaches to interaction and can help individuals to be more open-minded to issues, as they learn more about the issue under consideration. Rosenberg's work suggests that the development of deliberative democracy is likely, at best, to be slow. It is unlikely that people will gain deliberative capacities simply through their involvement in deliberative events unless there is systematic effort by facilitators to imbue participants with appropriate psychological facilities. Related to this, Bächtiger and Wegmann highlight Pincione and Tesón's (2006) theory of discourse failure as a societal phenomenon that occurs because of the rational ignorance of the citizens and their cognitive errors which, in particular, indicate the danger of partisan polarisation. Psychological investigations into deliberative democracy are increasing and more evidence here should be part of the future of deliberative democracy.

Political deliberation across divides

As well as the structural obstacles to the achievement of a deliberative system connected to capitalism and inequality, and the psychological problems, another area which is seen as making political deliberation difficult, relates to various types of divisions in societies. Divisions caused by ethnicity, different levels of expertise and political affiliations are considered by writers in the book. In Chapter 5, Manlio Cinalli and Ian O'Flynn take up the issue of cultural and ethnic differences and their impact on deliberation. Their research suggests that deliberation between individuals from different ethnic and cultural backgrounds is possible. Value pluralism is not necessarily exclusionary, and different values are combinable through deliberation. They give evidence of such deliberation happening, and provide a framework for understanding this. Similarly to Cinali and O'Flynn, Maia Setälä, in Chapter 9, focuses on mediated and dispersed deliberation across geographic divides. She warns of the potential dangers of 'enclave deliberation' and of groups of like-minded people talking 'past each other'. Her chapter suggests that determined efforts have to be made to incorporate what we might term 'enclave groups' into the policy process. Brown addresses the possibility of deliberation across epistemic divides. He argues that technical questions should be dealt with by experts but that political questions should be addressed by a combination of lay citizens and experts, ideally through hybrid bodies. Halpin and Cintula consider another potential divide that might undermine deliberative democracy, that between the representatives of 'civil society groups' involved in the public policy process and members of such groups. They suggest that there may be ways to reconcile potential differences in this area without the group representatives being prevented from deliberating among themselves or group members feeling left out of, and disconnected from, the policy process. More work on these problems is needed, however.

Over the last quarter of a century or more, there has been a growth in the importance of international governmental institutions, such as the European Union, the International Monetary Fund and the World Bank, and of international summits, meetings and conferences, such as the various events associated with climate change and the workings of the international finance system. There are debates about how far the various institutions of 'global governance' undermine the power of different nation states. Despite continued academic differences on that question, however, there seems little doubt that international bodies have more influence over states than was the case for much of the twentieth century. If important decisions are now being taken by international bodies of various kinds, rather than by nation states acting on their own, this has implications for democracy that generally has developed within nation states (Bohman, 2007; Smith and Brassett, 2008; Dryzek, 2010). Questions of deliberation in international bodies are taken up in the chapters by Bächtiger and Wegmann, Setälä, Steiner and Elstub. In considering deliberation at the level of the European Union, one of the obstacles addressed is the question of a sense of community across the twenty-seven member states, though it is stressed that deliberation is not completely lacking in the European Union. Deliberative opinion polling has been used across the whole European Union but the impact of the polls on EU decision-making and on popular feelings towards the European Union have been limited, if not negligible. If instituting citizen deliberation at the national level is difficult, the problems are magnified at the international level. The larger and more divided the system, the greater the challenges to ensure it is deliberative. At the same time, a systemic approach makes achieving a transnational or global deliberative system more attainable.

Ways forward

A number of authors, as well as outlining existing evidence on the state of deliberative democracy and the literature on specific issues, also suggest ways forward for deliberative democracy to address and overcome these issues.

Bächtiger and Wegmann argue that the way forward does not lie in denying the big differences which divide people politically or promoting a 'gentleman's club' type of politics where people from a restricted social background consider issues in a calm way and reach a consensus. Instead, they call for a 'noble politics' where those involved will come from diverse social backgrounds and will have passionate and conflicting views about political issues. This would help to take deliberative politics closer to existing politics in liberal democracies. It would also help to meet the demands of the mass media. They argue that such a politics could still demand of participants that they accept some classical deliberative virtues and would exclude the total closed-mindedness of the participants and a total unwillingness to be swayed by the better argument. It can, of course, be questioned whether such a proposal is not already included in ideas about how liberal democratic politics should work. Some might ask, if this is all deliberative democracy amounts to, is there such a thing as *deliberative democracy*?

While Bächtiger and Wegmann argue strongly that, in moving forward, deliberative democracy should forget ideas of reaching consensus between participants, Rosenberg argues exactly the opposite. For Rosenberg, the individual psychological dispositions that deliberative democracy demands will be furthered if participants know that they are expected to reach a consensus at the end of their deliberations. One of the key requirements, for Rosenberg, of deliberation is the willingness and the ability of individuals to see things from others' perspectives. That is why, as well as supporting consensus decision-making, Rosenberg calls for 'deliberative events' to include a role-playing exercise where each participant is asked to play a role with which he or she is not familiar. Cinali and O'Flynn's evidence indicates, however, that, although different values are compatible, they might remain incommensurable, making consensus unlikely.

While Blakeley argues that deliberation can and should play only a limited role in democracy, especially in capitalist societies, McLaverty argues that, for deliberative democracy to advance, moves towards greater equality will be needed. He is far from sanguine about the chances of this happening, however. Given the divisions between people that are found in societies, Setälä's argument, that it is important for 'enclave public spheres' to be connected to 'strong' decision-making public spheres, is of considerable significance. This may already happen in some nation states but, in those public policy decision-making arenas where it does not, there is a need for more theoretical and practical work to arrive at ways in which this can be achieved.

Steiner suggests ways in which the policy process might be opened up to the public. He supports the deliberation day idea of Ackerman and Fishkin (2004ab) where people will be able to deliberate about the policy proposals of different parties. He suggests randomly selected mini-publics comprising party members should attend meetings where parties determine their policy approaches.

Randomly selected mini-publics could also be involved, he suggests, at the draft legislation stage. These mini-publics could be consulted, along with experts, before legislation is prepared. For him, a series of randomly selected mini-publics, drawn form different geographical areas, could be consulted during the progression of policy. The suggestions would not replace representative democracy but would add public deliberative elements to it. The proposals would not build on existing public sphere and civil society activity but would rely heavily on state-promoted public deliberation initiatives. Elstub argues, however, that a greater comparative understanding of what can be expected of the different types of mini-public is required before such recommendations for sequencing them can be made. Furthermore, it might be asked, following Blakeley and McLaverty, why should any of Steiner's suggestions be implemented, given the structural obstacles standing in the way of such suggestions? Others might think that postponing the promotion of deliberative democratic institutions until after the elimination of capitalism and inequality would be putting it off to wait for a utopian future that will never arrive, and that deepening democracy within the structural constraints of liberal democracy is still a worthy enterprise, and can, indeed, contribute to overcoming these structural obstacles.

We do not claim that this book has resolved these ten key issues affecting deliberative democracy. We do claim to have advanced understanding in these important areas. Without doubt, if deliberative democracy is to progress further, become normal practice, and be approximated in a system, then further consideration of these ten issues must be part of the future of deliberative democracy. There is a need to build on the research and insights included in this book, as part of the ongoing effort to realise the full potential of democracy.

References

Abelson, R. P., E. Aronson, W. J. McGuire, T. M. Newcomb, M. J. Rosenberg, and P. H. Tannebaum (eds) (1968), *Theories of Cognitive Consistency: A Sourcebook*, Chicago: McNally.

Ackerman, B. and J. Fishkin (2004a), *Deliberation Day*, New Haven, CT: Yale University Press.

Ackerman, B. and J. Fishkin (2004b), 'For a smarter public. Deliberation day', *The American Prospect*, 1 January.

Alcaide, S. (2011), 'Movimiento 15-M: los ciudadanos exigen reconstruir la democracia', *El País*, 17 May, <http://politica.elpais.com/politica/2011/05/16/actualidad/1305578500_751064.html> (last accessed 6 June 2011).

Alvarez, P. (2012), 'Unión general de precarios', *El País*, 2 May, <http://ccaa.elpais.com/ccaa/2012/05/02/madrid/1335941551_220061.html> (last accessed 7 May 2012).

Anderson, E. (2011), 'Democracy, public policy, and lay assessments of scientific testimony', *Episteme*, 8: 2, 144–64.

Andersen, V. N. and K. M. Hansen (2007), 'How deliberation makes better citizens: The Danish deliberative poll on the euro', *European Journal of Political Research* 46: 4, 531–56.

Aristotle [350 BC] (1962), *The Politics*, London: Penguin.

Artal, R. M. (2011), 'El futuro siempre fue incierto', *El País*, 17 May, <http://politica.elpais.com/politica/2011/05/17/actualidad/1305614269_048313.html> (last accessed 8 June 2011).

Atkinson, M. M. and W. D. Coleman (1989), 'Strong states and weak states: Sectoral policy networks in advanced capitalist economies', *British Journal of Political Science*, 19: 1, 47–67.

Baber, W. and R. Bartlett (2005), *Deliberative Environmental Politics: Democracy and Ecological Rationality*, Cambridge, MA: MIT Press.

Bächtiger, A. (2011), 'Contestatory deliberation', paper presented at the 2010 Annual Meeting of the American Political Science Association, Washington DC, 2–5 September, and the Conference on Epistemic Democracy, Yale University, October 2011.

Bächtiger, A. and D. Hangartner (2007), 'Institutions, culture, and deliberative ideals: A theoretical and empirical inquiry', paper presented at the Annual Meeting of the American Political Science Association, Chicago, 30 August–2 September.

Bächtiger, A., and D. Hangartner (2010), 'When deliberative theory meets empirical political science: Theoretical and methodological challenges in political deliberation', *Political Studies*, 58: 4, 609–29.

Bächtiger, A., S., Niemeyer, M. Neblo, R. M. Steenbergen and J. Steiner (2010), 'Disentangling diversity in deliberative democracy: Competing theories, their blind spots and complementarities', *The Journal of Political Philosophy*, 18: 1, 32–63.

Bächtiger, A., M. Spörndli, M. R. Steenbergen, and J. Steiner (2005), 'The deliberative dimension of legislatures', *Acta Politica*, 40: 2, 225–38.

Bächtiger, A. and J. Steiner (2004), 'Switzerland: Territorial cleavage management as paragon and paradox', in A. Ugo and N. Bermeo (eds), *Federalism and Territorial Cleavages*, Baltimore, MD: Johns Hopkins University Press, pp. 27–54.

Bäckstrand, K., J. Khan, A. Kronsell, and E. Lövbrand (eds) (2010), *Environmental Politics and Deliberative Democracy: Examining the Promise of New Modes of Governance*, Cheltenham: Edward Elgar Publishing.

Barabas, J. (2004), 'How deliberation affects policy opinions', *American Political Science Review*, 98: 4, 687–701.

Barber, B. (1984), *Strong Democracy: Participatory Politics for a New Age*, Berkeley, CA: University of California Press.

Barker, E. (1951), *Principles of Social and Political Theory*, Oxford: Clarendon Press.

Barker, E. (ed.) (1978), *The Politics of Aristotle*, Oxford: Oxford University Press.

Barroso, F. J. (2011), 'La Junta Electoral de Madrid prohíbe la concentración en la Puerta del Sol', *El País*, 18 May, <http://politica.elpais.com/politica/2011/05/16/actualidad/1305579962_497160.html> (last accessed 6 June 2011).

Barry, B. (2006), 'Democracy needs dialogue and deliberation – not political blocs', in H. Afshar (ed.), *Democracy and Islam*, London: Hansard Society, pp. 22–4.

Bartlett, F. C. (1932), *Remembering: A Study in Experimental and Social Psychology*, Cambridge: Cambridge University Press.

Bättig, M., and T. Bernauer (2009), 'National institutions and global public goods: Are democracies more cooperative in climate change policy?', *International Organization*, 63: 2, 281–308.

Bau, A. (2012), 'Agenda setting and democratic innovation: The case of the Sustainable Communities Act (2007)', *Politics*, 32: 1, 10–20.

Bauer, M. (2008*)*, 'Survey research and the public understanding of science', in M. Bucchi and B. Trench (eds), *Handbook of Public Communication on Science and Technology*, London: Routledge, pp. 111–30.

Beatty, J. (2006), 'Masking disagreement among experts', *Episteme*, 3: 1–2, 52–67.

Bell, S. and A. Hindmoor (2009), *Rethinking Governance: Bringing the State Back In*, Cambridge: Cambridge University Press.

Benhabib, S. (1996), 'Toward a deliberative model of democratic legitimacy', in S. Benhabib (ed.), *Democracy and Difference: Contesting the Boundaries of the Political*, Princeton, NJ: Princeton University Press, pp. 67–94.

Benhabib, S. (2002), *The Claims of Culture: Equality and Diversity in the Global Era*, Princeton, NJ: Princeton University Press.

Berlin, I. (1969), *Four Essays on Liberty*, Oxford: Oxford University Press.

Berlin, I. (1991), *The Crooked Timber of Humanity*, London: Fontana.

Bessette, J. (1980), 'Deliberative democracy: The majoritarian principle in American government', in R. Goodwin and W. Shambra (eds), *How Democratic is the Constitution?*, Washington, DC: American Enterprise Institute, pp. 102–16.

Blakeley, G. (2005), 'Democracy', in G. Blakeley and V. Bryson (eds), *Marx and Other Four-Letter Words*, London: Pluto Press, pp. 192–208.

Blanchar, C. (2011), 'Aliviar las hipotecas ya es prioridad', *El País*, 15 November, <http://politica.elpais.com/politica/2011/11/15/actualidad/1321388219_720902.html> (last accessed 9 May 2012).

Blaug, R. (1997), 'Between fear and disappointment: Critical, empirical and political uses of Habermas', *Political Studies*, 45: 1, 100–17.

Bloor, D. (1976), *Knowledge and Social Imagery*, London and Boston, MA: Routledge and Kegan Paul.

Bogas, J. (2009), 'Captivated or complacent audiences assessing deliberative quality in competitive and consensus systems', seminar paper, University of Leiden.

Bohman, J. (1995), 'Public reason and cultural pluralism: Political liberalism and the problem of moral conflict', *Political Theory*, 23: 2, 253–79.

Bohman, J. (1996), *Public Deliberation: Pluralism, Complexity and Democracy*, Cambridge, MA: MIT Press.

Bohman, J. (1998), 'Survey article: The coming of age of deliberative democracy', *The Journal of Political Philosophy*, 6: 4, 400–25.

Bohman, J. (1999), 'Democracy as inquiry, inquiry as democratic: Pragmatism, social science, and the cognitive division of labor', *American Journal of Political Science*, 43: 2, 590–607.

Bohman, J. (2000), 'The division of labor in democratic discourse: Media, experts and deliberative democracy', in A. Costain and S. Chambers (eds), *Deliberation, Democracy and the Media*, Lanham, MD: Rowman and Littlefield, pp. 47–64.

Bohman, J. (2007), *Democracy Across Borders: From Demos to Demoi*, Cambridge, MA: MIT Press.

Boykoff, M. and J. Boykoff (2004), 'Balance as bias: Global warming and the US prestige press', *Global Environmental Change*, 14: 2, 125–36.

Brassett, J., and W. Smith (2010), 'Deliberation and global civil society: agency, arena, affect', *Review of International Studies*, 36: 2, 413–30.

Brewer, M. B. (2001), 'The many faces of social identity: Implications for political psychology', *Political Psychology*, 22: 1, 115–25.

Brown, G. (2007), 'Speech to the National Council of Voluntary Organisations on politics' <http://news.bbc.co.uk/1/hi/uk_politics/6976445.stm> (last accessed 14 January 2013).

Brown, M. B. (2006), 'Citizen panels and the concept of representation', *Journal of Political Philosophy*, 14: 2, 203–25.

Brown, M. B. (2008), 'Fairly balanced: The politics of representation on government advisory committees', *Political Research Quarterly*, 61:4, 547–60.

Brown, M. B. (2009), *Science in Democracy: Expertise, Institutions, and Representation*, Cambridge, MA: MIT Press.

Bucchi, M. (2008), 'Of deficits, deviations and dialogues: Theories of public communication of science', in M. Bucchi and B. Trench (eds), *Handbook of Public Communication of Science and Technology*, New York: Routledge, pp. 57–76.

Burke, E. (1854), 'Speech to the electors of Bristol', in *The Works of the Right Honourable Edmund Burke*, vol. 1, London: Henry J. Bohn, pp. 446–8.

Cabinet Office (2001), 'Government memorandum in response to the public administration select committee's sixth report on public participation: Issues and innovations', in House of Commons Select Committee on Public Administration, *Public Participation: Issues and Innovations: The Government's Response to the Public Administration Select Committee's Sixth Report of Session 2000–01*, London: HMSO.

Calhoun, C. (1996), 'Introduction', in C. Calhoun (ed.), *Habermas and the Public Sphere*, Cambridge, MA: MIT Press, pp. 1–48.

Callon, M., P. Lascoumes, Y. Barthe (2009), *Acting in an Uncertain World: An Essay on Technical Democracy*, Cambridge, MA: MIT Press.

Carson, L. and C. M. Hendriks, (2008), 'Can the market help the forum? Negotiating the commercialization of deliberative democracy', *Policy Science*, 41: 3, 293–313.

Chambers, S. (1996), *Reasonable Democracy*, Ithaca, NY: Cornell University Press.

Chambers, S. (2003), 'Deliberative democratic theory', *Annual Review of Political Science*, 6, 307–26.

Chambers, S. (2005), 'Measuring publicity's effect: Reconciling empirical research and normative theory', *Acta Politica*, 40: 2, 255–66.

Chambers, S. (2009), 'Rhetoric and the public sphere: has deliberative democracy abandoned mass democracy?', *Political Theory*, 37: 3, 323–50.

Chapman, L. J. and J. P. Chapman (1969), 'Illusory correlation as an obstacle to the use of valid psychodiagnostic signs', *Journal of Abnormal Psychology*, 74: 3, 271–80.

Chen, D. S., and C. Y. Deng (2007), 'Interaction between citizens and experts in public deliberation: A case study of consensus conferences in Taiwan', *East Asian Science, Technology and Society*, 1: 1, 77–97.

Cinalli, M. and I. O'Flynn (2013), 'Public deliberation, network analysis and the political integration of Muslims in Britain', *British Journal of Politics and International Relations*, forthcoming.

Cohen, J. (1996), 'Procedure and substance in deliberative democracy', in S. Benhabib (ed.), *Democracy and Difference: Contesting the Boundaries of the Political*, Princeton, NJ: Princeton University Press, pp. 95–119.

Cohen, J. and J. Rogers (2003), 'Power and reason', in A. Fung and E. O. Wright (eds), *Deepening Democracy*, London: Verso, pp. 237–55.

Cohen, J. and C. F. Sabel (2005), 'Global democracy', *NYU Journal of International Law and Politics*, 37: 4, 763–97.

Collins, H., and R. Evans (2007), *Rethinking Expertise*, Chicago: University of Chicago Press.

Congreso de los Diputados (2011), Diario de sesiones del Congreso de los Diputados. Pleno y Diputación Permanente, No. 256, 28 June. <http://www.congreso.es/public_oficiales/L9/CONG/DS/PL/PL_256.PDF#page=3> (last accessed 5 July 2011).

Connolly, W. (2005), *Pluralism*, Durham, NC: Duke University Press.

Coote, A. and J. Lenaghan, (1997), *Citizens' Juries: Theory into Practice*, London: Institute for Public Policy Research.

Crepaz, M. and J. Steiner (2012), *European Democracies*, 8th edn, New York: Pearson.

Crosby, N. and D. Nethercut (2005), 'Citizens juries: Creating a trustworthy voice of the people', in J. Gastil and P. Levine (eds), *The Deliberative Democracy Handbook: Strategies for Effective Civic Engagement in the 21st Century*, San Francisco: Jossey-Bass, pp. 111–19.

Crowder, G. (2002), *Liberalism and Value Pluralism*, London: Continuum.

Cué, C. E. (2011), 'Los indignados agitan la campaña y los partidos les piden el voto', *El País*, 19 May. <http://politica.elpais.com/politica/2011/05/19/actualidad/1305788356_860217.html> (last accessed 6 June 2011).

Culpepper, P. (2001), 'Employers' associations, public policy, and the politics of decentralized cooperation in Germany and France', in P. A. Hall and D. Soskice (eds), *Varieties of Capitalism: The Institutional Foundations of Comparative Advantage*, New York: Oxford University Press, pp. 275–306.

Culpepper, P. (2003), *Creating Cooperation: How States Develop Human Capital in Europe*, Ithaca, NY: Cornell University Press.

Dahl, R. A. (1989), *Democracy and its Critics*, New Haven, CT and London: Yale University Press.

Dahl, R. A. (1999), 'Can international organizations be democratic?', in I. Shapiro and C. Hacker-Cordón (eds), *Democracy's Edges*, Cambridge: Cambridge University Press, pp. 19–36.

Dalton, R. (2004), *Democratic Challenges, Democratic Choices: The Erosion of Political Support in Advanced Industrial Democracies*, Oxford: Oxford University Press.

Dalton, R. (2006), *Citizen Politics: Public Opinion and Political Parties in Advanced Industrial Democracies*, Washington, DC: CQ Press.

Davidson, S. and S. Elstub (2013), 'Deliberative and participatory democracy in the UK', *British Journal of Politics and International Relations*, forthcoming.

Davidson, S. and A. Stark, (2011), 'Institutionalising public deliberation: Insights from the Scottish Parliament', *British Politics*, 6: 2, 155–86.

Davidson, S., A. Stark, and G. Heggie (2011), 'Best laid plans … The institutionalisation of public deliberation in Scotland', *The Political Quarterly*, 82: 3, 379–88.

Davies, C., M. Wetherell, and E. Barnett (2006), *Citizens at the Centre: Deliberative Participation in Healthcare Decisions*, London: The King's Fund.

Deitelhoff, N. (2009), 'The discursive process of legalization: charting islands of persuasion in the ICC case', *International Organization*, 63: 1, 33–65.

Delannoi, G, O. Dowlen, and P. Stone (2012), 'The lottery as a democratic institution', paper presented at The Lottery as a Democratic Institution: A Workshop, Trinity College Dublin, 11–12 October.

Delli Carpini, M. X., F. L. Cook and L. R. Jacobs (2004), 'Public deliberation, discursive participation and citizen engagement: A review of the empirical literature', *Annual Review of Political Science*, 7: 3, 15–44.

Delli Carpini, M. X. and S. Keeter (1996), *What Americans Know about Politics and Why It Matters*, New Haven, CT: Yale University Press.

Democracia Real Ya (2011), 22 May,< http://www.democraciarealya.es/prensa/> (last accessed 15 September 2011).

Democracia Real Ya (2011), < http://www.democraciarealya.es/adhesiones/> (last accessed 20 September 2011).

Dewey, J. (1927), *The Public and Its Problems*, New York: Henry Holt.

Dolezal, M., M. Helbling and S. Hutter (2010), 'Debating Islam in Austria, Germany and Switzerland: Ethnic citizenship, church–state relations and right-wing populism', *West European Politics*, 33: 2, 171–90.

Dorling, D. (2010), *Injustice: Why Social Inequality Persists*, Bristol: Policy Press.

Druckman, J. N. and K. R. Nelson (2003), 'Framing and deliberation: How citizens' conversations limit elite influence', *American Journal of Political Science*, 47: 4, 729–45.

Dryzek, J. (1996), *Democracy in Capitalist Times: Ideals, Limits and Struggles*, New York: Oxford University Press.

Dryzek, J. (2000), *Deliberative Democracy and Beyond*, Oxford: Oxford University Press.

Dryzek, J. (2005), 'Deliberative democracy in divided societies. Alternatives to agonism and analgesia, *Political Theory*, 33: 2, 218–42.

Dryzek, J. (2006), *Deliberative Global Politics*, Cambridge: Polity.

Dryzek, J. (2007), 'Theory, evidence, and the tasks of deliberation', in S. W. Rosenberg (ed.), *Deliberation, Participation and Democracy: Can the People Govern?*, Basingstoke: Palgrave, pp. 237–50.

Dryzek, J. S. (2009), 'Democratization as deliberative capacity building', *Comparative Political Studies*, 42: 11, 1379–1402.

Dryzek, J. S. (2010), *Foundations and Frontiers of Deliberative Governance*, Oxford: Oxford University Press.

Dryzek, J., A. Bächtiger and K. Milewicz (2011), 'Toward a deliberative global citizens' assembly', *Global Policy* 2: 1, 33–42.

Dryzek, J. and R. Goodin (2006), 'Deliberative impacts: The macro-political uptake of mini-publics, *Politics and Society* 34: 2, 19–244.

Dryzek, J. and S. Niemeyer (2006), 'Reconciling pluralism and consensus as political ideals', *American Journal of Political Science*, 50: 3, 634–49.

Dryzek, J. and S. Niemeyer (2010), 'Representation', in J. Dryzek *Foundations and Frontiers of Deliberative Governance*, Oxford: Oxford University Press, pp. 42–65.

Dür, A. (2008), 'Measuring interest group influence in the EU: A note on methodology', *European Union Politics*, 9: 4, 559–76.

Dworkin, R. (2006a), 'Moral pluralism', in R. Dworkin, *Justice in Robes*, Cambridge, MA: Harvard University Press, pp. 105–16.

Dworkin, R. (2006b), *Is Democracy Possible Here?: Principles for a New Political Debate*, Princeton NJ: Princeton University Press.

EFE (2012), 'Democracia Real Ya se constituye como asociación', *El País*, 22 April, <http://politica.elpais.com/politica/2012/04/22/actualidad/335113954_5544 11.html (last accessed 9 May 2012).

Eilperin, J. (2006), *Fight Club Politics: How Partisanship is Poisoning the House of Representatives*, Lanham, MD: Rowman and Littlefield.

Ekeli, K. S. (2005), 'Giving a voice to posterity – Deliberative democracy and representation of future people', *Journal of Agricultural and Environmental Ethics*, 18: 5, 429–50.

Elola, J. (2012a), "Hackbogados' contra el euríbor', *El País*, 26 February, <http://economia.elpais.com/economia/2012/02/25/actualidad/1330161352_392075. html> (last accessed 3 May 2012).

Elola, J. (2012b), 'La silenciosa expansión del 15-M', *El País*, 5 May, <http://politica. elpais.com/politica/2012/05/05/actualidad/1336234920_810740.html> (last accessed 9 May 2012).

El País (2011a), 'El Parlamento andaluza tramite una iniciativa legislativa del 15-M', *El País*, 7 September, <http://politica.elpais.com/politica/2011/09/07/actualidad/ 1315414155_545769.html> (last accessed 20 September 2011).

El País (2011b), 'Hasta 8.5 millones de españoles apoyan el Movimiento 15-M', 3 August, <http://politica.elpais.com/politica/2011/08/03/actualidad/13123886 49_737959.html> (last accessed 26 September).

El País (2011c), 'El 73% cree que los indignados tienen razón', 23 October, <http:// politica.elpais.com/politica/2011/10/23/actualidad/1319392784_983542.html> (last accessed 3 May 2012).

El País (2011d), 'José Bono considera que la Ley Electoral es una norma "disparatada"', 2 December, <http://politica.elpais.com/politica/2011/12/02/actualidad/1322 815899_601661.html> (last accessed 3 May 2012).

Elster, J. (1998), 'Deliberation and constitution making', in J. Elster (ed.), *Deliberative Democracy*, Cambridge: Cambridge University Press, pp. 97–122.

Elstub, S. (2006), 'A double edged sword: The increasing diversity of deliberative democracy', *Contemporary Politics*, 12: 3–4, 301–20.

Elstub, S. (2008), *Towards a Deliberative and Associational Democracy*, Edinburgh: Edinburgh University Press.

Elstub, S. (2010a), 'The third generation of deliberative democracy', *Political Studies Review*, 8: 3, 291–307.

Elstub, S. (2010b), 'Linking micro deliberative democracy and decision-making: Trade-offs between theory and practice in a partisan citizen forum', *Representation*, 46: 3, 309–24.

Elstub, S. (2013), 'Deliberative pragmatic equilibrium review: A framework for comparing institutional devices and their enactment of deliberative democracy in the UK', *British Journal of Politics and International Relations*, forthcoming.

Esterling, K. M., A. Fung and T. Lee (2010), 'How much disagreement is good for democratic deliberation: The CaliforniaSpeaks health care reform experiment', available at <http://ssrn.com/abstract=1401151 or http://dx.doi.org/10.2139/ssrn.1401151> (last accessed 21 September 2012).

Ezrahi, Y. (1980), 'Utopian and pragmatic rationalism: The political context of scientific advice', *Minerva*, 18: 1, 11–31.

Falk, R. and A. Strauss (2001), 'Toward global parliament', *Foreign Affairs*, 80, 212–20.

Farrar, C., J. Fishkin, D. P. Green, C. List, R. Luskin and E. L. Paluck (2010), 'Disaggregating deliberation's effects: An experiment within a deliberative poll', *British Journal of Political Science*, 40: 2, 333–47.

Farrell, D., E. O'Malley, and J. Suiter (2012), 'Deliberative democracy in action Irish-style: The 2011 *We the Citizens* pilot citizens' assembly', *Irish Political Studies*, forthcoming.

Fenno, R. (1973), *Congressmen in Committees*, Boston, MA: Little, Brown.

Ferguson, N. (2011), 'The global temper tantrum', *Newsweek*, 158: 3, 18 July, 27.

Festenstein, M. (2002), 'Deliberation, citizenship and identity', in D'Entrèves (ed.), *Democracy as Public Deliberation: New Perspectives*, Manchester: Manchester University Press, pp. 88–111.

Festenstein, M. (2004), 'Deliberative democracy and two models of pragmatism', *European Journal of Social Theory*, 7: 3, 291–306.

Festinger, L. (1957), *A Theory of Cognitive Dissonance*, Stanford, CA: Stanford University Press.

15-M News (2011a), 'Decálogo de Acampada Valencia', Edition 1, 5 June, <http://madrid.tomalaplaza.net/periodico-15m-news/> (last accessed 10 September 2011).

15-M News (2011b), 'Encuentro estatal en Madrid #interacampadas', Edition 1, 5 June, <http://madrid.tomalaplaza.net/periodico-15m-news/> (last accessed 10 September 2011).

15-M News (2011), 'Peticiones de los indignados de Cáceres', Edition 2, 15 June, <http://madrid.tomalaplaza.net/files/2011/06/15-M-News-2.pdf> (last accessed 28 September 2011).

15-M News (2011), Especial Llegada de la Marcha Popular Indignada', 20 July, <http://madrid.tomalaplaza.net/files/2011/07/15M-ESPECIAL1.pdf> (last accessed 28th September 2011).

Finnis, J. (1997), 'Communsuration and public reason', in R. Chang (ed.), *Incommensurability, Incomparability and Practical Reason*, Cambridge, MA: Harvard University Press, pp. 215–33.

Fischer, F. (2000), *Citizens, Experts, and the Environment: The Politics of Local Knowledge*, Durham, NC: Duke University Press.

Fiske, S. and S. E. Taylor (1991), *Social Cognition*, New York: McGraw-Hill.

Fishkin, J. S. (1991), *Democracy and Deliberation: New Directions for Democratic Reform*, London: Yale University Press.

Fishkin, J. S. (1997), *The Voice of the People: Public Opinion and Democracy*, New Haven, CT: Yale University Press.

Fishkin, J. S. (2006), 'Realising deliberative democracy: Strategies for democratic consultation', in E. Lieb and B. He (eds), *The Search for Deliberative Democracy in China*, Basingstoke: Palgrave, pp. 37–52.

Fishkin, J. S. (2009), *When the People Speak: Deliberative Democracy and Public Consultation*, Oxford: Oxford University Press.

Fishkin, J. and C. Farrar, (2005), 'Deliberative polling: from experiment to community resource', in J. Gastill and P. Levine (eds), *The Deliberative Democracy Handbook*, San Francisco: Jossey-Bass, pp. 68–80.

Fishkin, J., B. He, and A. Siu (2006), 'Public consultation through deliberation in China: The first Chinese deliberative poll', in J. Gastill and P. Levine (eds), *The Deliberative Democracy Handbook*, San Francisco: Jossey-Bass, pp. 229–44.

Fishkin, J. and R. C. Luskin (2000), 'The Quest for Deliberative Democracy', in M. Saward (ed.), *Democratic Innovation: Deliberation, Representation and Association*, London: Routledge, pp. 17–27.

Fishkin, J. S. and R. C. Luskin (2005), 'Experimenting with a democratic ideal: deliberative polling and public opinion', *Acta Politica* 40: 3, 284–98

Foucault, M. (1990), *The History of Sexuality*, London: Penguin.

Fournier, P., H. van der Kolk, K. Carty, A. Blais, and J. Rose (2011), *When Citizens Decide: Lessons from Citizen Assemblies on Electoral Reform*, Oxford: Oxford University Press.

Fraser, N. (1992), 'Rethinking the public sphere: A contribution to the critique of actually existing democracy', in C. Calhoun (ed.), *Habermas and the Public Sphere*, Cambridge, MA: MIT Press, pp. 109–42.

Fraser, N. (2005), 'Reframing justice in a globalizing world', *New Left Review*, 36, 69–88.

French, D. and M. Laver (2009), 'Participation, bias, durable opinion shifts and sabotage through withdrawal in citizens' juries', *Political Studies*, 57: 422–50.

Frölich-Steffen, S. (2006), 'Rechtspopulistische herausforderer in konkordanzdemokratien. erfahrungen aus Österreich, der Schweiz und den Niederlanden', in F. Decker (ed.), *Populismus. Gefahr für die Demokratie oder nützliches Korrektiv?*, Wiesbaden: VS Verlag für Sozialwissenschaften: pp. 144–64.

Fung, A. (2003), 'Survey article: Recipes for public spheres: eight institutional design choices and their consequences', *Journal of Political Philosophy*, 11: 3, 388–67.

Fung, A. (2007), 'Democratic theory and political science: A pragmatic method of constructive engagement', *American Political Science Review*, 101: 3, 443–58.

Fung, A. and E. O. Wright (2003a), 'Countervailing power in empowered participatory governance', in A. Fung and E. O. Wright (eds), *Deepening Democracy: Institutional Innovation in Empowered Participatory Governance*, London: Verso, pp. 259–89.

Fung, A. and E. O. Wright (2003b), 'Thinking about empowered participatory governance', in A. Fung and E. O. Wright (eds), *Deepening Democracy: Institutional Innovation in Empowered Participatory Governance*, London: Verso, pp. 3–42.

Funtowicz, S. O. and J. R. Ravetz (1993), 'Science for the post-normal age', *Futures*, 25: 7, 739–55.

Furedi, F. (2005), *The Politics of Fear*, London: Continuum.

Galarraga, N. (2011), 'El 15-M pretende revitalizarse con protestas en más de 60 ciudades', *El País*, 14 October, <http://politica.elpais.com/politica/2011/10/14/actualidad/1318622901_205874.html> (last accessed 9 May 2012).

Galbraith, J. K. (1993), *The Culture of Contentment*, London: Penguin.

Garea, F. (2011a), 'El Escaño 351', *El País*, 14 August, <http://politica.elpais.com/politica/2011/08/14/actualidad/1313343760_653017.html> (last accessed 20 September 2011).

Garea, F. (2011b), 'Apoyo a la indignación del 15-M', *El País*, 5 June, <http://elpais.com/diario/2011/06/05/espania/130722481_850215.html> (last accessed 20 September 2011).

Gastil, J. and J. P. Dillard (1999), 'Increasing political sophistication through public deliberation', *Political Communication*, 16: 1, 3–23.

Gerber, M., A. Bächtiger and S. Shikano (2011), 'The European deliberative citizen in action? Evidence from a transnational deliberative poll (Europolis)', paper presented at the sixth European Consortium for Political Research General Conference, Reykjavik, 25–27 August.

Gerken, H. (2005), 'Second order diversity', *Harvard Law Review* 118: 4, *Harvard Public Law Working Paper No. 108*, <http://ssrn.com/abstract=600163> (last accessed 12 May 2012).

Gibson, R. K. and S. Miskin (2002) 'Australia Decides? The role of the media in deliberative polling', in J. Warhusrt and M. Mackerras (eds), *Constitutional Politics*, St Lucia, Brisbane: Queensland Press, 163–76.

Gilligan, C. (1982), *In a Different Voice*, Cambridge, MA: Harvard University Press.

Gladwell, M. (2010), 'Small Change', *New Yorker*, 86: 30, 42–9.

Globescan (2012), 'Economic system seen as unfair: Global poll', BBC World Service Poll, <http://www.globescan.com/images/images/pressreleases/bbc2012_economics/BBC12_Economics.pdf> (last accessed 9 May 2012).

Goodin, H. J. and D. Stein (2009), 'The use of deliberative discussion to enhance the critical thinking abilities of nursing students', *Journal of Public Deliberation*, 5: 1, 1–18.

Goodin, R. E. (2005), 'Sequencing deliberative moments', *Acta Politica*, 40: 2, 182–96.

Goodin, R. E. (2008), *Innovating Democracy: Democratic Theory and Practice after the Deliberative Turn*, Oxford: Oxford University Press.

Goodin, R. E. and S. R. Ratner (2011), 'Democratizing international law', *Global Policy* 2: 3, 241–7.

Grant, W. (2001), 'Pressure politics: From "insider" politics to direct action?', *Parliamentary Affairs*, 54: 2, 337–48.

Gray, J. (1995a), *Enlightenment's Wake: Politics and Culture at the Close of the Modern Age*, London: Routledge.

Gray, J. (1995b), *Isaiah Berlin*, London: Fontana.

Gray, J. (2000), *Two Faces of Liberalism*, Cambridge: Polity.

Griffin, M. (2011), 'Developing deliberative minds – Piaget, Vygotsky and the deliberative democratic citizen', *Journal of Public Deliberation*, 7: 1, 1–27.

Grönlund, K. and M. Setälä (2007), 'Political trust, satisfaction and voter turnout', *Comparative European Politics*, 5, 400–22.

Gutmann, A. and D. Thompson (1996), *Democracy and Disagreement*, London: Harvard University Press.

Gutmann, A. and D. Thompson (2004), *Why Deliberative Democracy?*, Princeton, NJ: Princeton University Press.

Habermas, J. (1970), *Toward a Rational Society: Student Protest, Science, and Politics*, Boston, MA: Beacon Press.

Habermas, J. (1984), *The Theory of Communicative Action*, Vol. 1, *Reason and the Rationalization of Society*, Boston, MA: Beacon Press.

Habermas, J. (1986), *The Theory of Communicative Action*, Vol. 1, Cambridge: Polity Press.

Habermas, J. (1989), *The Theory of Communicative Action*, Vol. 2, Cambridge: Polity Press.

Habermas, J. (1990), *Moral Consciousness and Communicative Action*, Cambridge: Polity Press.

Habermas, J. (1992), *The Structural Transformation of the Public Sphere: An Inquiry Into a Category of Bourgeois Society*, Cambridge: Polity Press.

Habermas, J. (1996), *Between Facts and Norms*, Cambridge: Polity Press.

Habermas, J. (1998), 'Reconciliation through the public use of reason', in C. Cronin and P. De Greiff (eds), *The Inclusion of the Other*, Cambridge: Polity, pp. 49–73.

Habermas, J. (2005), *The Postnational Constellation*, Cambridge: Polity.

Habermas, J. (2006), 'Political communication in media society: Does democracy still enjoy an epistemic dimension? The impact of normative theory on empirical research', *Communication Theory*, 16: 4, 11–426.

Hackett, P. and P. Hunter (2011), *Who Governs Britain? A Profile of MPs in the New Parliament*, London: The Smith Institute, <http://www.smith-institute.org.uk/publications.html?page=2> (last accessed 2 August 2011).

Haidt, J. (2001), 'The emotional dog and its rational tail: A social intuitionist approach to moral reasoning', *Psychological Review*, 108: 4, 814–34.

Haidt, J. (2007), 'The new synthesis in moral psychology', *Science*, 316: 5827, 998–1002.

Halpin, D. (2010), *Groups, Democracy and Representation*, Manchester: Manchester University Press.

Hamil, R., T. D. Wilson and R. E. Nisbett (1980), 'Insensitivity to sample bias: Generalizing from atypical cases', *Journal of Personality and Social Psychology*, 39: 4, 578–89.

Hammack, P. L. (2008), 'Narrative and the cultural psychology of identity', *Personality and Social Psychology Review*, 12: 3, 222–47.

Hardwig, J. (1985), 'Epistemic dependence', *The Journal of Philosophy*, 82: 7, 335–49.

Hastie, R, S. D. Penrod and Pennington, N. (1983), *Inside the Jury*, Cambridge, MA: Harvard University Press.

Hay, C. (2007), *Why We Hate Politics*, Cambridge: Polity.

He, B. and M. E. Warren (2011), 'Authoritarian deliberation: The deliberative turn in Chinese Political Development', *Perspectives on Politics*, 9: 2, 269–89.

Heider, F. (1958), *The Psychology of Interpersonal Relations*, Hillsdale, NJ: Lawrence Erlbaum Associates.

Held, D. (1995), *Democracy and the Global Order: From the Modern State to Cosmopolitan Governance*, Cambridge: Polity.

Held, D., and A. Fane Hervey (2009), 'Democracy, climate change and global govern-ance', Policy Network Paper, <http://www.policy-network.net/publications_detail.aspx?ID=3406> (last accessed 19 July 2012).

Hendriks, C. (2002), 'Institutions of deliberative democratic processes and interest groups: Roles, tensions and incentives', *Australian Journal of Public Administration*, 61: 1, 64–75.

Hendriks, C. (2005), 'Consensus conferences and planning cells: Lay citizen delibera-tions', in J. Gastil and P. Levine (eds), *The Deliberative Democracy Handbook: Strategies for Effective Civic Engagement in the 21st Century*, San Francisco: Jossey-Bass, pp. 80–110.

Hendriks, C. (2006), 'Integrated deliberation: Reconciling civil society's dual role in deliberative democracy', *Political Studies*, 54: 3, 486–508.

Hendriks, C., J. Dryzek and C. Hunold (2007), 'Turning up the heat: Partisanship in deliberative innovation', *Political Studies*, 55: 2, 362–83.

Heradsveit, D. and G. M. Bonham (1996), 'Attribution theory and Arab images of the gulf war', *Political Psychology*, 17: 2, 271–92.

Hibbing, J. R. and E. Theiss-Morse (2002), *Stealth Democracy: Americans' Beliefs About How Government Should Work*, Cambridge: Cambridge University Press.

Hickerson, A. and J. Gastil (2008), 'Assessing the difference critique of deliberation: Gender, emotion and the jury experience', *Communication Theory*, 18: 2, 281–303.

Hjarvard, S. (2008), 'The mediatization of society. A theory of the media as agents of social and cultural change', *Nordicom Review*, 29: 2, 105–34.

Holzinger, K. (2004), 'Bargaining through arguing. An empirical analysis based on speech act theory, *Political Communication*, 21: 2, 195–222.

Hooghe, M. (1999), 'The rebuke of Thersites. Deliberative democracy under conditions of inequality', *Acta Politica*, 34: 4, 287–301.

Huitema, D., M. Kerkhof, and U. Pesch (2007), 'The nature of the beast: are citizens´ juries deliberative or pluralist?', *Policy Science*, 40: 4, 287–311.

Hüller, T. (2010), 'Playground or democratisation? New participatory procedures at the European Commission', *Swiss Political Science Review*, 16: 1, 77–107.

Hunold, C. (2006), 'Corporatism, pluralism and democracy: toward a deliberative theory of bureaucratic accountability', *Governance*, 14: 3, 151–67.

IDEA International (2009), 'Voter turnout', Stockholm: IDEA International, <www. idea.int/vt/> (last accessed 8 August 2011).

Irwin, A., and B. Wynne (1996), *Misunderstanding Science? The Public Reconstruction of Science and Technology*, Cambridge: Cambridge University Press.

Jacobs, L., F. L. Cook, and M. X Delli Carpini (2009), *Talking Together: Public Deliberation and Political Participation in America*, Chicago: University of Chicago Press.

James, M. R. (2008), 'Descriptive representation in the British Coumbia Citizens' Assembly', in M. E. Warren and H. Pearse (eds), *Designing Deliberative Democracy. The British Columbia Citizens' Assembly*, Cambridge: Cambridge University Press, pp. 106–26.

Jasanoff, S. (1990), *The Fifth Branch: Science Advisors as Policy Makers*, Cambridge, MA: Harvard University Press.

Jasanoff, S., G. E. Markle, J. C. Petersen, and T. Pinch (eds) (1995), *Handbook of Science and Technology Studies*, Thousand Oaks CA: Sage Publications.

John, P., S. Cotterill, A. Moseley, L. Richardson, G. Smith, G. Stoker, and C. Wales, (2011), *Nudge, Nudge, Think, Think: Experimenting with Ways to Change Civic Behaviour*, London: Bloomsbury Academic.

Jones, P. (2003), 'Toleration and neutrality: Compatible ideals?', in D. Castiglione and C. McKinnon (eds), *Toleration, Neutrality and Democracy*, Dordrecht: Kluwer, pp. 97–110.

Jones, P. (2006), 'Toleration, value-pluralism and the fact of pluralism', *Critical Review of International Social and Political Philosophy*, 9: 2, 189–210.

Jordan, G. (2007), 'Policy without learning: Double devolution and abuse of the deliberative idea', *Public Policy and Administration*, 22: 1, 48–73.

Jordan, G. and D. Halpin, (2004), 'Olson triumphant? Explaining the growth of a small business organisation', *Political Studies*, 52: 3, 431–49.

Junn, J., T. Mendelberg and E. Czaja (2011), 'Race and the group bases of public opinion', in A. J. Berinsky (ed.), *New Directions in Public Opinion*, London: Routledge, pp. 119–28.

Junquera, N. (2011), 'Jóvenes ... y no tan jóvenes indignados', *El País*, 19 May, <http://politica.elpais.com/politica/2011/05/19/actualidad/1305817490_432066.html> (last accessed 5 June 2011).

Kahan, D. M. (2010), 'Fixing the communications failure', *Nature*, 463 (21 January): 296–97.

Kahneman, D. (2010), *Thinking, Fast and Slow*, New York: Farrar, Straus and Giroux.

Karpowitz, C. F., C. Raphael and A. S. Hammond (2009), 'Deliberative democracy and inequality: Two cheers for enclave deliberation among the disempowered', *Politics & Society*, 37: 4, 576–615.

Keeley, G. (2011), 'MPs put their bank cards on the table to restore faith in politics', *The Times*, 9 September.

Kegan, R. (1982), *The Evolving Self: Problem and Process in Human Development*, Cambridge, MA: Harvard University Press.

Kegan, R. (1994), *In Over Our Heads: The Mental Demands of Modern Life*, Cambridge, MA: Harvard University Press.

Kelley, H. H. (1973), 'The Processes of Causal Attribution', *American Psychologist*, 28: 2, 107–28.

Kerr, N. L., R. J. MacCoun and G. P. Kramer (1996), 'Bias in judgment: Comparing individuals and groups', *Psychological Review*, 103: 4, 687–719.

Kleinman, D. L., J. A. Delborne and A. A. Anderson (2011), 'Engaging citizens: The high cost of citizen participation in high technology', *Public Understanding of Science*, 20: 2, 221–40.

Knoke, D. and J. Kuklinsky (1982), *Network Analysis*, London: Sage.

Kohlberg, L. (1981/4), *Essays on Moral Development*: Vols 1 and 2, New York: Harper & Row.

Kohn, M. (2000), 'Language, power, and persuasion: Toward a critique of deliberative democracy', *Constellations*, 7: 3, 408–29.

'Konsensusdemokratie im Wandel: Eine Re-Analyse von Lijpharts Studie für die Schweiz von 1997 bis 2007', *Schweizerische Zeitschrift für Politikwissenschaft*, 14: 1, 1–47.

Koopmans, R. and P. Statham (1999), 'Political claims analysis: Integrating protest event and political discourse approaches', *Mobilization*, 4: 2, 203–22.

Kriesi, H. (2005), 'Argument-based strategies in direct-democratic votes: The Swiss experience', *Acta Politica*, 40: 2, 299–316.

Kusch, M. (2007), 'Towards a political philosophy of risk: Experts and publics in deliberative democracy', in T. Lewens (ed.), *Risk: Philosophical Perspectives*, London: Routledge, 131–55.

Landwehr, C. (2010), 'Discourse and coordination: Modes of interaction and their roles in political decision-making', *The Journal of Political Philosophy*, 18: 1, 101–22.

Lane, M. (2011), 'When the experts are uncertain: Scientific knowledge and the ethics of democratic judgment', paper presented at the Edmond J. Safra Center for Ethics, Harvard University, December.

Lassman, P. (2011), *Pluralism*, Cambridge: Polity.

Latour, B. (1987), *Science in Action: How to Follow Scientists and Engineers through Society*, Cambridge, MA: Harvard University Press.

Leet, M. (1998), 'Jurgen Habermas and deliberative democracy', in A. Carter and G. Stokes (eds), *Liberal Democracy and its Critics*, Cambridge: Polity, pp. 77–97.

Leib, E. J. (2004), *Deliberative Democracy in America: A Proposal for a Popular Branch of Government*, University Park, PA: Pennsylvania State University Press.

Lightbody, R. (2012), 'Towards a DePER Understanding of Public Hearings: Sequencing Public Hearings in a Deliberative Policy Process', paper presented at the Deepening Democracy: Participation, Deliberation or Both? Conference, University of Bradford, 12–14 September.

Limón, R. (2011), 'Pero qué quieren?', *El País*, 19 May. <http://politica.elpais.com/politica/2011/05/19/22m/1305801136_256482.html> (last accessed 5 June 2011).

Lindell, M (2011), 'Same but different: Similarities and differences in the implementation of deliberative mini-publics', paper presented at the 2011 European Consortium for Political Research General Conference, University of Reykjavik, Iceland, 24–27 August.

Lindsay, A. D. (1929), *The Essentials of Democracy*, Oxford: Oxford University Press.

Loftus, E. F. (1996), *Eyewitness Testimony*, Cambridge, MA: Harvard University Press.

Loftus, E. F. (1997), 'Creating false memories', *Scientific American*, 277: 3, 70–5.

Lowndes, V., L. Pratchett and G. Stoker (2006), 'Diagnosing and remedying the failings of official participation schemes: the CLEAR framework', *Social Policy and Society*, 5: 2, 281–91.

Luria, A. R. (1978), *Cognitive Development: Its Cultural and Social Foundations*, Cambridge, MA: Harvard University Press.

Luskin, R. C., J. S. Fishkin and R. Jowell (2002), 'Considered opinions: Deliberative polling in Britain', *British Journal of Political Science*, 32: 3, 455–87.

McAffee, N. (2000), *Habermas, Kristeva and Citizenship*, Ithaca, NY: Cornell University Press.

McArthur, L. A. (1972), 'The how and what of why: Some determinants and consequences of causal attribution', *Journal of Personality and Social Psychology*, 22: 2, 171–93.

McArthur, L. Z. (1981), 'What grabs you? The role of attention in impression formation and causal attribution', in E. T. Higgins, C. P. Herman and I. P. Zanna (eds), *Social Cognition: The Ontario Symposium*, Vol. 1, Hillsdale, NJ: Erlbaum, pp. 201–41.

MacCoun, R. J. (2006), 'Psychological constraints on transparency in legal and government decision making', *Swiss Political Science Review*, 12: 3, 112–23.

McFarland, A. S. (1993), *Cooperative Pluralism: The National Coal Policy Experiment*, Lawrence, KS: University of Kansas Press.

McIver, S. (1997), *An Evaluation of the King's Fund Citizens' Juries Programme*, Birmingham: Health Services Management Centre.

MacKenzie, M. K. and M. E. Warren (2012), 'Two trust-based uses of minipublics in democratic systems', in J. Parkinson and J. Mansbridge (eds), *Deliberative Systems: Deliberative Democracy at the Large Scale*, Cambridge: Cambridge University Press, pp. 95–124.

Mackie, G. (2003), *Democracy Defended*, Cambridge: Cambridge University Press.

McLaverty, P. (2009), 'Is deliberative democracy the answer to representative democracy's problems? A consideration of the UK Labour government's programme of citizens' juries', *Representation*, 45: 4, 379–89.

McLaverty, P. and D. Halpin (2008), 'Deliberative drift: The emergence of deliberation in the policy process', *International Political Science Review*, 29: 2, 197–214.

McLaverty, P. and I. MacLeod (2012), 'Combining participatory and deliberative Democracy', paper presented at the Deepening Democracy: Participation, Deliberation or Both? Conference, University of Bradford, 12–14 September.

MacLean, S., and M. M. Burgess (2010), 'In the public interest: Assessing expert and stakeholder influence in public deliberation about biobanks', *Public Understanding of Science*, 19: 4, 486–96.

Macpherson, C. B. (1977), *The Life and Times of Liberal Democracy*, Oxford: Oxford University Press.

McQuail, D. (1992), *Media Performance: Mass Communication and the Public Interest*, London: Sage.

Maginn, P. (2007), 'Deliberative democracy or discursively biased? Perth's dialogue with the city initiative', *Space and Polity*, 11: 3, 331–52

Mann, T. E. and N. J. Ornstein (2006), *The Broken Branch: How Congress Is Failing America And How to Get It Back on Track*, Oxford: Oxford University Press.

Manin, B. (1987), 'On legitimacy and political deliberation', *Political Theory*, 15: 3, 338–68.

Manin, B. and J. L. Martí (2010), 'The place of self-interest and the role of power in deliberative democracy', *The Journal of Political Philosophy*, 18: 1, 64–100.

Mansbridge, J. (1980), *Beyond Adversary Democracy*, Chicago: University of Chicago Press.

Mansbridge, J. (1992), 'A deliberative theory of interest representation', in M. Petracca (ed.), *The Politics of Interests: Interest Groups Transformed*, Oxford: Westview Press, pp. 32–57.

Mansbridge, J. (2007) '"Deliberative democracy" or "democratic deliberation"?', in S. W. Rosenberg (ed.), *Deliberation, Participation and Democracy: Can the People Govern?*, Basingstoke: Palgrave, pp. 251–71.

Mansbridge, J. (2010a), 'Everyday talk goes viral', paper presented at the Annual Meeting of the American Political Science Association, Washington, DC, 2–5 September.

Mansbridge, J. (2010b), 'Deliberative polling as the gold standard', *The Good Society*, 19: 1, 55–62.

Mansbridge, J., J. Bohman, C. Chambers, D. Estlund, A. Føllesdal, A. Fung, C. Lafont, B. Manin, and J. L. Marti (2010), 'The place of self-interest and the role of power in deliberative democracy', *Journal of Political Philosophy*, 18: 1, 64–100.

Mansbridge, J., J. Bohman, S. Chambers, T. Christiano, A. Fung, J. Parkinson, D. Thompson and M. E. Warren (2011), 'A systemic approach to deliberative democracy', paper presented at the Workshop on the Frontiers of Deliberation, European Consortium for Political Research Joint Sessions, St Gallen, Switzerland, 12–17 April.

Martin, L. and G. Vanberg (2005), 'Coalition policymaking and legislative review', *American Political Science Review*, 99: 1, 93–106.

Matheson, D. (2005), 'Conflicting experts and dialectical performance: Adjudication heuristics for the layperson', *Argumentation*, 19: 2, 145–58.

Marx, K. (1973), *Surveys from Exile*, Harmondsworth: Penguin.

Maxwell, R. (2006), 'Muslims, South Asians and the British mainstream: A national identity crisis?', *West European Politics*, 29: 4, 736–56.

Mead, E. and D. Stasavage (2006), 'Two effects of transparency on the quality of deliberation', *Swiss Political Science Review*, 12: 3, 123–33.

Meer, N. (2006), '"Get off your knees": Print media public intellectuals and Muslims in Britain', *Journalism Studies*, 7: 1, 35–59.

Mendelberg, T. (2001), *The Race Card*, Princeton, NJ: Princeton University Press.

Mendelberg, T. (2002), 'The deliberative citizen: Theory and evidence', in M. X. Delli Carpini, L. Huddy and R. Y. Shapiro (eds), *Political Decision-Making, Deliberation and Participation*, San Diego: Elsevier Science, pp. 201–41.

Mendelberg, T. and C. Karpowitz (2007), 'How people deliberate about justice: Groups, gender, and decision rules', in S. Rosenberg (ed.), *Deliberation, Participation and Democracy*, Basingstoke: Palgrave, pp. 101–29.

Mendelberg, T. and J. Oleske (2000), 'Race and public deliberation', *Political Communication*, 17: 2, 169–91.

Mercier, H. and H. Landemore (2012), 'Reasoning is for arguing: Understanding the successes and failures of deliberation', *Political Psychology*, 33: 2, 243–58.

Miliband, R. (1973), *The State in Capitalist Society*, London: Quartet Books.

Mill, J. S. (1951), *Considerations on Representative Government*, in H. B. Acton (ed.), *Utilitarianism, Liberty and Representative Government*, London: Dent, pp. 187–482.

Mill, J. S. (2009), *On the Subjugation of Women*, London: Hesperus.

Miller, D. (1992), 'Deliberative democracy and social choice', *Political Studies*, 40 (issue supplement), 54–76.

Miller, D. (2000), 'Is deliberative democracy unfair to disadvantaged groups?', in D. Miller, *Citizenship and National Identity*, Cambridge: Polity, pp. 142–60.

Miller, D. and M. Walzer (eds) (1995), *Pluralism, Justice and Equality*, Oxford: Oxford University Press.

Mooney, C. and S. Kirshenbaum (2009), *Unscientific America: How Scientific Illiteracy Threatens our Future*, New York: Basic Books.

Moore, A. (2012), 'Following from the front: Theorizing deliberative facilitation', *Critical Policy Studies*, 6: 2, 146–62.

Morrell, M. E. (2005), 'Deliberation, democratic decision-making and internal political efficacy', *Political Behavior*, 27: 1, 49–69

Mouffe, C. (1999), 'Deliberative democracy of agonistic pluralism?', *Social Research*, 66: 3, 745–58.

Mouffe, C. (2000), *The Democratic Paradox*, London: Verso.

Mouffe, C. (2005), *On the Political*, London: Routledge.

Muhlberger, P. (2005), 'The virtual agora project: A research design for studying democratic deliberation', *Journal of Public Deliberation*, 1: 1, 1–13.

Muñoz, L. A. (2011), 'La acampada quiere convertirse en un Parlamento digital', *El País*, 1 June, <http://politica.elpais.com/politica/2011/06/01/actualidad/1306937364_783254.html> (last accessed 5 June 2011).

Mutz, D. (2006), *Hearing the Other Side*, Cambridge: Cambridge University Press.

National Science Board (2012), 'Science and technology: Public attitudes and understanding', *Science and Engineering Indicators 2012*, Arlington VA: National Science Foundation (National Science Board, 12 January), <http://www.nsf.gov/statistics/seind12/c7/c7h.htm> (last accessed 19 July 2012).

Naurin, D. (2007), 'Backstage behavior? Lobbyists in public and private settings in Sweden and the European Union', *Comparative Politics*, 39: 2, 209–28.

Neblo, M. A., K. M. Esterling, R. P. Kennedy, D. M. J. Lazer, and A. E. Sokhey (2010), 'Who wants to deliberate – and why?', *American Political Science Review*, 104: 3, 566–83.

Newey, G. (2001), *After Politics: the Rejection of Politics in Contemporary Liberal Philosophy*, Basingstoke: Palgrave Macmillan.

Niemeyer, S. (2011), 'The emancipatory effect of deliberation: empirical lessons from mini-publics, *Politics & Society*, 39: 1, 103–40.

Niemeyer, S. (2012), 'From the minipublic to a deliberative system: is scaling up deliberation possible?', forthcoming in A. Bächtiger, K. Grönlund, and M. Setälä (eds), *Deliberative Mini-Publics: Promises, Practices and Pitfalls*, Colchester: ECPR Press.

Niemeyer, S. and J. Dryzek (2007), 'The ends of deliberation: Meta-consensus and inter-subjective rationality as ideal outcomes', *Swiss Political Science Review*, 13: 4, 497–526.

Nisbet, M. C. (2009), 'Communicating climate change: Why frames matter to public engagement', *Environment*, 51: 2, 12–23.

Noelle-Neumann, E. (1984), *The Spiral of Silence: Public Opinion – Our Social Skin*, Chicago: University of Chicago Press.

Öberg, P., T. Svensson,, P. Christiansen,, A. Nørgaard,, H. Rommetvedt, and G. Thesen (2011), 'Disrupted exchange and declining corporatism: Government authority and interest group capability in Scandinavia', *Government and Opposition*, 46: 3, 365–91.

O'Flynn, I. and G. Sood (2012), 'Deliberative polls and other mini-publics: A constructive critique', forthcoming in A. Bächtiger, K. Grönlund, and M. Setälä (eds), *Deliberative Mini-Publics. Promises, Practices and Pitfalls*, Colchester: ECPR Press.

Painter, M. and J. Pierre (2005), 'Unpacking policy capacity: Issues and themes, in M. Painter and J. Pierre (eds), *Challenges to State Policy Capacity: Global Trends and Comparative Perspectives*, Basingstoke: Palgrave, pp. 1–18.

Papadopoulos, Y. (2003), 'Cooperative forms of governance: problems of democratic accountability in complex environments', *European Journal of Political Research*, 42: 4, 473–501.

Parkinson, J. (2003), 'Legitimacy problems in deliberative democracy', *Political Studies* 51: 1, 180–96.

Parkinson, J. (2004), 'Hearing voices: negotiating representation claims in public deliberation', *British Journal of Politics and International Relations*, 6: 3, 370–88.

Parkinson, J. (2006a), 'Rickety bridges: using the media in deliberative democracy', *British Journal of Political Science*, 36: 175–83.

Parkinson, J. (2006b), *Deliberating in the Real World: Problems of Legitimacy in Deliberative Democracy*, Oxford: Oxford University Press.

Parkinson, J. (2012), 'Democratizing deliberative systems', in J. Parkinson and J. Mansbridge (eds), *Deliberative Systems: Deliberative Democracy at the Large Scale*, Cambridge: Cambridge University Press.

Parkinson, J. and J. Mansbridge (eds) (2012), *Deliberative Systems*, Cambridge: Cambridge University Press, pp. 1–26.

Pateman, C. (2012), 'Participatory democracy revisited', *Perspectives on Politics*, 10: 1, 7–19.

Pattie, C., P. Seyd and P. Whiteley (2003), 'Civic attitudes and engagement in modern Britain', *Parliamentary Affairs*, 56: 4, 616–33.

Pattie, C., P. Seyd and P. Whiteley (2004), *Citizenship in Britain: Values, Participation and Democracy*, Cambridge: Cambridge University Press.

Pelletier, D., V. Kraak, C. McCullum, U. Uusitalo and R. Rich (1999), 'The shaping of collective values through deliberative democracy: An empirical study from New York's North Country', *Policy Sciences*, 32: 2, 103–31.

Peters, B. G. (2005), 'Policy instruments and policy capacity', in M. Painter and J. Pierre (eds), *Challenges to State Policy Capacity: Global Trends and Comparative Perspectives*, Basingstoke: Palgrave, pp. 73–91.

Peters, B., T. Schultz and A. Wimmel (2008), 'Contemporary journalism and its contribution to a discursive public sphere', in H. Wessler (ed.), *Public Deliberation and Public Culture: The Writings of Bernhard Peters, 1993–2005*, Basingstoke: Palgrave Macmillan, pp. 134–59.

Pettigrew, T. F. (1998), 'Intergroup contact theory', *Annual Review of Psychology*, 49, 65–85.

Pérez-Lanzac, C. (2011) 'Indignados y acampados', *El País*, 17 May, <http://politica.elpais.com/politica/2011/05/17/actualidad/1305623988_837783.html> (last accessed 5 June 2011).

Phillips, A. (1995), *The Politics of Presence*, Oxford: Clarendon Press.

Phillips, A. (1999), *Which Equalities Matter?*, Cambridge: Polity.

Pielke, R. A., Jr (2007), *The Honest Broker: Making Sense of Science in Policy and Politics*, Cambridge: Cambridge University Press.

Pimbert, M. P. and T. Wakeford (2002), 'Prajateerpu: A citizens jury / scenario workshop on food and farming futures for Andhra Pradesh, India', London: IIED <http://www.diversefoodsystems.org/lfs_docs/Prajateerpu.pdf> (last accessed 24 June 2010).

Pincione, G. and F. R. Tesón (2006), *Rational Choice and Democratic Deliberation: A Theory of Discourse Failure*, Cambridge: Cambridge University Press.

Powell, M. and M. Colin (2008), 'Meaningful citizen engagement in science and technology: What would it really take?', *Science Communication*, 30: 1, 126–36.

Price, D. (2000), 'Choices without reasons: citizens' juries and policy evaluation', *Journal of Medical Ethics*, 26: 4, 272–6.

Price, V. and J. N. Cappella (2002), 'Online deliberation and its influence: The electronic dialogue project in Campaign 2000', *IT and Society*, 1: 1, 303–20.

Przeworski, A. (1998), 'Deliberation and ideological domination', in J. Elster (ed.), *Deliberative Democracy*, Cambridge: Cambridge University Press, pp. 140–60.

Quattrone, G. A. and A. Tvesky (1984), 'Causal versus diagnostic contingencies: On self-deception and the voter's illusion', *Journal of Personality and Social Psychology*, 46: 2, 237–48.

Rawls, J. (1993), *Political Liberalism*, New York: Columbia University Press.

Rawls, J. (1995), 'Reply to Habermas', *Journal of Philosophy*, 92: 3, 132–80.

Rawls, J. (1996), *Political Liberalism*, 2nd ed., New York: Columbia University Press.

Rawls, J. (1997), 'The idea of public reason revisited', *The University of Chicago Law Review*, 64: 3, 765–806.

Reinisch, C. and J. Parkinson (2007), 'Swiss *landsgemeinden*: A deliberative democratic evaluation of two outdoor parliaments', paper presented at the European Consortium for Political Research Joint Sessions, Helsinki, Finland, May 2007.

Renn, O., T. Webler, and P. M. Wiedeman (1995), *Fairness and Competence in Citizen Participation: Evaluating Models for Environmental Discourse*, Dordrecht, Netherlands: Kluwer Academic.

Richardson, H. S. (2002), *Democratic Autonomy. Public Reasoning about the Ends of Policy*, Oxford: Oxford University Press.

Richardson, H. S. (2010), 'Public opinion and popular will', in D. Kahane, D. Weinstock, D. Leydet and M. Williams (eds), *Deliberative Democracy in Practice*, Vancouver, Canada: University of British Columbia Press, pp. 177–93.

Risse, T. (2000), 'Let's argue! Communicative action in world politics', *International Organization*, 54: 1, 1–39.

Rosenberg, S. W. (2002), *The Not So Common Sense: How People Judge Social and Political Life*, New Haven, CA: Yale University Press.

Rosenberg, S. W. (ed) (2007a), *Deliberation, Participation and Democracy: Can the People Govern?*, Basingstoke: Palgrave.

Rosenberg, S. W. (2007b), 'Rethinking democratic deliberation: The limits and potential of citizen participation', *Polity*, 39: 3, 335–60.

Rosenberg, S. W. and G. Wolfsfeld (1977), 'International conflict and the problem of attribution', *Journal of Conflict Resolution*, 21: 1, 75–103.

Ross, L. (1977), 'The intuitive psychologist and his shortcomings: Distortions in the attribution process', in L. Berkowitz (ed.), *Advances in Experimental Social Psychology 10*, New York: Academic Press, pp. 173–220.

Rothstein, B. (1998), *Just Institutions Matter: The Moral and Political Logic of the Universal Welfare State*, Cambridge: Cambridge University Press.

Ryfe, D. M. (2005), 'Does deliberative democracy work?', *Annual Review of Political Science*, 8, 49–71.

Saalfeld, T. (2000), 'Members of parliament and governments in Western Europe:

Agency relations and problems of oversight', *European Journal of Political Research*, 37: 3, 353–76.

Saíz, E. (2011), 'El movimiento 15-M, del anonimato al "trending topic"', *El País*, 17 May, <http://politica.elpais.com/politica/2011/05/17/actualidad/1305634388_860978.html> (last accessed 5 June 2011).

Saleh, S. (2011), 'Me llamo Bea y soy inquilina', *El País*, 14 December, <http://ccaa.elpais.com/ccaa/2011/12/14/madrid/1323851215_319460.html> (last accessed 9 May 2012).

Saleh, S. and Pérez-Lanzac, C. (2011), 'Un campamento con calles y baños portátiles', *El País*, 19 May, <http://www.elpais.com/articulo/espana/campamento/calles/banos/portatiles/elpepuesp/20110519elpepunac_16/Tes> (last accessed 12 September 2011).

Sanders, L. (1997), 'Against deliberation', *Political Theory*, 25: 3, 347–76.

Sanders, L. (2010), 'Making Deliberation Cooler', *The Good Society*, 19: 1, 41–7.

Sarewitz, D. (2004), 'How science makes environmental controversies worse', *Environmental Science and Policy*, 7: 5, 385–403.

Sarewitz, D. (2011), 'Does climate change knowledge really matter?', *Wiley Interdisciplinary Reviews: Climate Change*, 2: 4, 475–81.

Saward, M. (2003), 'Enacting democracy', *Political Studies*, 51: 1, 161–79.

Scholte, J. A. (2005), *Globalization: A Critical Introduction*, 2nd edn, Basingstoke: Palgrave Macmillan.

Schumpeter, J. (1952), *Capitalism, Socialism and Democracy*, London: Unwin University Books.

Schweiger, D. M., W. R. Sandberg and J. W. Ragan (1986), 'Group approaches for improving strategic decision making: a comparative analysis of dialectical inquiry, devil's advocacy, and consensus', *The Academy of Management Journal*, 29: 1, 51–71.

Scott, J. (2000), *Social Network Analysis: A Handbook*, London: Sage.

Scottish Government Social Research Group (2009), *Social Science Method Series* Guide 1: *Deliberative Methods*, <http://www.soctland.gov.uk/Resources/Doc/175356/0091392.pdf> (last accessed 20 September 2012).

Setälä, M. (2010), 'Designing issue-focused forms of citizens participation', paper presented at the conference on *Democracy – A Citizen Perspective*, Åbo, 25–7 May.

Setälä, M., K. Grönlund, K. Herne, (2010), 'Citizen deliberation on nuclear power: A comparison of two decision-making methods', *Political Studies*, 58: 4, 688–714.

Shapiro, I. (1999), 'Enough of deliberation', in S. Macedo (ed.), *Deliberative Politics*, New York: Oxford University Press, pp. 28–38.

Shapiro, I. (2003), *The State of Democratic Theory*, Princeton, NJ: Princeton University Press.

Sintomer, Y. (2010), 'Random selection, republican self-government, and deliberative democracy', *Constellations*, 17: 3, 472–87.

Smith, G. (2000), 'Toward deliberative institutions', in M. Saward (ed.), *Democratic*

Innovation: Deliberation, Representation and Association, London: Routledge, pp. 29–39.

Smith, G. (2003), *Deliberative Democracy and the Environment*, London: Routledge.

Smith, G. (2005), *Beyond the Ballot: 57 Democratic Innovations from Around the World*, London: Power Inquiry.

Smith, G. (2009), *Democratic Innovations: Designing Institutions for Citizen Participation*, Cambridge: Cambridge University Press.

Smith, G. and C. Wales (2000), 'Citizens' juries and deliberative democracy', *Political Studies*, 48: 1, 51–65.

Smith, W. and J. Brassett (2008), 'Deliberation and global governance: liberal, cosmopolitan, and critical perspectives', *Ethics & International Affairs*, 22: 1, 69–92.

Snyder, M. and W. B. Swann (1978), 'Hypothesis-testing processes in social interaction', *Journal of Personality and Social Psychology*, 36: 11, 1202–12.

Spörndli, M. (2004), *Diskurs und Entscheidung. Eine empirische Analyse kommunikativen Handelns im deutschen Vermittlungsausschuss*, Wiesbaden, Germany: VS Verlag für Sozialwissenschaften.

Squires, J. (2002), 'Deliberation and decision-making: Discontinuity in the two-track model', in M. P. d'Entréves (ed.), *Democracy as Public Deliberation: New Perspectives*, Manchester: Manchester University Press, pp. 133–56.

Stasavage, D. (2007), 'Polarization and publicity: Rethinking the benefits of deliberative democracy', *The Journal of Politics*, 69: 1, 59–72.

Steiner, J. (2012), *The Foundations of Deliberative Democracy: Empirical Research and Normative Implications*, Cambridge: Cambridge University Press.

Steiner, J., A. Bächtiger, M. Spörndli and M. Steenbergen (2004), *Deliberative Politics in Action: Analysing Parliamentary Discourse*. Cambridge: Cambridge University Press.

Steiner, J. and R. H. Dorff (1980), *A Theory of Political Decision Making. Interparty Decision Making in Switzerland*, Chapel Hill, NC: University of North Carolina Press.

Stewart, J., E. Kendell and A. Coote (1994), *Citizens' Juries*, London: IPPR.

Stoker, G. (2006), *Why Politics Matters: Making Democracy Work*, Basingstoke: Palgrave.

Stone, P. (2010), 'Three Arguments for Lotteries', *Social Science Information*, 49: 2, 147–63.

Stone, D., B. Patton and S. Heen (1999), *Difficult Conversation: How to Discuss What Matters Most*, New York: Viking/Penguin.

Streeck, W. (2011), 'The crises of democratic capitalism', *New Left Review*, 71, 5–29.

Streeck, W. (2012), 'Markets and peoples', *New Left Review*, 73, 63–71.

Strodtbeck, F. L., R. James, and C. Hawkins (1957), 'Social status in jury deliberations', *American Sociological Review*, 22: 7, 13–719.

Strom, K. (2000), 'Delegation and accountability in parliamentary democracies', *European Journal of Political Research*, 37: 3, 261–89.

Sturgis, P., C. Roberts, C. and N. Allum (2005), 'A different take on the deliberative poll: Information, deliberation and attitude constraint', *Public Opinion Quarterly*, 69: 1, 30–65.

Suleng, K. (2012), 'Qué ha sido del 15-M?', *El País*, 15 April, <http://ccaa.elpais.com/ccaa/2012/04/15/valencia/1334523268_446184.html> (last accessed 3 May 2012).

Sunstein, C. R. (2002), 'The law of group polarization', *Journal of Political Philosophy*, 10: 2, 175–95.

Sunstein, C. R. (2007), *Republic.com 2.0*, Princeton, NJ: Princeton University Press.

Sunstein, C. R. (2009), *Going to Extremes. How Like Minds Unite and Divide*, Oxford: Oxford University Press.

Sunstein, C. R. and R. Thaler (2008), *Nudge: Improving Decisions about Health, Wealth and Happiness*, New Haven CT: Yale University Press.

Tajfel H. (1981), *Human Groups and Social Categories: Studies in Social Psychology*, Cambridge: Cambridge University Press.

Tarrow, S. (1994), *Power in Movement*, Cambridge: Cambridge University Press.

Taylor, S. E. and S. T. Fiske (1978), 'Salience, attention, and attribution: Top of the head phenomena', in L. Berkowitz (ed.), *Advances in Experimental Social Psychology*, Vol. 11, New York: Academic Press, pp. 249–88.

Therborn, G. (1977), 'The rule of capital and the rise of democracy', *New Left Review*, 1/103, 3–41.

Therborn, G. (ed.) (2006), *Inequalities of the World*, London: Verso.

Thompson, D. (2008), 'Deliberative democratic theory and empirical political science', *Annual Review of Political Science*, 11, 497–520.

Tucker, A. (2008), 'Pre-emptive democracy: Oligarchic tendencies in deliberative democracy', *Political Studies*, 56: 1, 127–47.

Turiel, E. (1983), *The Development of Social Knowledge: Morality and Convention*, Cambridge: Cambridge University Press.

Turner, S. P. (2003), *Liberal Democracy 3.0: Civil Society in an Age of Experts*, London and Thousand Oaks, CA: Sage Publications.

Tversky, A. and D. Kahneman (1982), *Judgment under Uncertainty: Heuristics and Biases*, Eugene, OR: Oregon Research Institute.

Uhlmann, E. L., D. A. Pizarro, D. Tannenbaum and P. H. Ditto (2009), 'The motivated use of moral principles', *Judgment and Decision Making*, 4: 6, 479–91.

Uhr, J. (1998), *Deliberative Democracy in Australia*, Cambridge: Cambridge University Press.

Ulbert, C. and Risse, T. (2005), 'Deliberately changing the discourse: what does make arguing effective?', *Acta Politica*, 40: 3, 351–67.

Vanberg, V. and J. M. Buchanan (1989), 'Interests and theories in constitutional choice', *Journal of Theoretical Politics*, 1: 1, 49–62.

Van Mill, D. (1996), 'The possibility of rational outcomes from democratic discourse and procedures', *The Journal of Political*, 53: 3, 734–52.

Vatter, A. (2008), 'Vom Extremtyp zum Normalfall? Die schweizerische Konsensusdemokratie in Wandel: Eine Re-Analyse von Lijphart's Studie für die Schweiz von 1997 bis 2007', *Schweizerische für Politikswissen-schaft*, 14: 1, 1–47.

Vygotsky, L. S. (1978), *Mind in Society: The Development of Higher Psychological Processes*, Cambridge, MA: Harvard University Press.

Walzer, M. (1983), *Spheres of Justice. A Defence of Pluralism and Equality*, Cambridge, MA: Harvard University Press.

Walzer, M. (1999), 'Deliberation, and what else?', in S. Macedo (ed.), *Deliberative Politics*, Oxford: Oxford University Press, pp. 58–69.

Warren, M. E. (1992), 'Democratic theory and self-transformation', *American Political Science Review*, 86: 1, 8–23.

Warren, M. E. (1996), 'Deliberative democracy and authority', *American Political Science Review*, 90: 1, 46–60.

Warren, M. E. (2002), 'Deliberative democracy', in G. Stokes and A. Carter (eds), *Democratic Theory Today*, Cambridge: Polity, pp. 173–202.

Warren, M. E. (2007), 'Institutionalizing deliberative democracy', in S. Rosenberg (ed.), *Deliberation, Participation and Democracy: Can the People Govern?*, Basingstoke: Palgrave, pp. 272–88.

Warren, M. E. and H. Pearse (2006), 'The separation of powers and democratic renewal of Westminster systems', paper presented at Yale University, 7 October.

Warren, M. E. and H. Pearse (eds.) (2008), *Designing Deliberative Democracy. The British Columbia Citizens' Assembly*, Cambridge: Cambridge University Press.

Wasserman, S. and K. Faust (1994), *Social Network Analysis: Methods and Applications*, Cambridge: Cambridge University Press.

Weale, A. (1999), *Democracy*, Basingstoke: Palgrave.

Weale, A., A. Bicquelet and J. Bara (2012), 'Debating abortion, deliberative reciprocity and parliamentary advocacy', *Political Studies*, 60: 3, 643–67.

Weber, E. (1998), *Pluralism by the Rules: Conflict and Cooperation in Environmental Regulation*, Washington, DC: Georgetown University Press.

Weingart, P. (1999), 'Scientific expertise and political accountability: Paradoxes of science in politics', *Science and Public Policy*, 26: 3, 151–61.

Weiss, L. (1998), *The Myth of the Powerless State: Governing the Economy in a Global Era*, Cambridge: Polity.

Wessler, H. (2008), 'Investigating deliberativeness comparatively', *Political Communication*, 25: 1, 1–22.

Wilkinson, R. and K. Pickett (2009), *The Spirit Level: Why More Equal Societies Almost Always Do Better*, London: Penguin.

Williams, M. S. (1998), *Voice, Trust and Memory: Marginalized Groups and the Failings of Liberal Representation*, Princeton, NJ: Princeton University Press.

Wood, E. M. (1995), *Democracy Against Capitalism*, Cambridge: Cambridge University Press.

Young, I. M. (1996), 'Communication and the other: Beyond deliberative democracy', in S. Benhabib (ed.), *Democracy and Difference*, Princeton, NJ: Princeton University Press, pp. 120–35.

Young, I. M. (2000), *Inclusion and Democracy*, Oxford: Oxford University Press.
Young, I. M. (2001), 'Activist challenges to deliberative democracy', *Political Theory*, 29: 5, 670–90.

Index

Discourse Quality Index, 139–40
discourses, contestation of, 34, 38–9, 175–6
discursive representation, 175–6
Ditto, Peter, 104–5
diversity, 5, 6, 10–11, 82–96, 98, 157–8,
    192–3
division of labour, 13, 56–7, 152, 190
draft legislation, 144–6, 195
Dryzek, John, 1, 7, 38–9, 90–1, 126–8, 130–1,
    139, 166, 173, 175, 183, 186

economic inequality, 9, 31, 35–6, 49
education, 9, 11, 35, 41–4, 48–9, 86, 126,
    127, 151, 192
Eilperin, Juliet, 133–4
election campaigns, 143
electoral reform, 24, 26–7, 28, 127–8, 169,
    181, 186
electoral turnout, 35, 125
elite deliberation, 4, 6, 76, 119–25, 133–4,
    190
elitism, 4, 6, 50, 54, 87, 163
Elstub, Stephen, 15, 48, 81, 166–88, 191, 193,
    195
emotion, 34, 42, 111, 115, 135, 147, 151
Empowered Participatory Governance (EPG),
    36–7
enclave deliberation, 156–65, 190, 192–3,
    194
England see United Kingdom
equality, 3, 8, 15, 20, 29, 31, 36–7, 42–3,
    46–8, 84–5, 158, 173–6, 191, 194; see also
    inequality
ethnic relations, 11, 82–3, 86–8, 91–5
ethnicity, 9, 39, 42, 82–3, 86–8, 91–5, 156,
    157, 161, 192
European Commission, 131, 163–4
European Council, 130
European Parliament, 163
European Union, 45, 130, 131, 147, 148, 161,
    163–4, 193
Europolis, 127, 163–4
evaluation, 52, 58–62, 104–6, 110–11, 112,
    116, 180
Evans, R., 59, 61
everyday talk, 17, 31, 55, 150, 159
evidence, 52, 53, 59, 61, 99, 104–5, 167
exclusion, 5, 29–30, 86, 96, 150–2, 157,
    162–3, 164–5, 177
exclusionary identities, 161, 162
exclusive states, 128, 183
expert bias, 60
experts, 9–10, 36, 50–67, 126, 156, 167, 168,
    169, 173, 177–8, 185, 191, 193

external exclusion, 150–1, 152, 157, 162, 163,
    165

Facebook, 21, 22, 23
facilitators, 14–15, 43–4, 48–9, 64–5, 116,
    126, 146, 160, 167, 168, 176, 180, 192
fairness, 52, 85, 149, 156
Falk, Richard, 130
false essentialism, 174, 175
false memories, 102
Federal Reserve Open Market Committee,
    140–1
Fenno, R., 134
Ferguson, Niall, 25
Festinger, Leon, 104
financial crisis, 21, 25
Finnis, John, 89
first-generation deliberative democracy, 1,
    4–5, 72
Fishkin, James S., 65, 119, 145–6, 168, 171,
    179, 194
Foucault, Michel, 29
framing, 62–3, 65–6, 81
France, 128, 164, 167, 183, 184
Fraser, Nancy, 25, 155, 156–8
Free Democratic Party (Switzerland), 142–3
Fung, A., 36–7, 187–8

Gastil, J., 109, 111
gender, 9, 39, 41, 42, 156, 157, 161
Gerber, M., 127
Gerken, Heather, 157
Germany, 77, 122, 123, 125, 139, 168
Gladwell, M., 23
globalisation, 11, 12, 44–5, 151–2; see also
    transnational institutions
Goodin, Robert E., 18, 111, 139, 140, 142–3,
    167, 182
Gramsci, Antonio, 42
Gray, John, 89, 95
Greece (ancient), 3, 29, 150, 167
Greece (modern), 21, 169, 184
Greenspan, Alan, 140
greeting, 6, 42, 43, 151
group deliberation, 10, 77–8, 110–11, 159–60,
    193
group polarisation, 159–62, 164–5
group size, 115, 171, 175, 180
Gutmann, Amy, 1, 5–6, 51, 53–4, 153, 154,
    165

Habermas, Jürgen, 1, 4–5, 13, 18, 22, 24,
    29–32, 38, 40, 48, 51, 54–6, 73, 129,
    137–8, 149, 151, 154–5, 157, 166